Pardon my Planet

Pardon my Planet

Omigawd! I've Become My Mother!

Vic Lee

**Andrews McMeel
Publishing**

Kansas City

ATTENTION: SCHOOLS AND BUSINESSES

Andrews McMeel books are available at quantity discounts with bulk purchase for educational, business, or sales promotional use. For information, please write to: Special Sales Department, Andrews McMeel Publishing, 4520 Main Street, Kansas City, Missouri 64111.

To Lisa Lynn—patient wife, reluctant muse.

To Tanner Tramp, Tango Seuss, Milo Squirts, Emily Wiggle, Beamba Regatza, and Loki Doke—our perfect children.

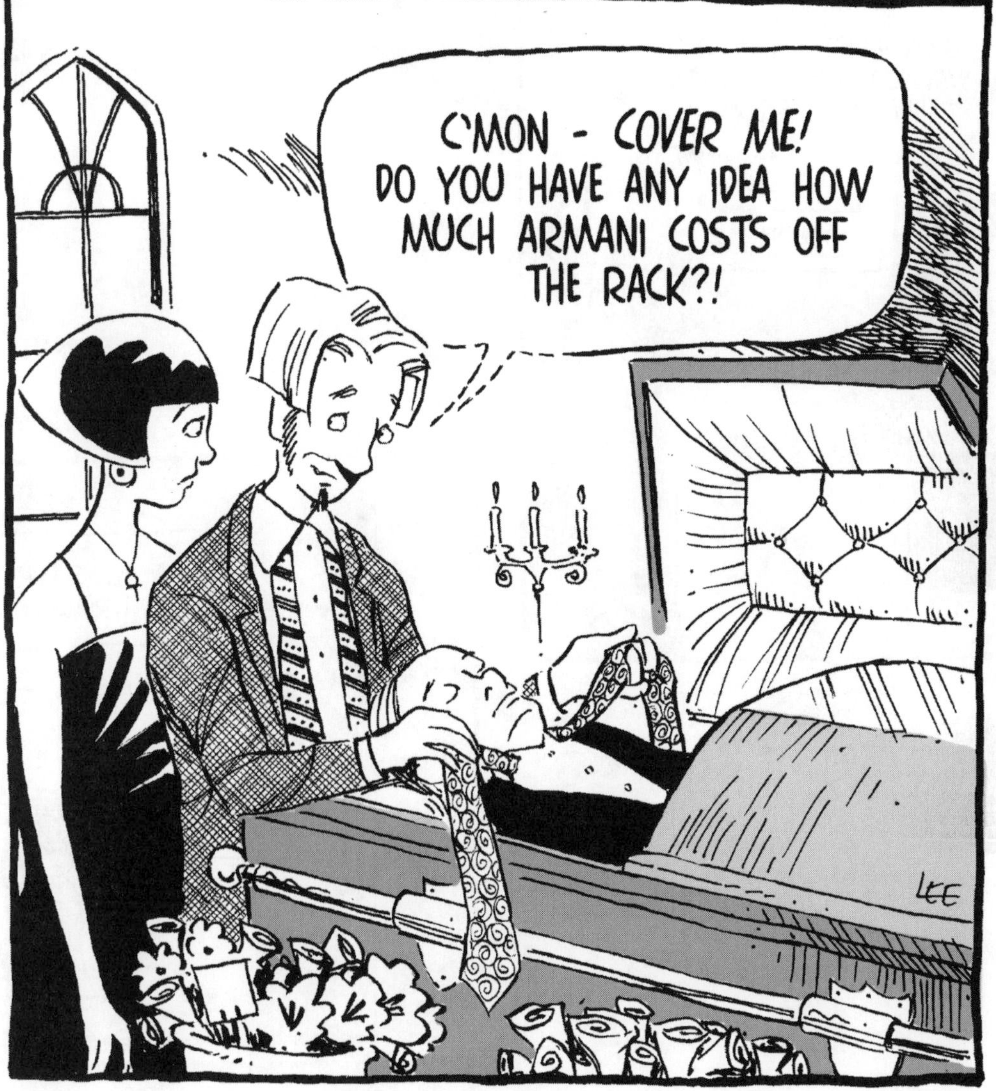
C'MON - COVER ME! DO YOU HAVE ANY IDEA HOW MUCH ARMANI COSTS OFF THE RACK?!
LEE

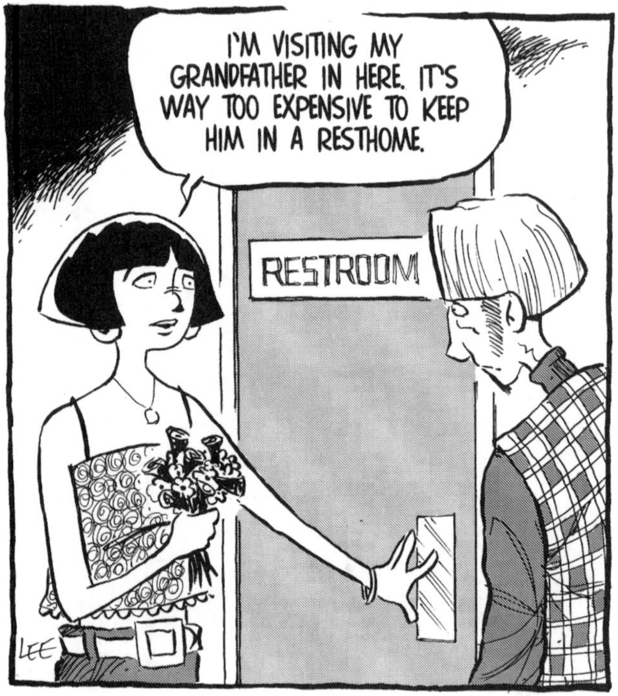
I'M VISITING MY GRANDFATHER IN HERE. IT'S WAY TOO EXPENSIVE TO KEEP HIM IN A RESTHOME.
RESTROOM
LEE

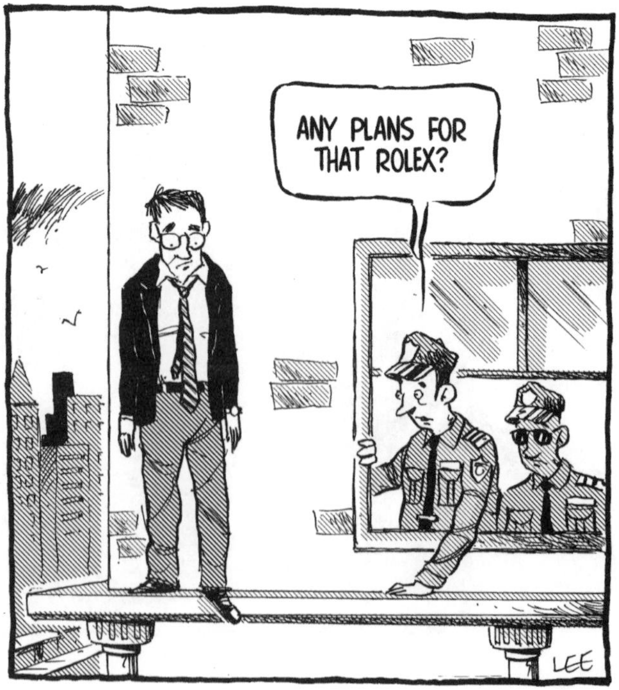
ANY PLANS FOR THAT ROLEX?
LEE

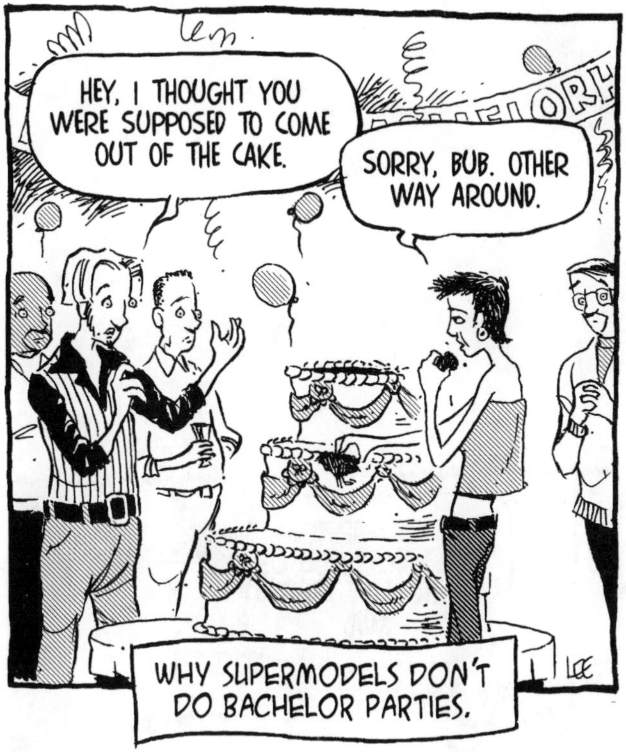
HEY, I THOUGHT YOU WERE SUPPOSED TO COME OUT OF THE CAKE.
SORRY, BUB. OTHER WAY AROUND.
WHY SUPERMODELS DON'T DO BACHELOR PARTIES.
LEE

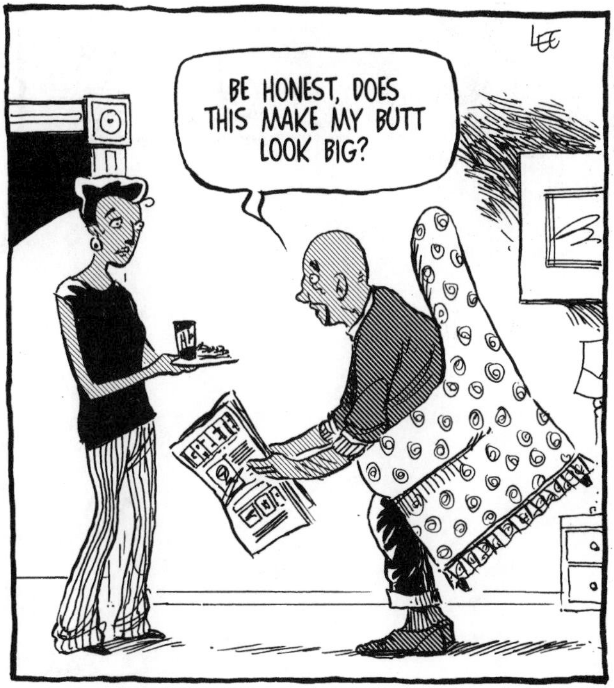
LEE
BE HONEST, DOES THIS MAKE MY BUTT LOOK BIG?

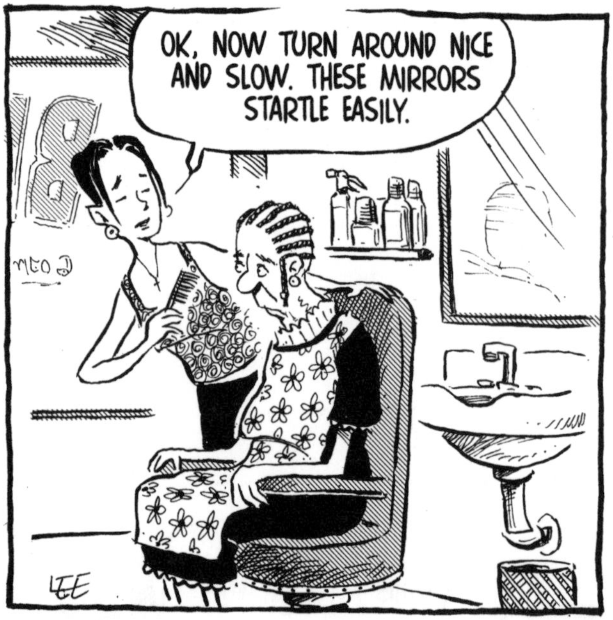
OK, NOW TURN AROUND NICE AND SLOW. THESE MIRRORS STARTLE EASILY.
LEE

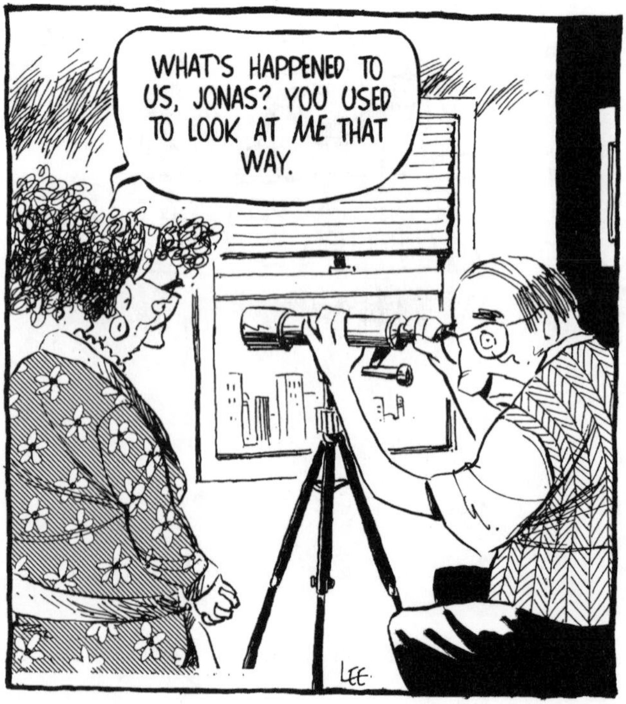
WHAT'S HAPPENED TO US, JONAS? YOU USED TO LOOK AT *ME* THAT WAY.
LEE

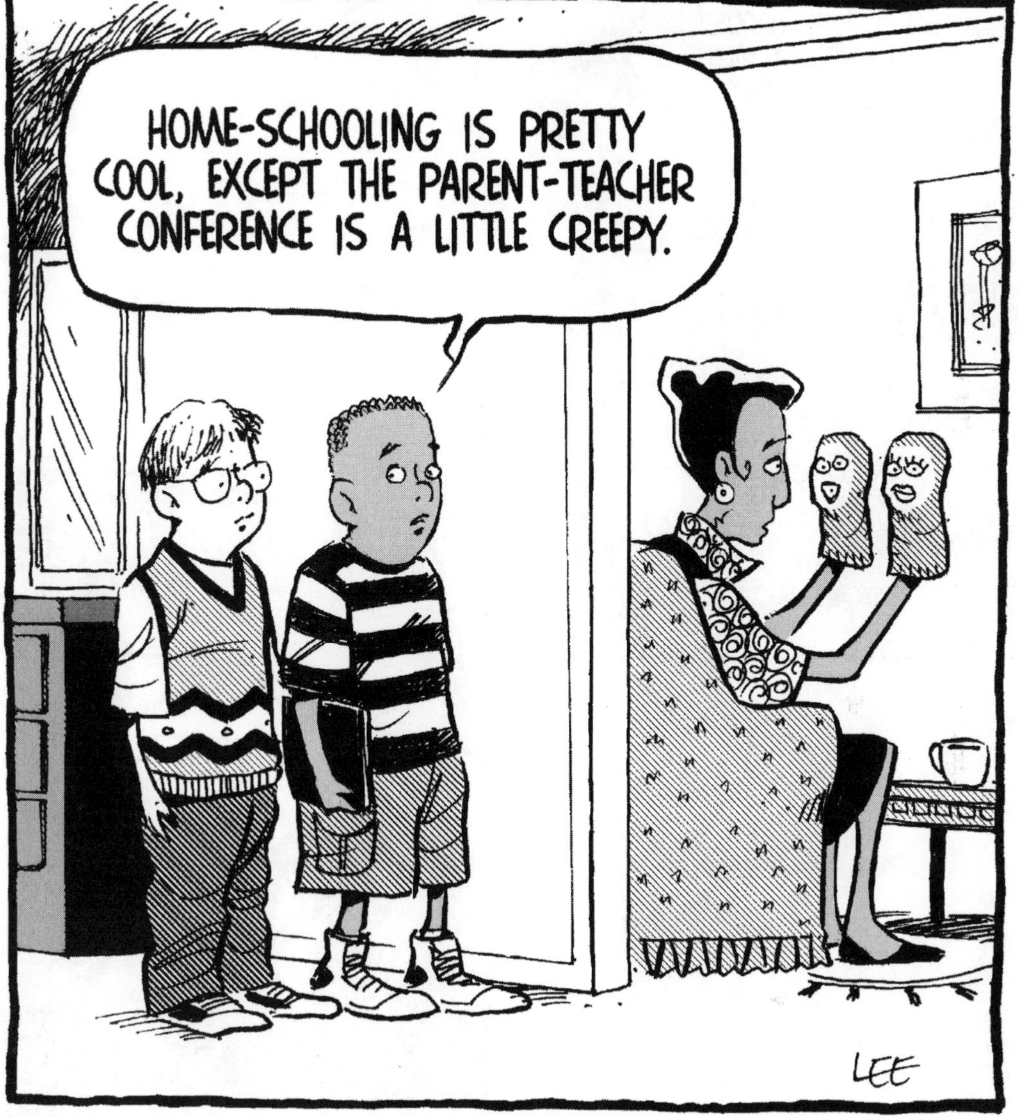
HOME-SCHOOLING IS PRETTY COOL, EXCEPT THE PARENT-TEACHER CONFERENCE IS A LITTLE CREEPY.
LEE

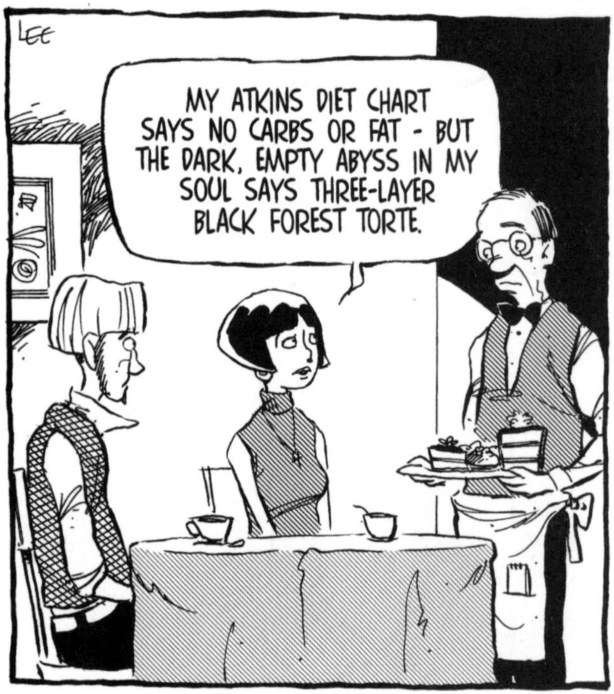
MY ATKINS DIET CHART SAYS NO CARBS OR FAT - BUT THE DARK, EMPTY ABYSS IN MY SOUL SAYS THREE-LAYER BLACK FOREST TORTE.

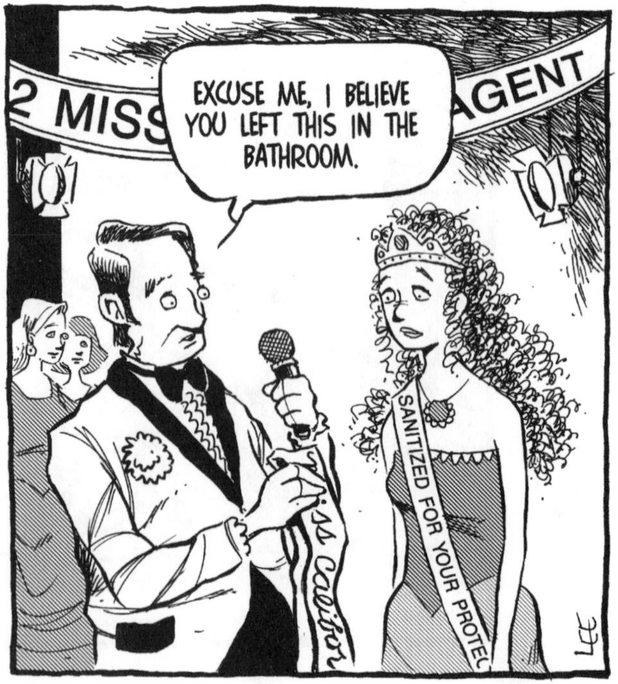
2 MISS
AGENT
EXCUSE ME, I BELIEVE YOU LEFT THIS IN THE BATHROOM.
SANITIZED FOR YOUR PROTEC

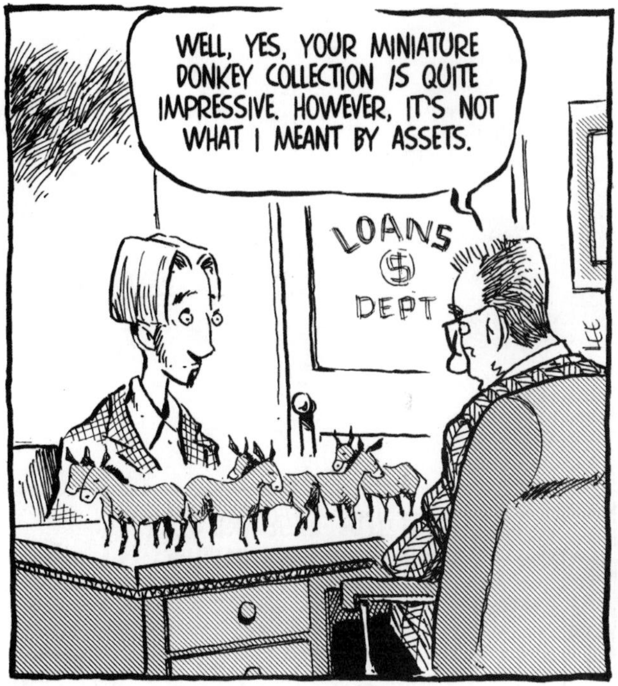
WELL, YES, YOUR MINIATURE DONKEY COLLECTION IS QUITE IMPRESSIVE. HOWEVER, IT'S NOT WHAT I MEANT BY ASSETS.
LOANS $ DEPT
LEE

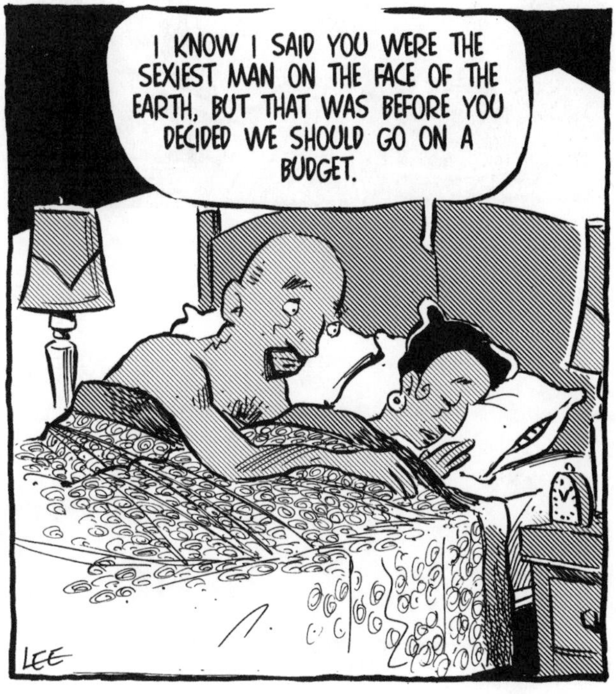
I KNOW I SAID YOU WERE THE SEXIEST MAN ON THE FACE OF THE EARTH, BUT THAT WAS BEFORE YOU DECIDED WE SHOULD GO ON A BUDGET.
LEE

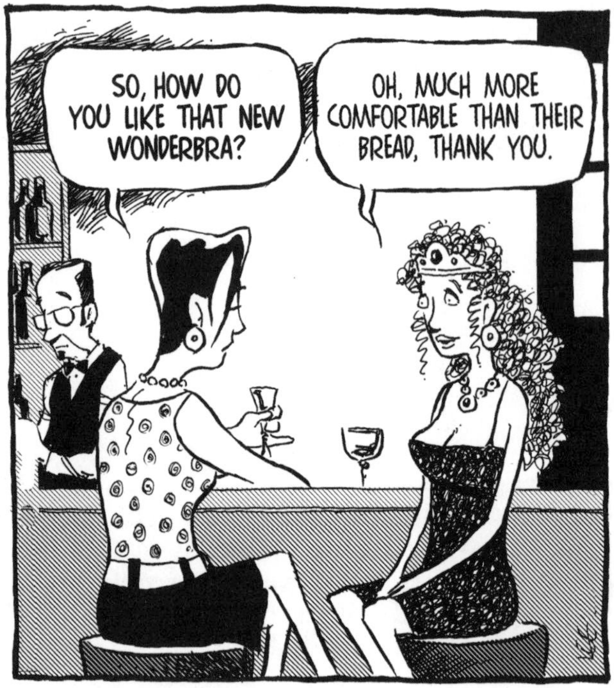
SO, HOW DO YOU LIKE THAT NEW WONDERBRA?
OH, MUCH MORE COMFORTABLE THAN THEIR BREAD, THANK YOU.
LEE

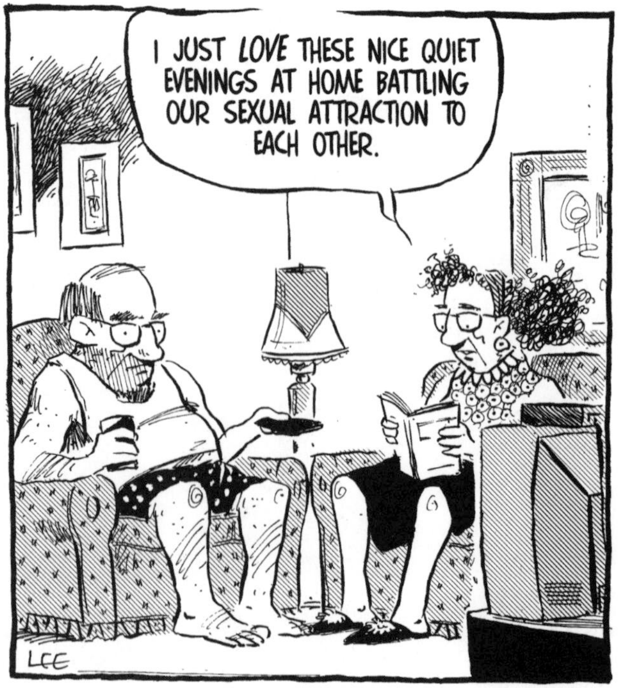
I JUST *LOVE* THESE NICE QUIET EVENINGS AT HOME BATTLING OUR SEXUAL ATTRACTION TO EACH OTHER.
LEE

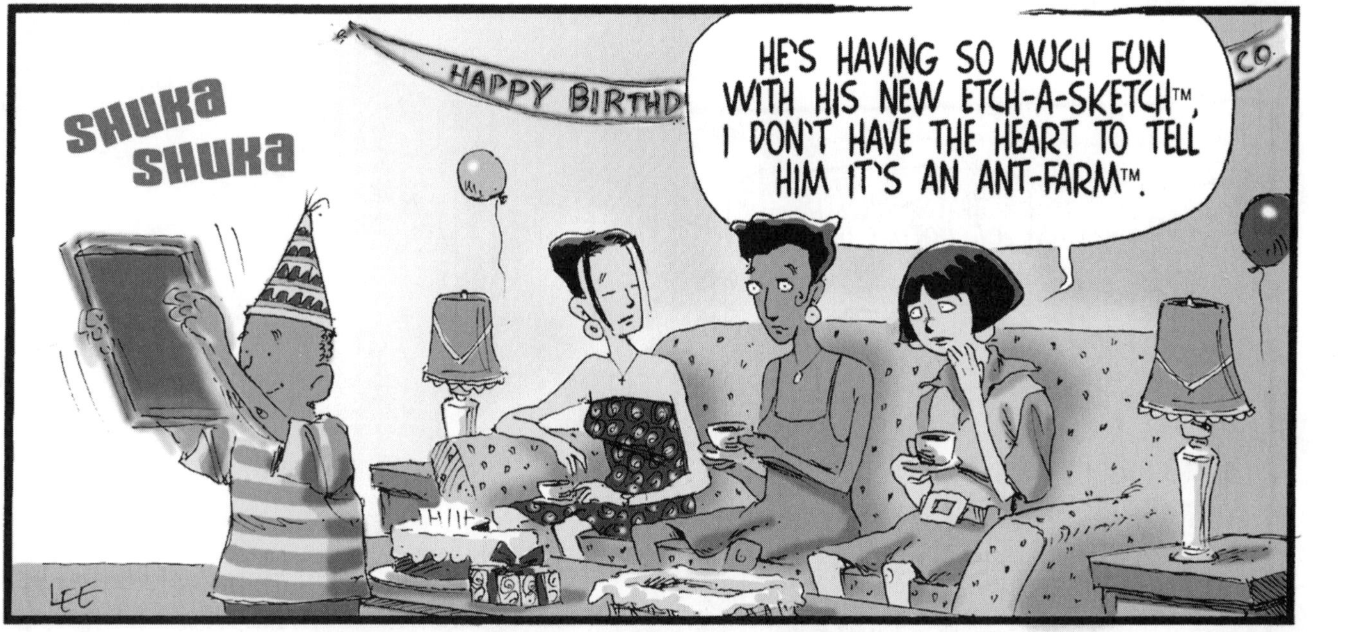
HAPPY BIRTHD
CO.
SHUKA SHUKA
HE'S HAVING SO MUCH FUN WITH HIS NEW ETCH-A-SKETCH™, I DON'T HAVE THE HEART TO TELL HIM IT'S AN ANT-FARM™.
LEE

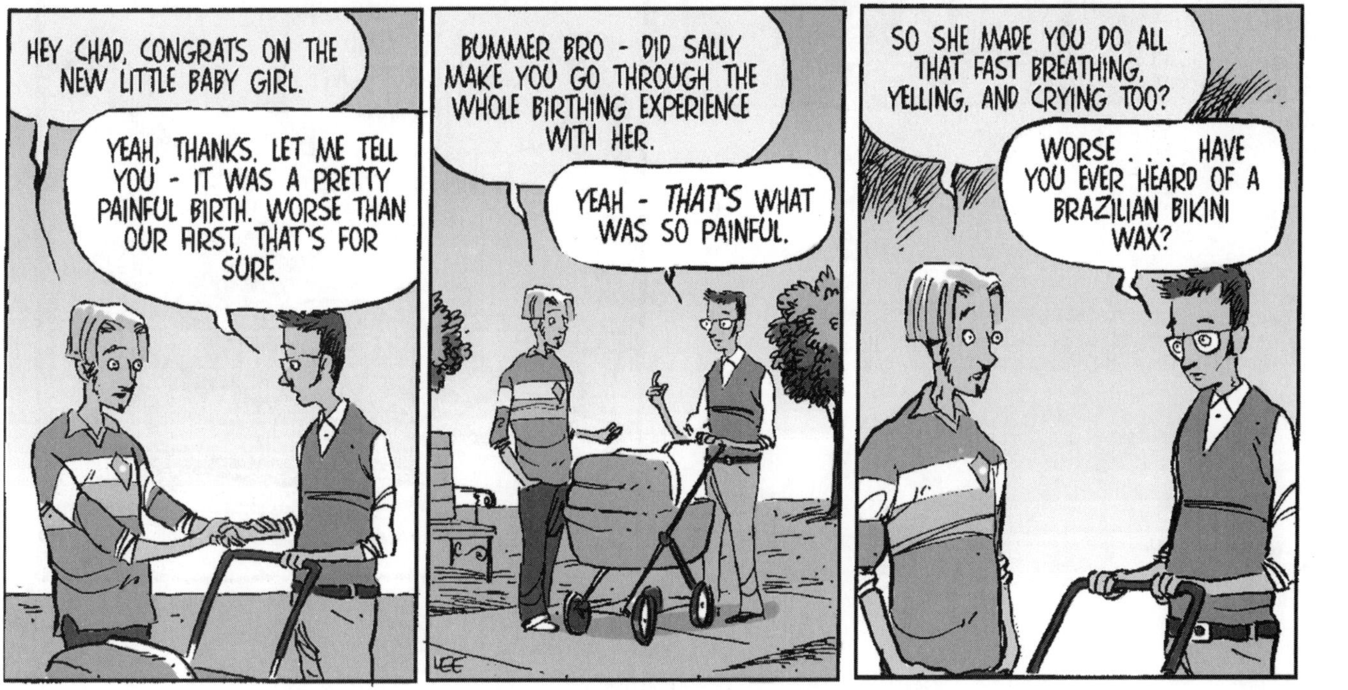
HEY CHAD, CONGRATS ON THE NEW LITTLE BABY GIRL.
YEAH, THANKS. LET ME TELL YOU - IT WAS A PRETTY PAINFUL BIRTH. WORSE THAN OUR FIRST, THAT'S FOR SURE.
BUMMER BRO - DID SALLY MAKE YOU GO THROUGH THE WHOLE BIRTHING EXPERIENCE WITH HER.
YEAH - *THAT'S* WHAT WAS SO PAINFUL.
LEE
SO SHE MADE YOU DO ALL THAT FAST BREATHING, YELLING, AND CRYING TOO?
WORSE . . . HAVE YOU EVER HEARD OF A BRAZILIAN BIKINI WAX?

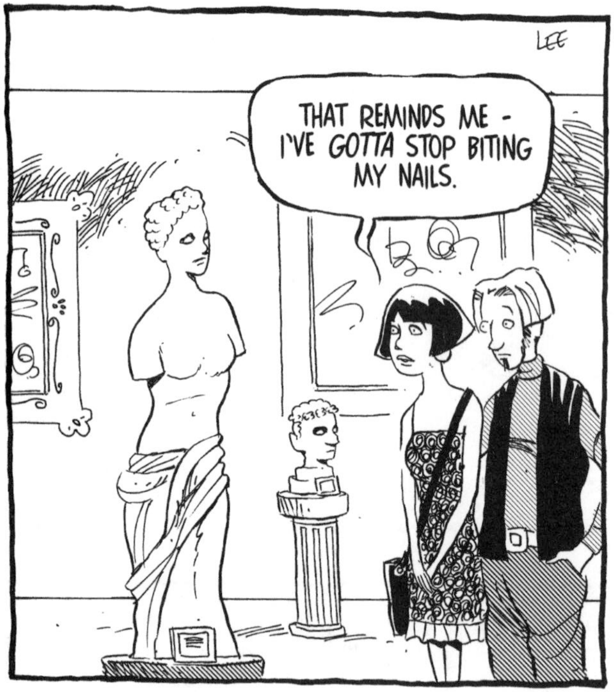
LEE
THAT REMINDS ME - I'VE *GOTTA* STOP BITING MY NAILS.

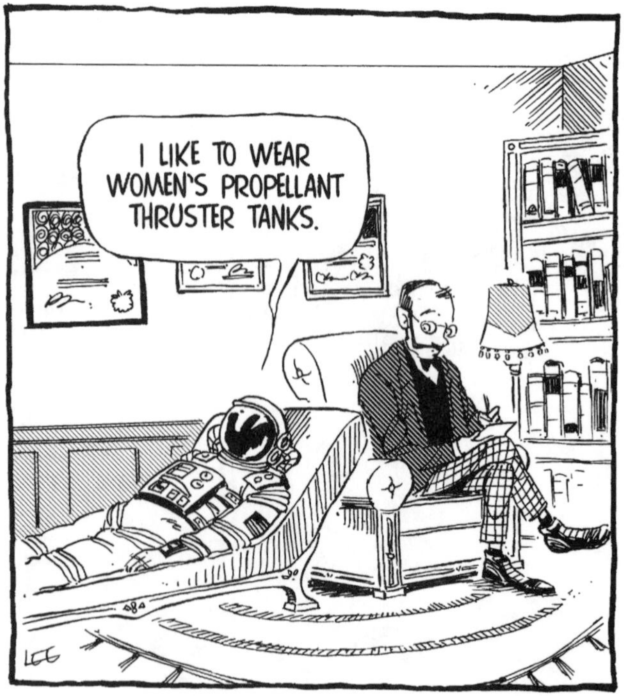
I LIKE TO WEAR WOMEN'S PROPELLANT THRUSTER TANKS.
LEE

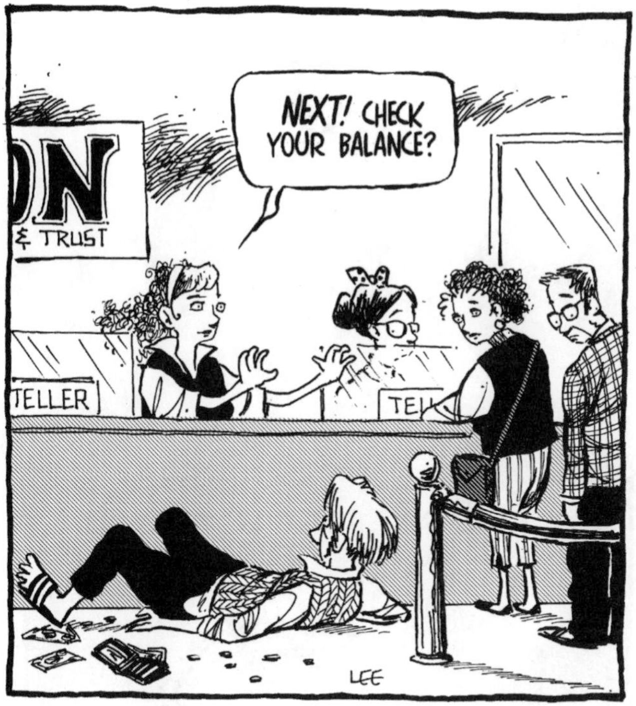
NEXT! CHECK YOUR BALANCE?
& TRUST
TELLER
LEE

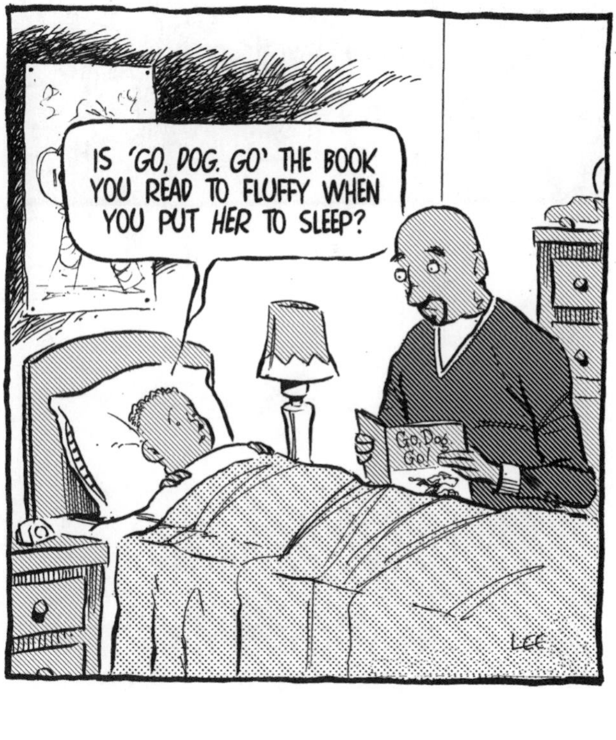
IS 'GO, DOG. GO' THE BOOK YOU READ TO FLUFFY WHEN YOU PUT HER TO SLEEP?
Go, Dog. Go!
LEE

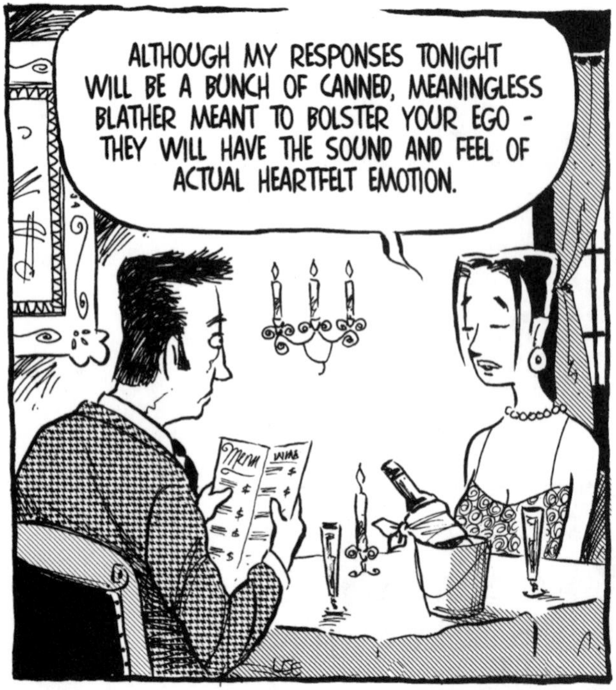
ALTHOUGH MY RESPONSES TONIGHT WILL BE A BUNCH OF CANNED, MEANINGLESS BLATHER MEANT TO BOLSTER YOUR EGO - THEY WILL HAVE THE SOUND AND FEEL OF ACTUAL HEARTFELT EMOTION.
LEE

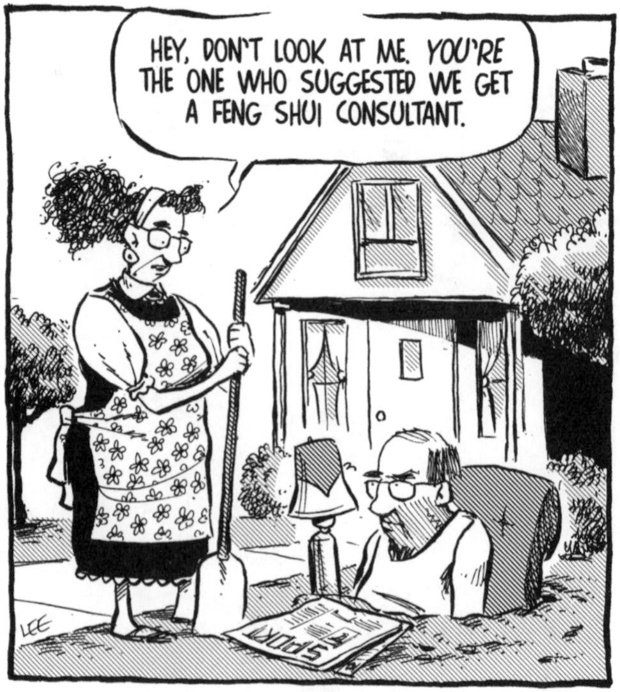
HEY, DON'T LOOK AT ME. *YOU'RE* THE ONE WHO SUGGESTED WE GET A FENG SHUI CONSULTANT.
SPORT
LEE

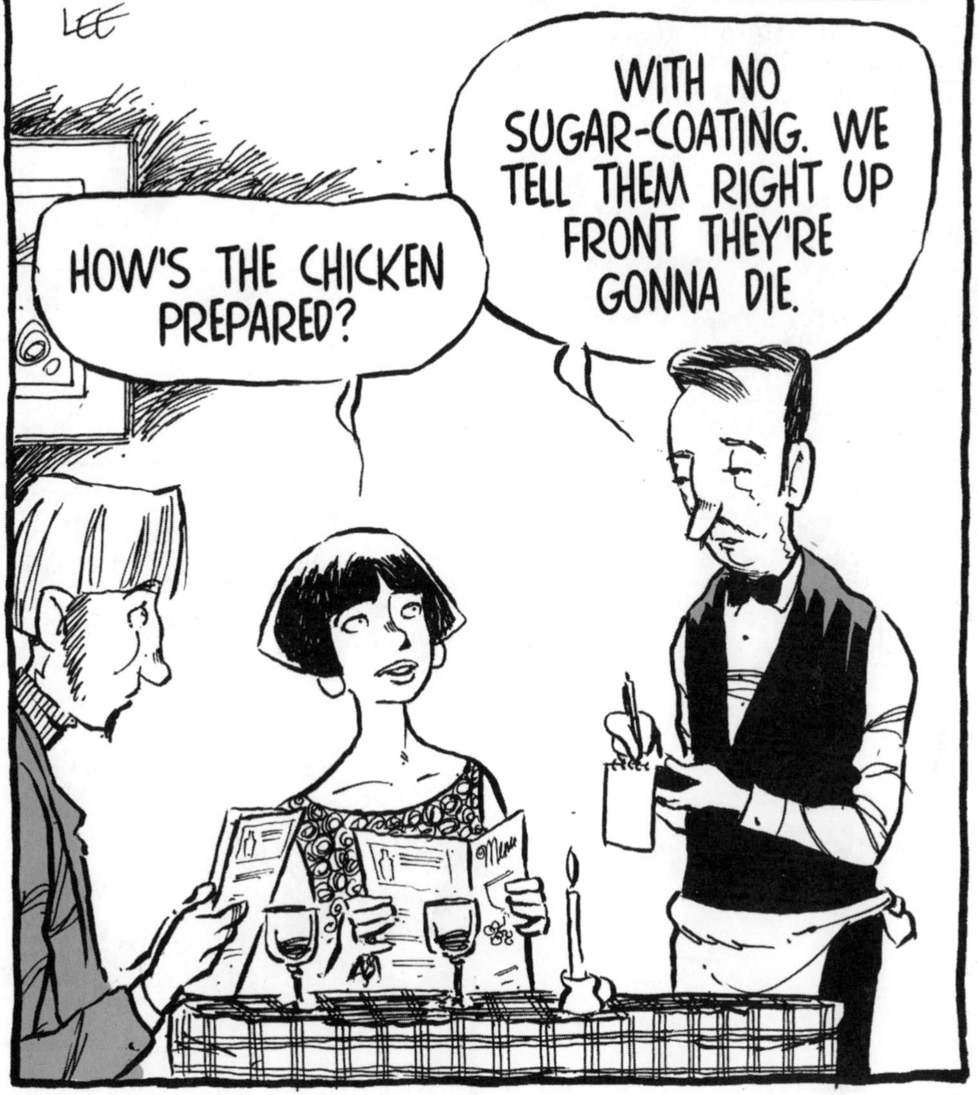
LEE
HOW'S THE CHICKEN PREPARED?
WITH NO SUGAR-COATING. WE TELL THEM RIGHT UP FRONT THEY'RE GONNA DIE.
Menu

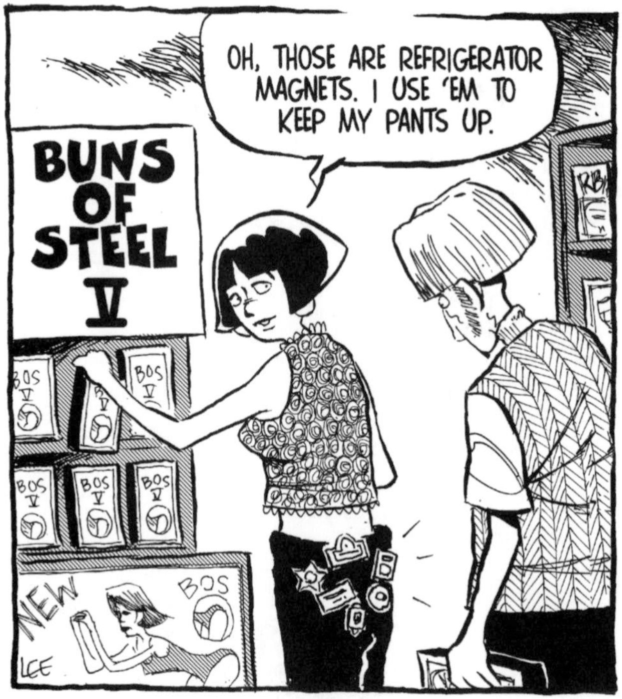
OH, THOSE ARE REFRIGERATOR MAGNETS. I USE 'EM TO KEEP MY PANTS UP.
BUNS OF STEEL V
NEW
BOS
LEE

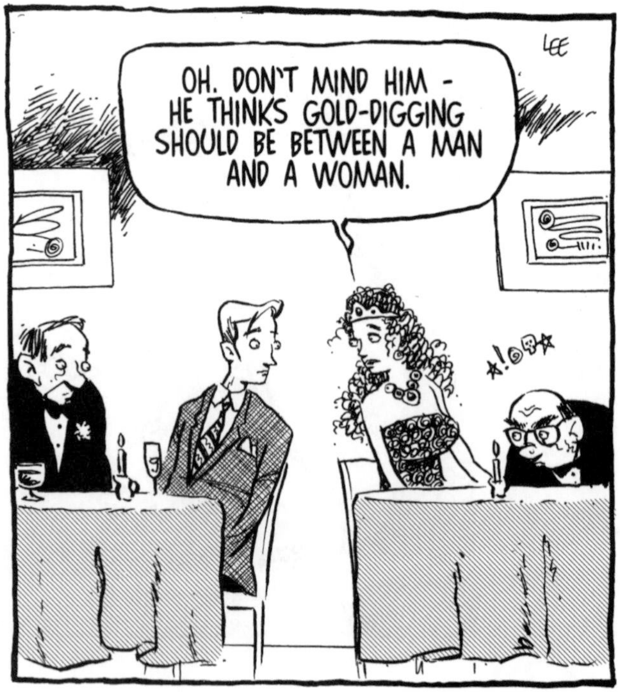
OH. DON'T MIND HIM - HE THINKS GOLD-DIGGING SHOULD BE BETWEEN A MAN AND A WOMAN.
LEE

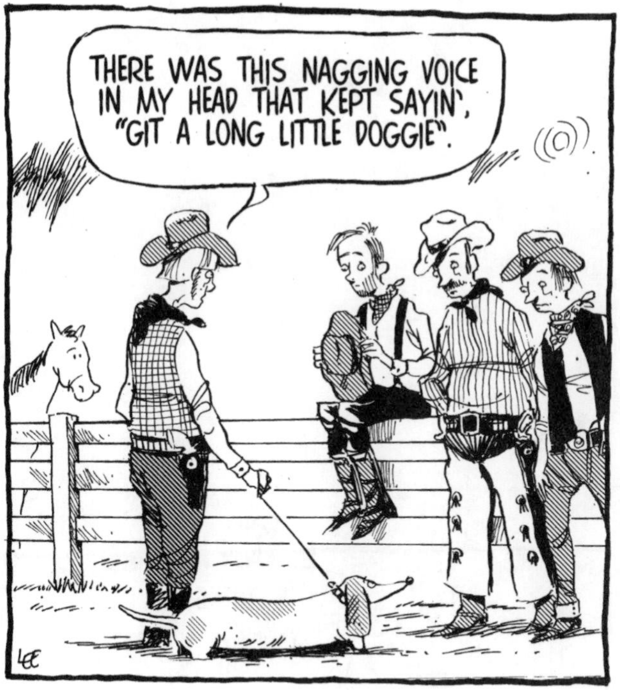
THERE WAS THIS NAGGING VOICE IN MY HEAD THAT KEPT SAYIN', "GIT A LONG LITTLE DOGGIE".
LEE

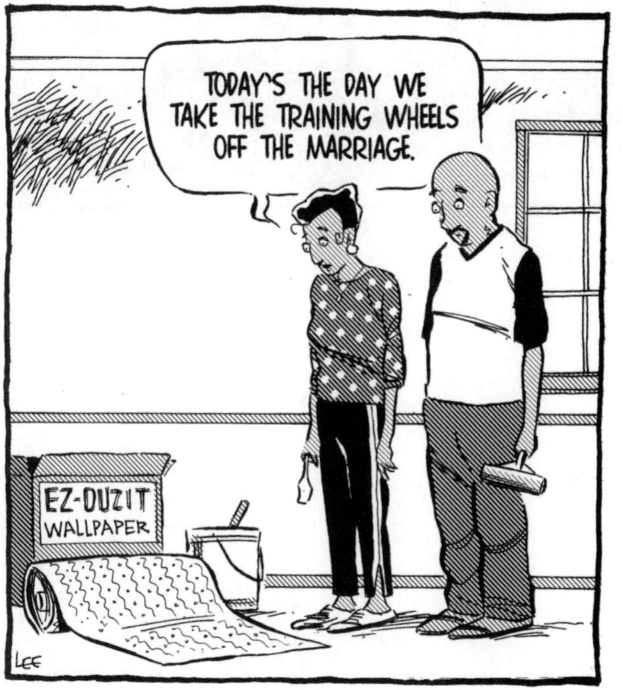
TODAY'S THE DAY WE TAKE THE TRAINING WHEELS OFF THE MARRIAGE.
EZ-DUZIT
WALLPAPER
LEE

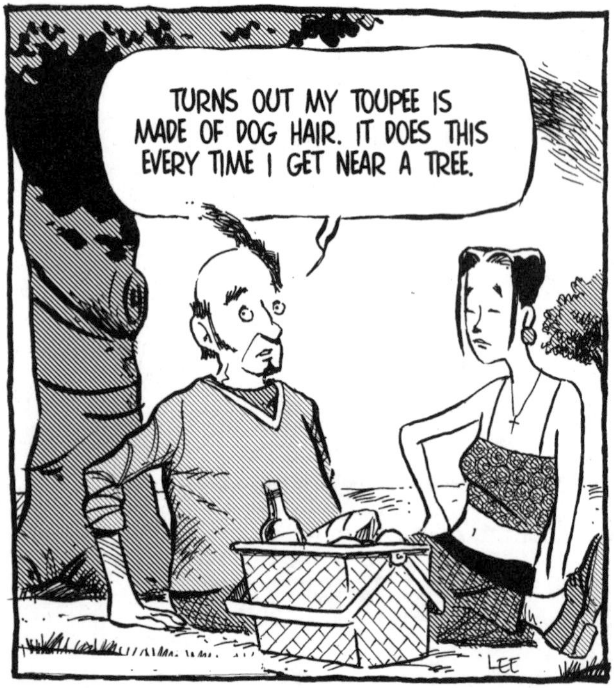
TURNS OUT MY TOUPEE IS MADE OF DOG HAIR. IT DOES THIS EVERY TIME I GET NEAR A TREE.
LEE

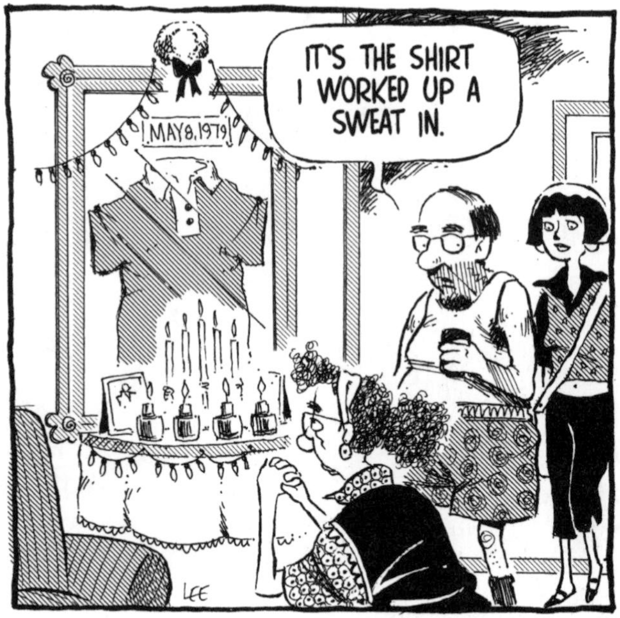
MAY 8, 1979
IT'S THE SHIRT I WORKED UP A SWEAT IN.
LEE

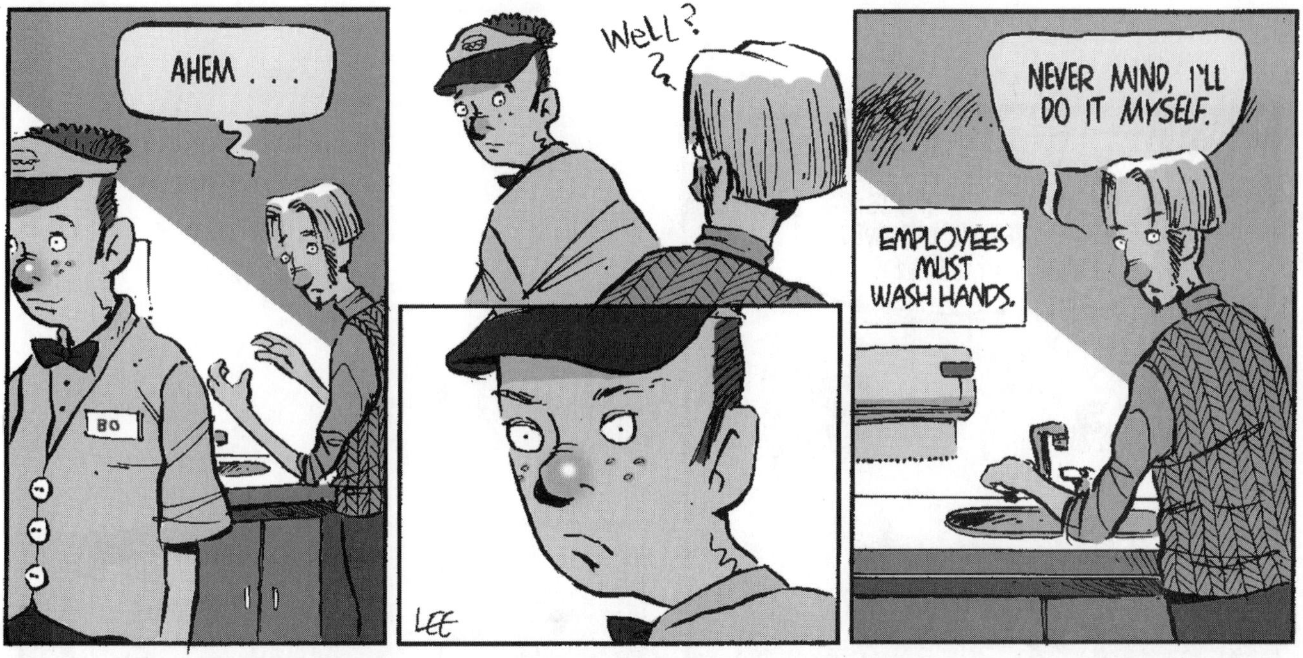
AHEM . . .
BO
WELL?
EMPLOYEES MUST WASH HANDS.
NEVER MIND, I'LL DO IT MYSELF.

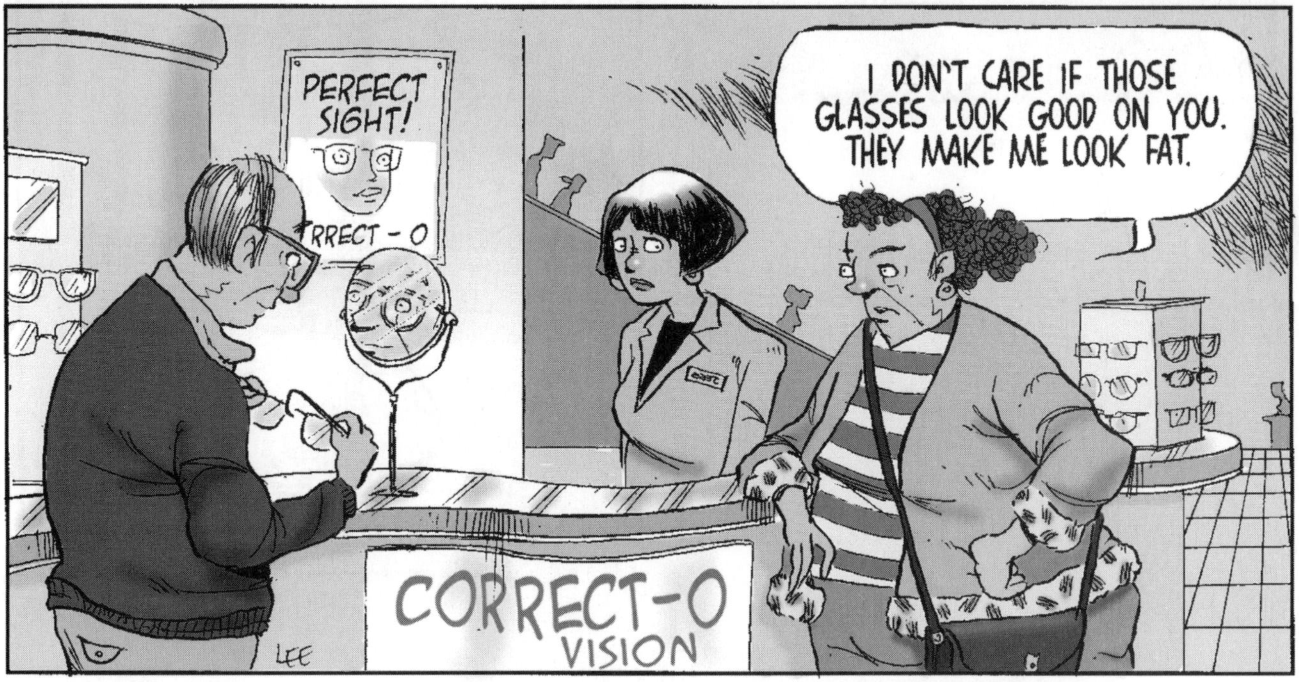
PERFECT SIGHT!
RRECT - O
I DON'T CARE IF THOSE GLASSES LOOK GOOD ON YOU. THEY MAKE ME LOOK FAT.
CORRECT-O VISION

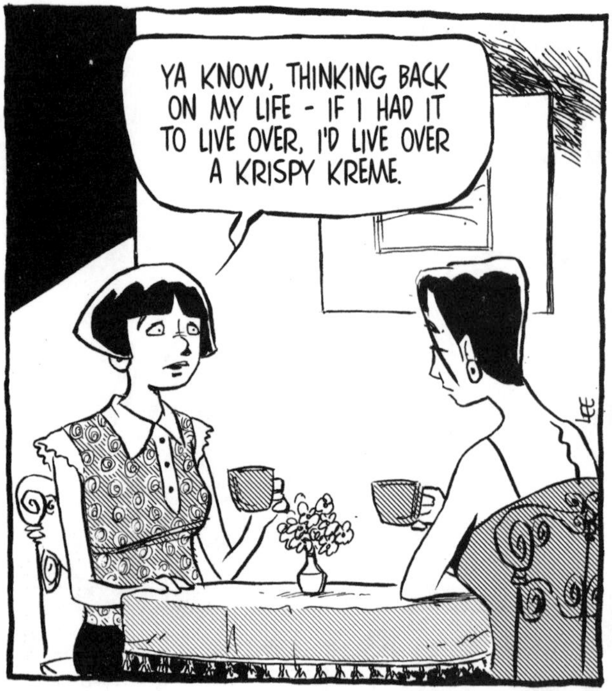
YA KNOW, THINKING BACK ON MY LIFE - IF I HAD IT TO LIVE OVER, I'D LIVE OVER A KRISPY KREME.

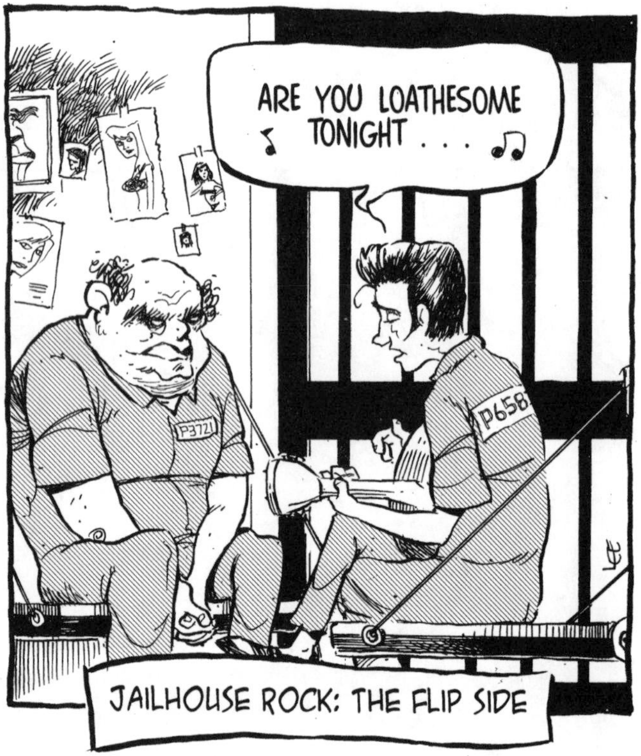
ARE YOU LOATHESOME TONIGHT . . .
P3721
P658
JAILHOUSE ROCK: THE FLIP SIDE

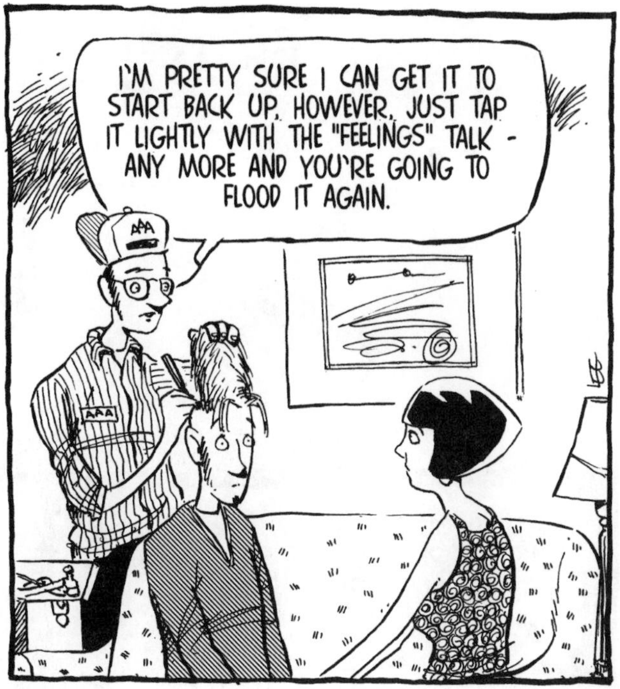
I'M PRETTY SURE I CAN GET IT TO START BACK UP. HOWEVER, JUST TAP IT LIGHTLY WITH THE "FEELINGS" TALK - ANY MORE AND YOU'RE GOING TO FLOOD IT AGAIN.
AAA
AAA
LEE

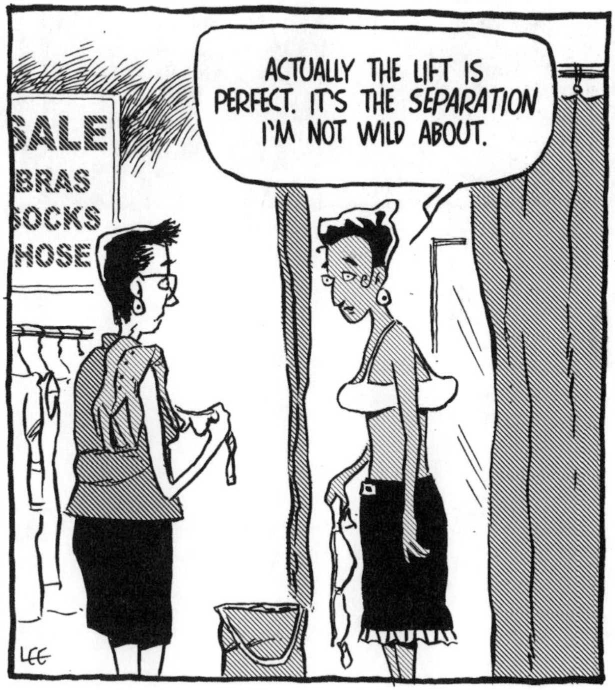
ACTUALLY THE LIFT IS PERFECT. IT'S THE *SEPARATION* I'M NOT WILD ABOUT.
SALE
BRAS
SOCKS
HOSE
LEE

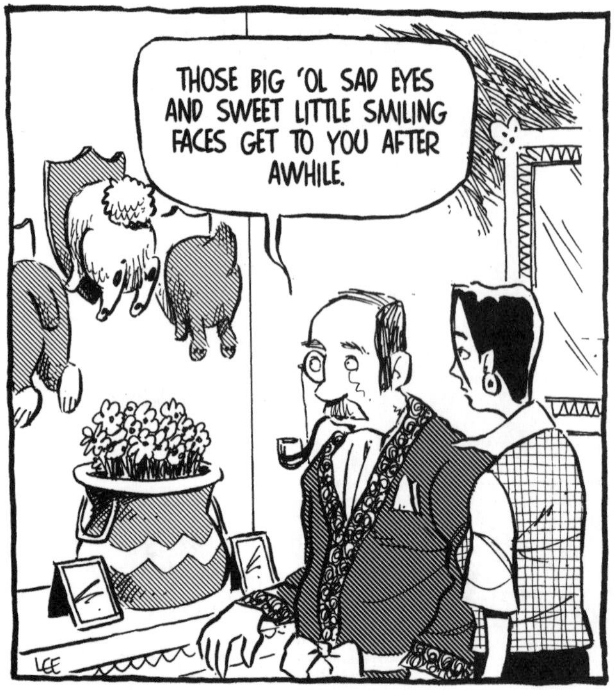
THOSE BIG 'OL SAD EYES AND SWEET LITTLE SMILING FACES GET TO YOU AFTER AWHILE.
LEE

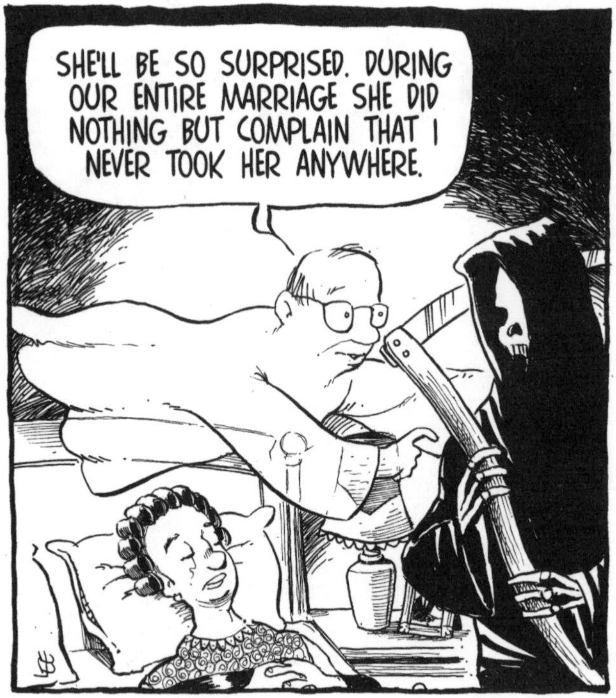
SHE'LL BE SO SURPRISED. DURING OUR ENTIRE MARRIAGE SHE DID NOTHING BUT COMPLAIN THAT I NEVER TOOK HER ANYWHERE.

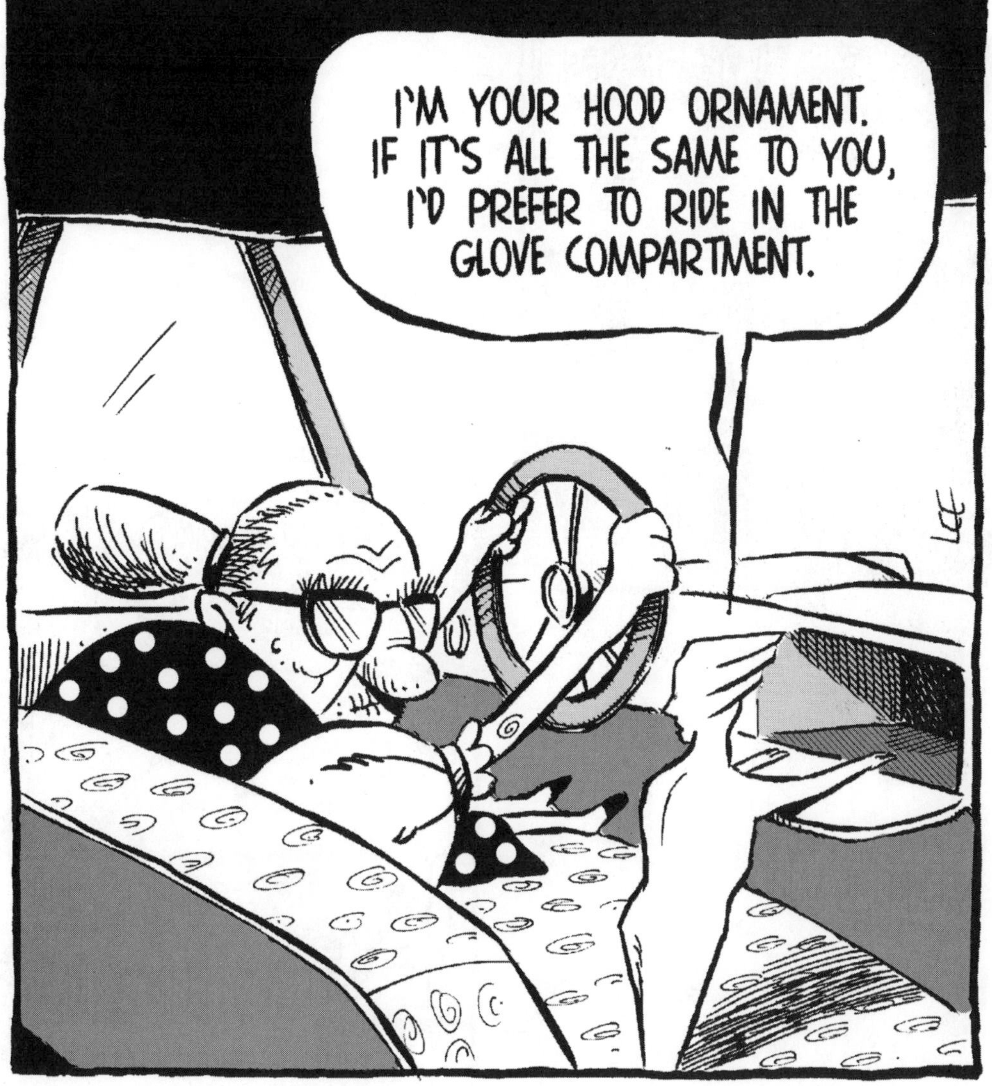
I'M YOUR HOOD ORNAMENT. IF IT'S ALL THE SAME TO YOU, I'D PREFER TO RIDE IN THE GLOVE COMPARTMENT.
LEE

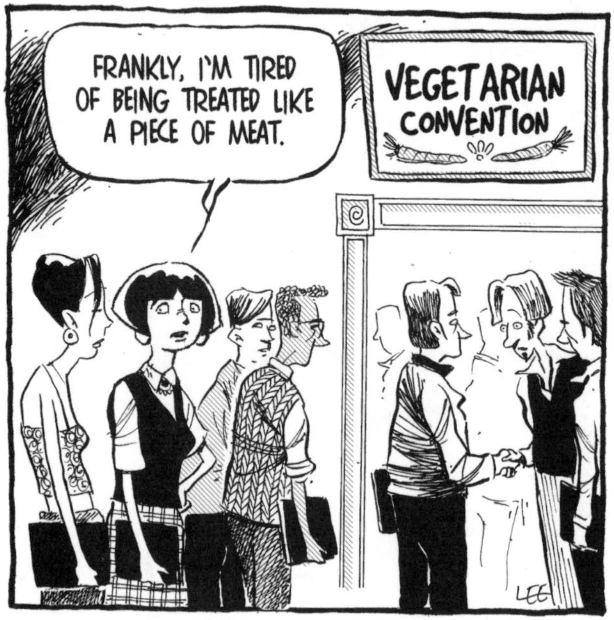
FRANKLY, I'M TIRED OF BEING TREATED LIKE A PIECE OF MEAT.
VEGETARIAN CONVENTION
LEE

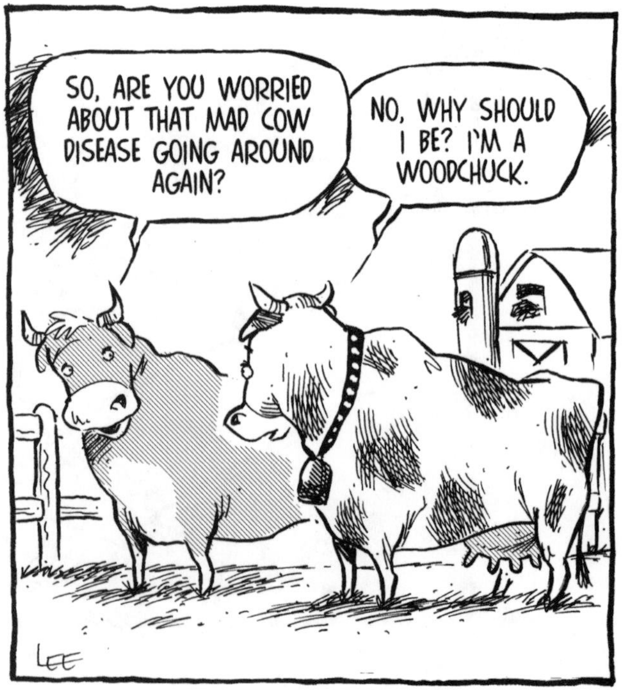
SO, ARE YOU WORRIED ABOUT THAT MAD COW DISEASE GOING AROUND AGAIN?
NO, WHY SHOULD I BE? I'M A WOODCHUCK.
LEE

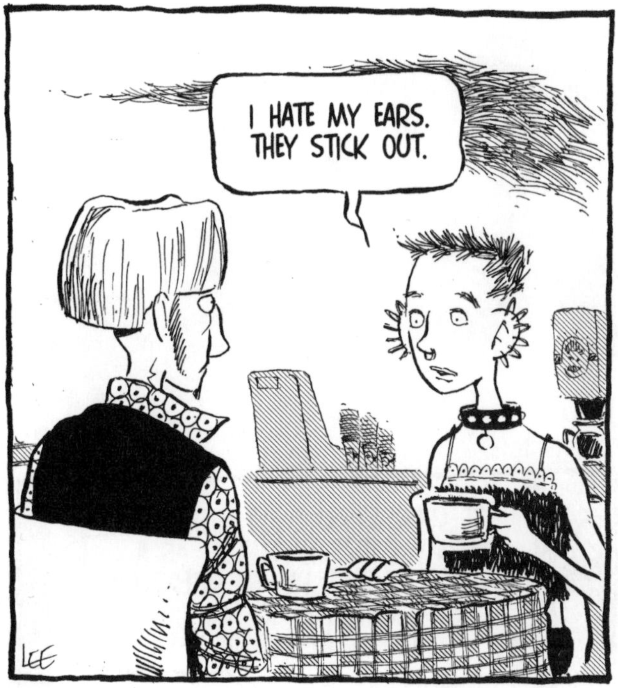
I HATE MY EARS. THEY STICK OUT.
LEE

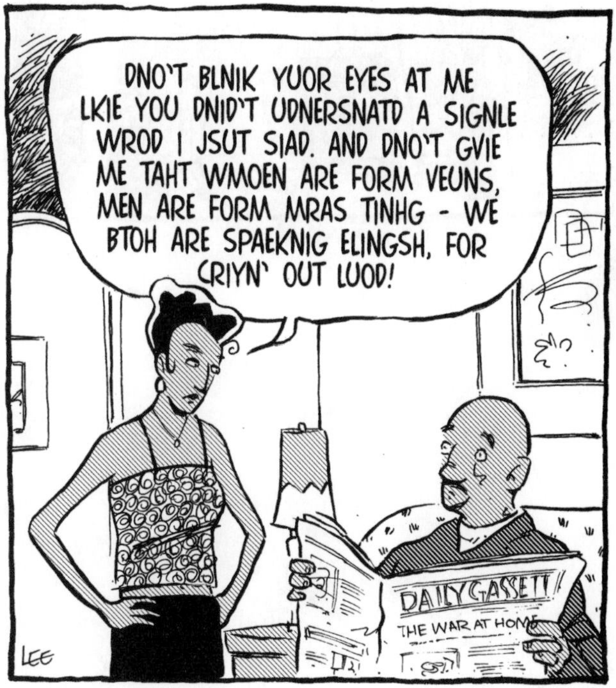
DNO'T BLNIK YUOR EYES AT ME LKIE YOU DNID'T UDNERSNATD A SIGNLE WROD I JSUT SIAD. AND DNO'T GVIE ME TAHT WMOEN ARE FORM VEUNS, MEN ARE FORM MRAS TINHG - WE BTOH ARE SPAEKNIG ELINGSH, FOR CRIYN' OUT LUOD!
DAILY GASSETT
THE WAR AT HOME
LEE

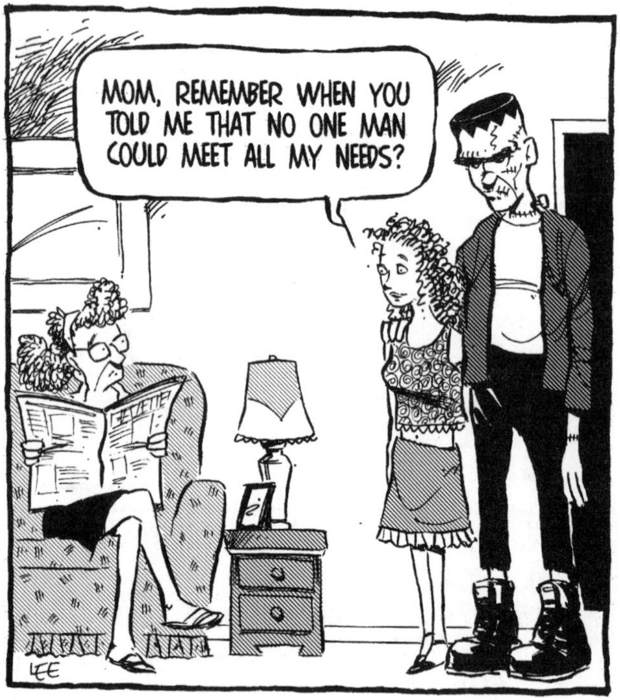
MOM, REMEMBER WHEN YOU TOLD ME THAT NO ONE MAN COULD MEET ALL MY NEEDS?
LEE

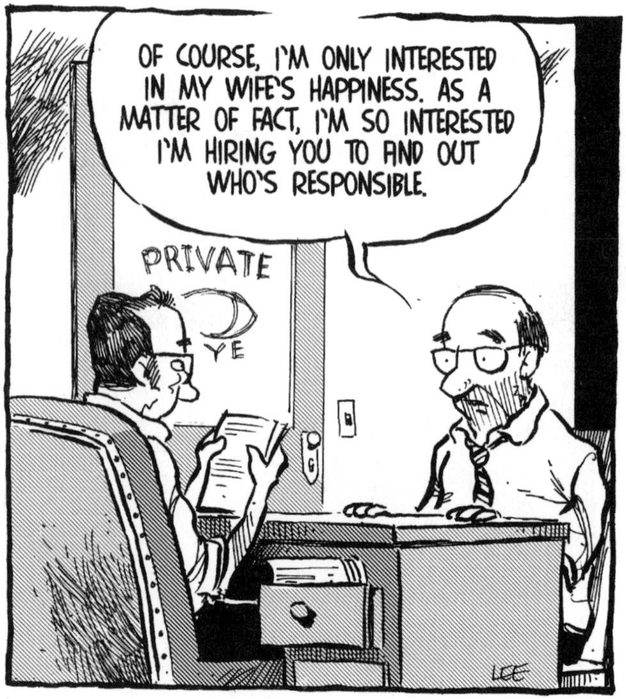
OF COURSE, I'M ONLY INTERESTED IN MY WIFE'S HAPPINESS. AS A MATTER OF FACT, I'M SO INTERESTED I'M HIRING YOU TO FIND OUT WHO'S RESPONSIBLE.
PRIVATE
YE
LEE

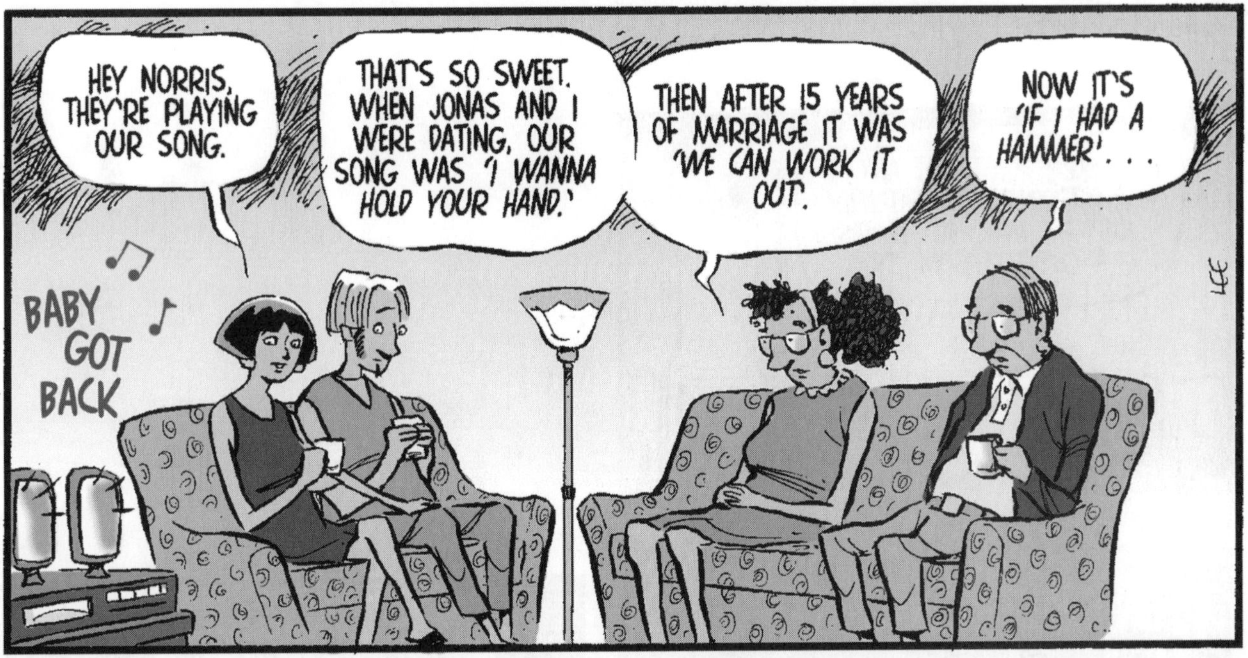
HEY NORRIS, THEY'RE PLAYING OUR SONG.
BABY GOT BACK
THAT'S SO SWEET. WHEN JONAS AND I WERE DATING, OUR SONG WAS 'I WANNA HOLD YOUR HAND.'
THEN AFTER 15 YEARS OF MARRIAGE IT WAS 'WE CAN WORK IT OUT'.
NOW IT'S 'IF I HAD A HAMMER'. . .
LEE

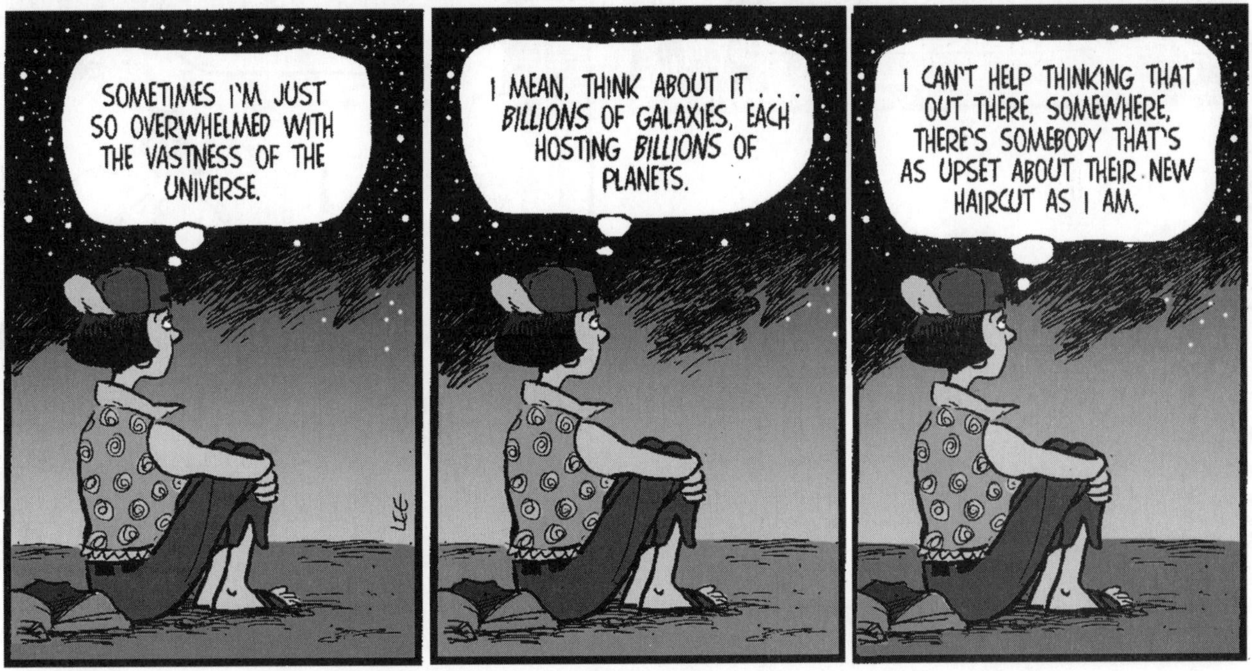
SOMETIMES I'M JUST SO OVERWHELMED WITH THE VASTNESS OF THE UNIVERSE.
LEE
I MEAN, THINK ABOUT IT . . . *BILLIONS* OF GALAXIES, EACH HOSTING *BILLIONS* OF PLANETS.
I CAN'T HELP THINKING THAT OUT THERE, SOMEWHERE, THERE'S SOMEBODY THAT'S AS UPSET ABOUT THEIR NEW HAIRCUT AS I AM.

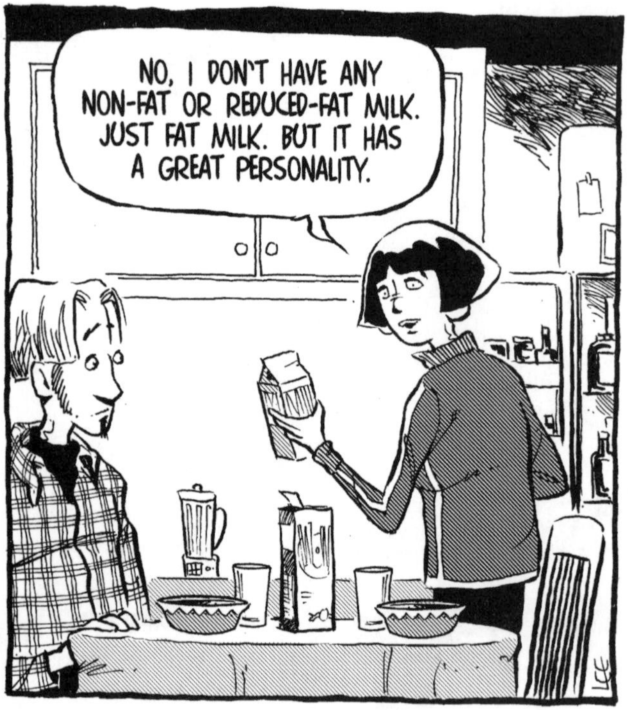
NO, I DON'T HAVE ANY NON-FAT OR REDUCED-FAT MILK. JUST FAT MILK. BUT IT HAS A GREAT PERSONALITY.
LEE

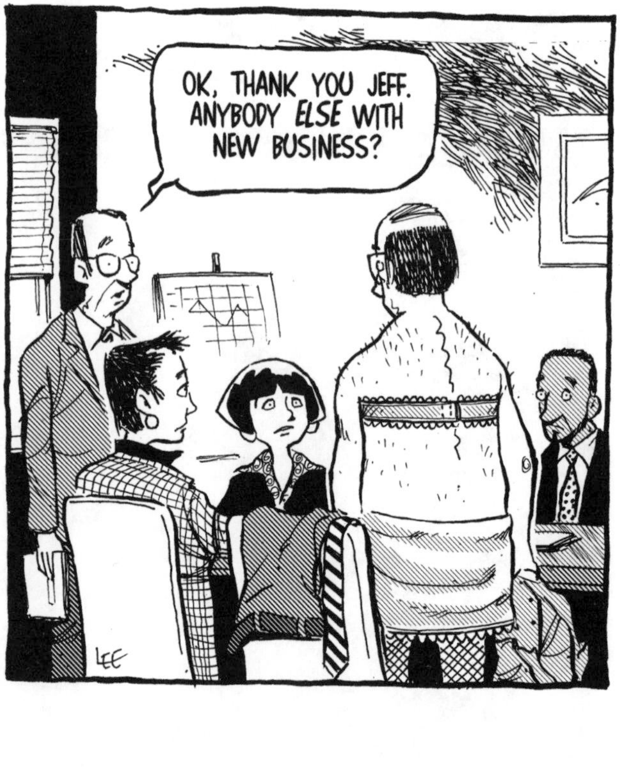
OK, THANK YOU JEFF. ANYBODY *ELSE* WITH NEW BUSINESS?
LEE

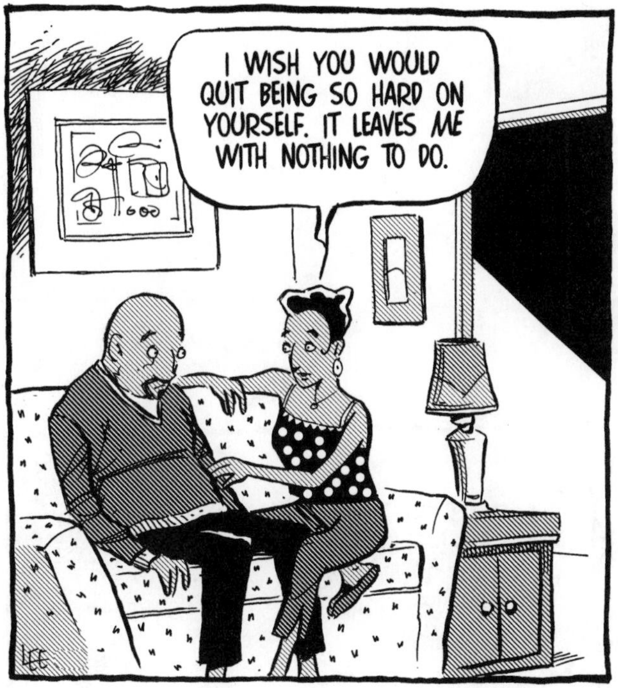
I WISH YOU WOULD QUIT BEING SO HARD ON YOURSELF. IT LEAVES ME WITH NOTHING TO DO.
LEE

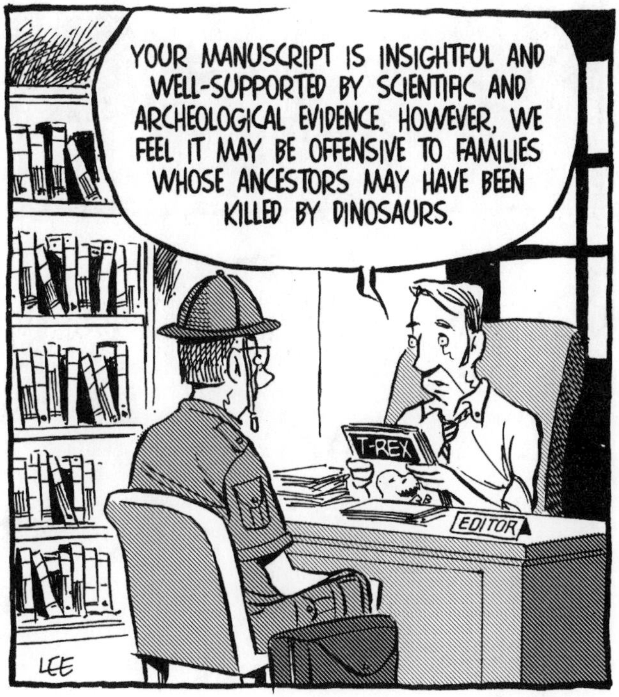
YOUR MANUSCRIPT IS INSIGHTFUL AND WELL-SUPPORTED BY SCIENTIFIC AND ARCHEOLOGICAL EVIDENCE. HOWEVER, WE FEEL IT MAY BE OFFENSIVE TO FAMILIES WHOSE ANCESTORS MAY HAVE BEEN KILLED BY DINOSAURS.
T-REX
EDITOR
LEE

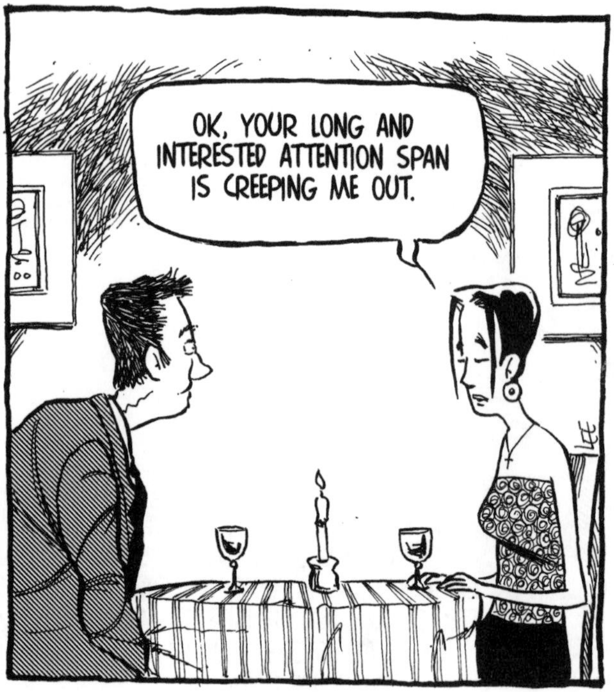
OK, YOUR LONG AND INTERESTED ATTENTION SPAN IS CREEPING ME OUT.
LEE

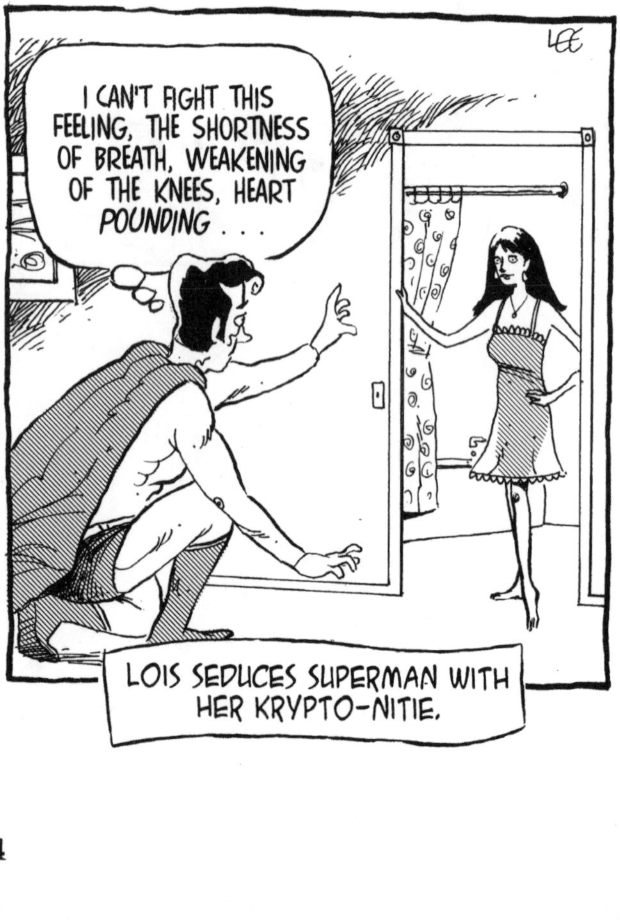
LEE
I CAN'T FIGHT THIS FEELING, THE SHORTNESS OF BREATH, WEAKENING OF THE KNEES, HEART *POUNDING* . . .

LOIS SEDUCES SUPERMAN WITH HER KRYPTO-NITIE.

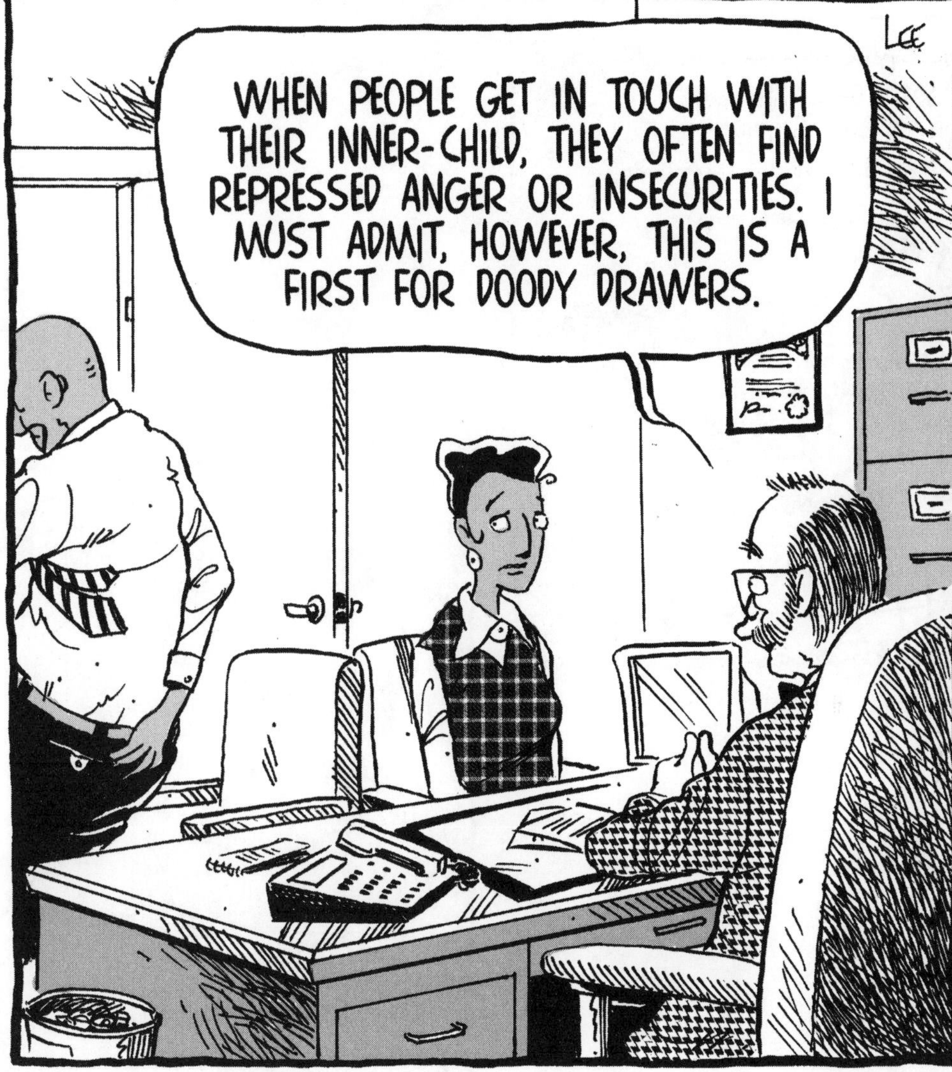
LEE
WHEN PEOPLE GET IN TOUCH WITH THEIR INNER-CHILD, THEY OFTEN FIND REPRESSED ANGER OR INSECURITIES. I MUST ADMIT, HOWEVER, THIS IS A FIRST FOR DOODY DRAWERS.

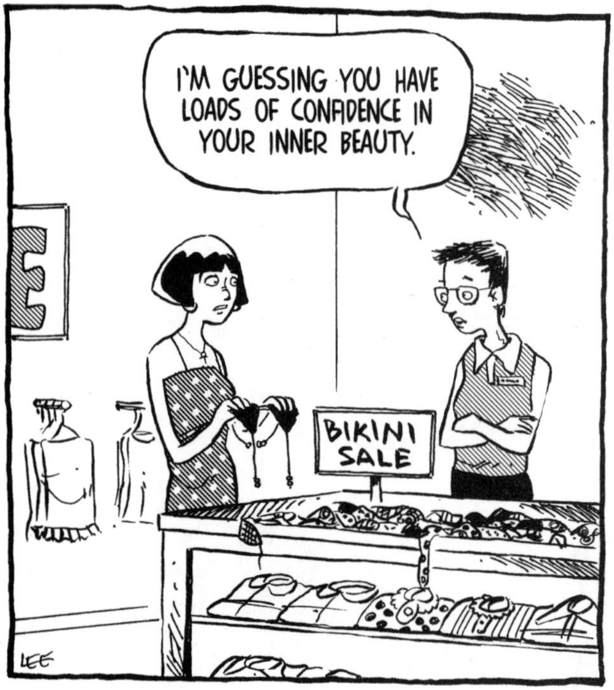
I'M GUESSING YOU HAVE LOADS OF CONFIDENCE IN YOUR INNER BEAUTY.
BIKINI SALE
LEE

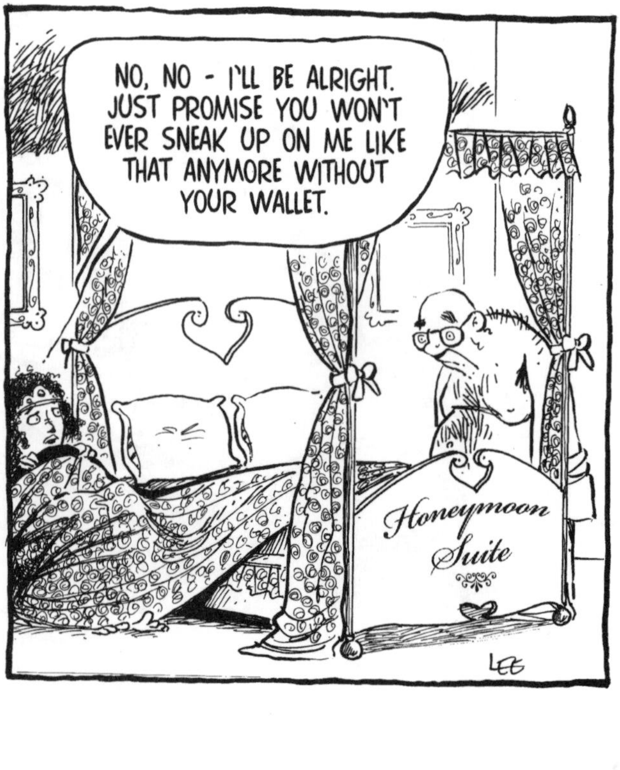
NO, NO - I'LL BE ALRIGHT. JUST PROMISE YOU WON'T EVER SNEAK UP ON ME LIKE THAT ANYMORE WITHOUT YOUR WALLET.
Honeymoon Suite
LEE

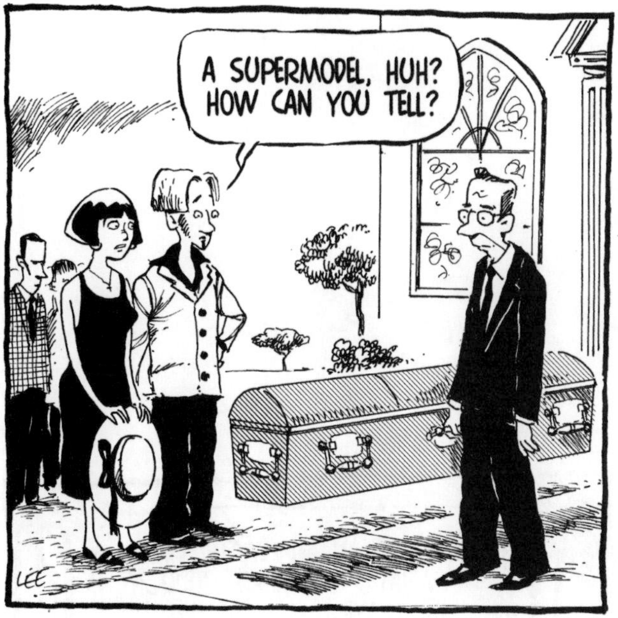
A SUPERMODEL, HUH? HOW CAN YOU TELL?
LEE

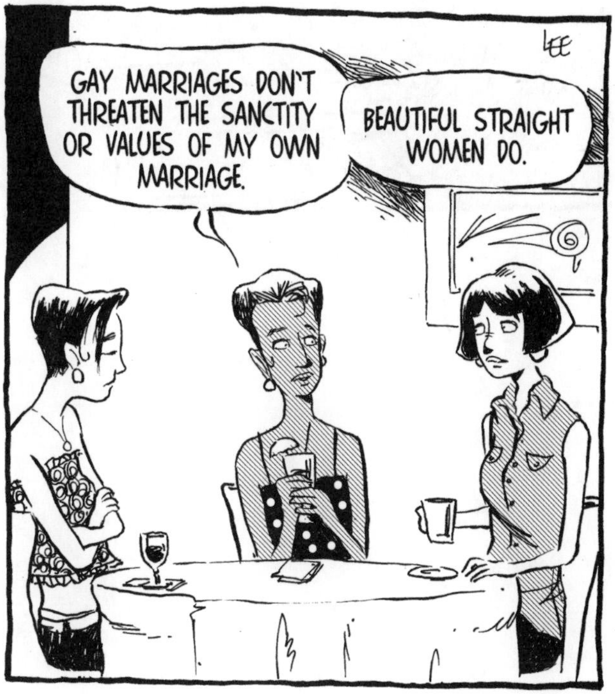
LEE
GAY MARRIAGES DON'T THREATEN THE SANCTITY OR VALUES OF MY OWN MARRIAGE.
BEAUTIFUL STRAIGHT WOMEN DO.

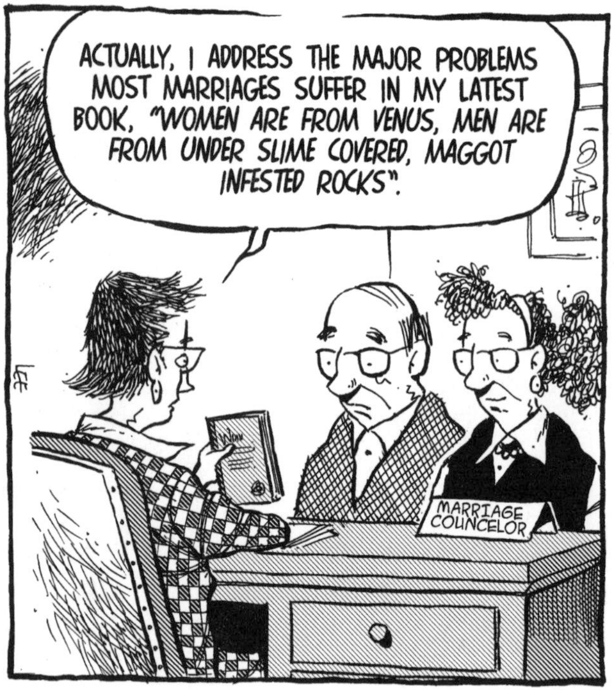
ACTUALLY, I ADDRESS THE MAJOR PROBLEMS MOST MARRIAGES SUFFER IN MY LATEST BOOK, "WOMEN ARE FROM VENUS, MEN ARE FROM UNDER SLIME COVERED, MAGGOT INFESTED ROCKS".
MARRIAGE COUNCELOR
LEE

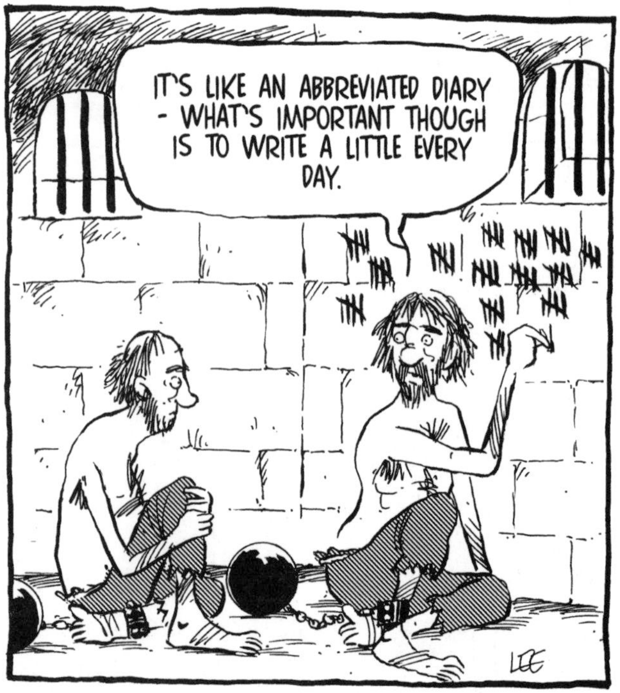
IT'S LIKE AN ABBREVIATED DIARY - WHAT'S IMPORTANT THOUGH IS TO WRITE A LITTLE EVERY DAY.
LEE

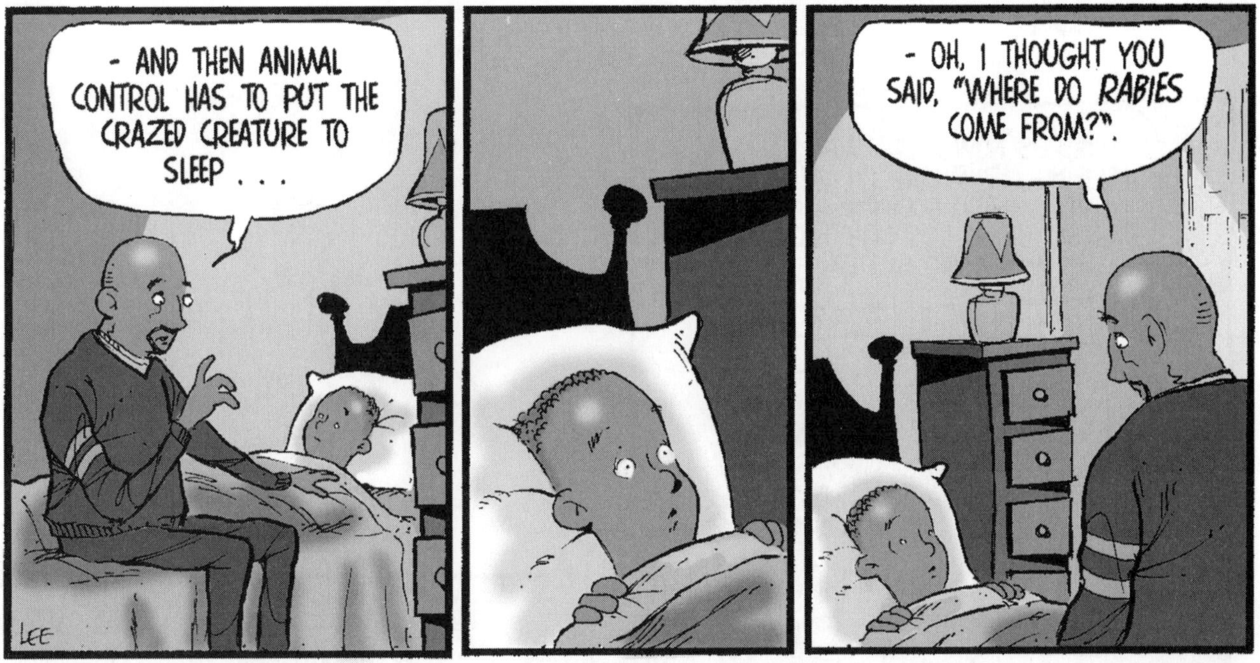
- AND THEN ANIMAL CONTROL HAS TO PUT THE CRAZED CREATURE TO SLEEP . . .
LEE
- OH, I THOUGHT YOU SAID, "WHERE DO RABIES COME FROM?".

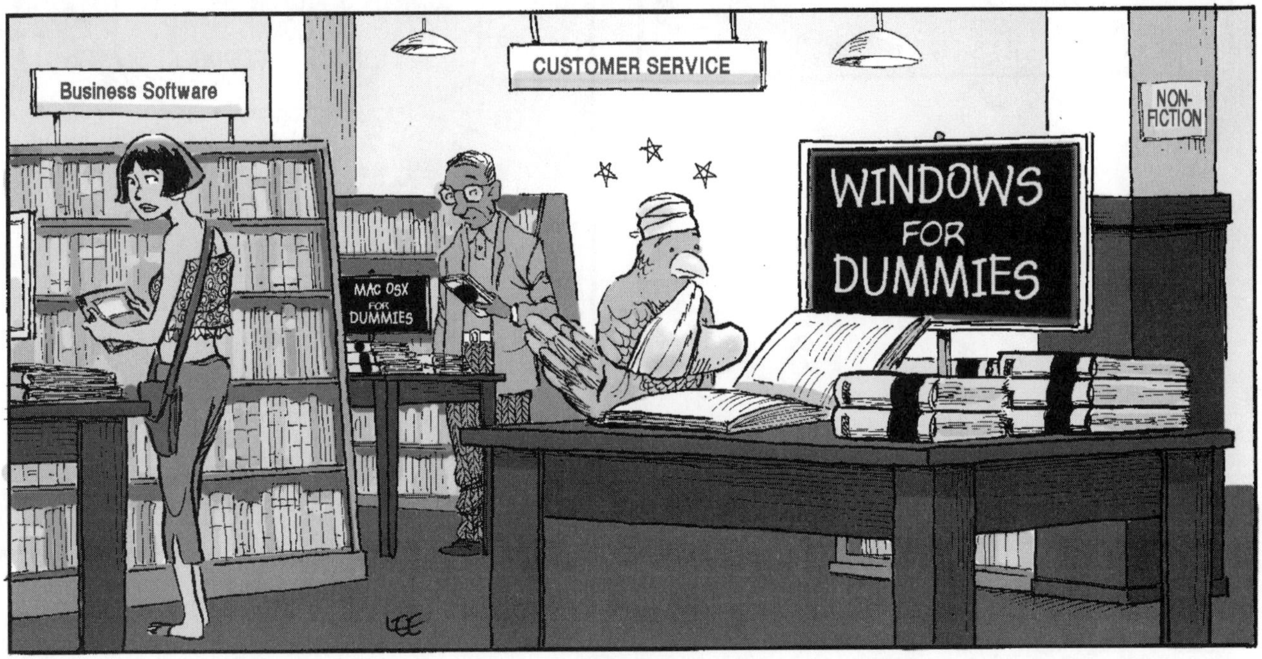
Business Software
CUSTOMER SERVICE
NON-FICTION
MAC OSX FOR DUMMIES
WINDOWS FOR DUMMIES
LEE

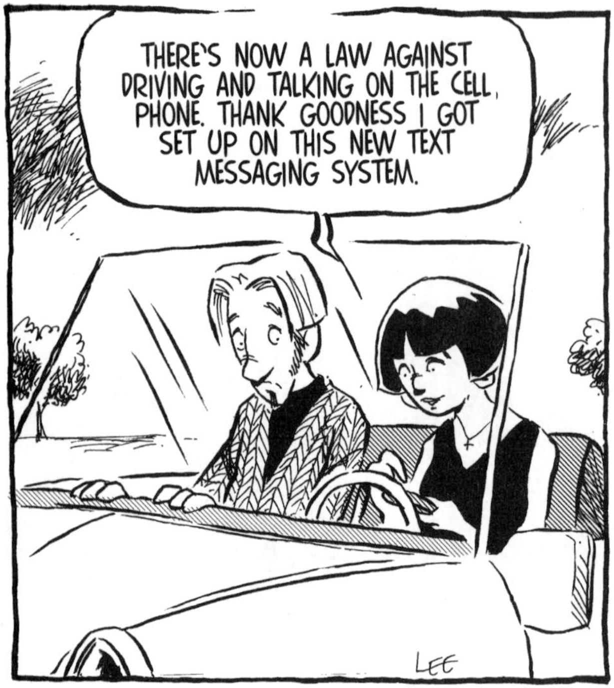
THERE'S NOW A LAW AGAINST DRIVING AND TALKING ON THE CELL PHONE. THANK GOODNESS I GOT SET UP ON THIS NEW TEXT MESSAGING SYSTEM.
LEE

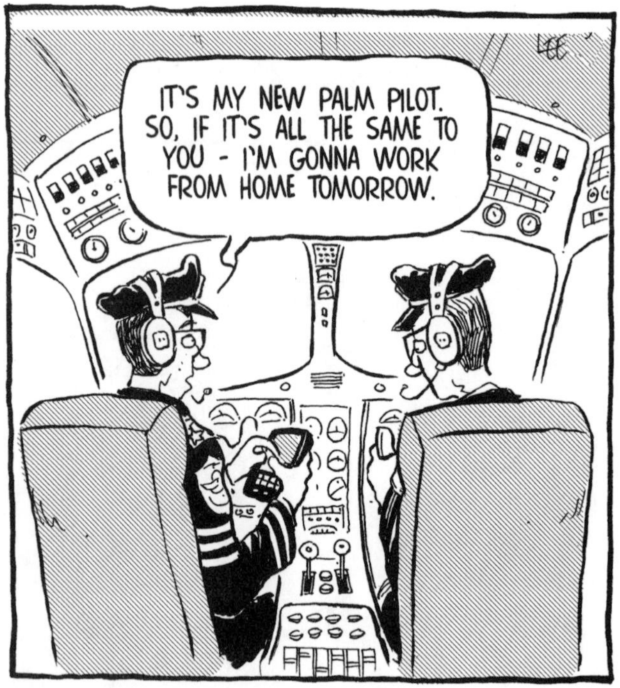
LEE
IT'S MY NEW PALM PILOT. SO, IF IT'S ALL THE SAME TO YOU - I'M GONNA WORK FROM HOME TOMORROW.

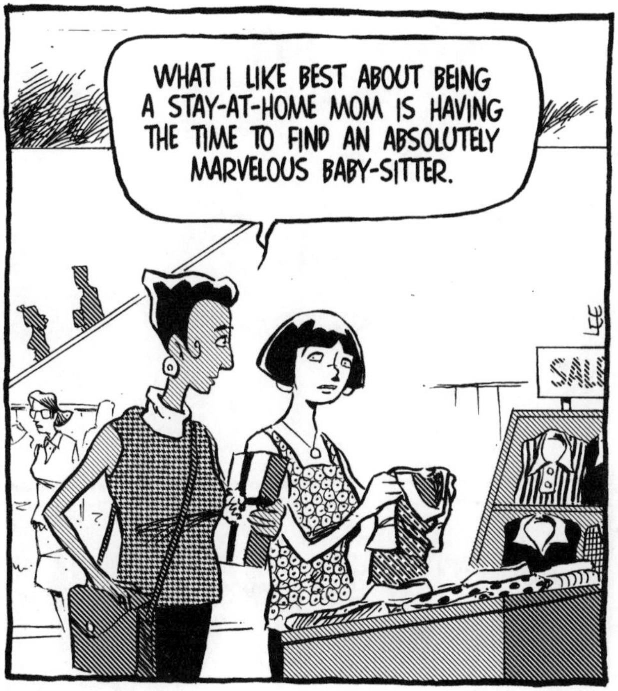
WHAT I LIKE BEST ABOUT BEING A STAY-AT-HOME MOM IS HAVING THE TIME TO FIND AN ABSOLUTELY MARVELOUS BABY-SITTER.
LEE

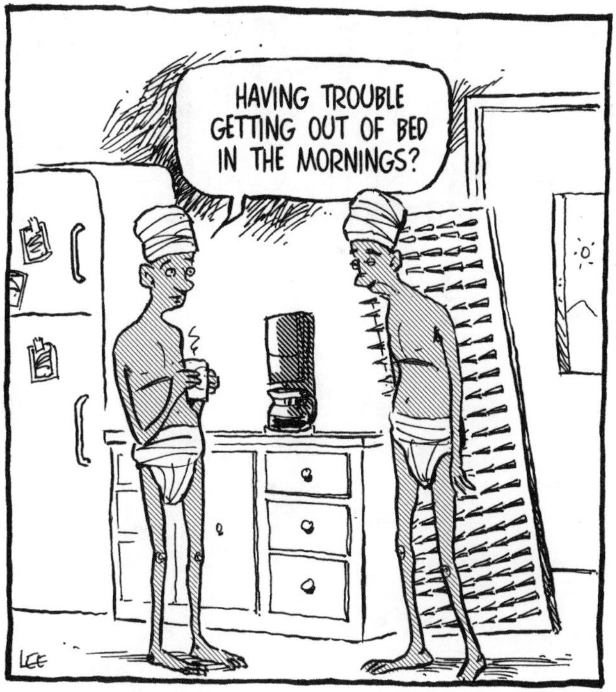
HAVING TROUBLE GETTING OUT OF BED IN THE MORNINGS?
LEE

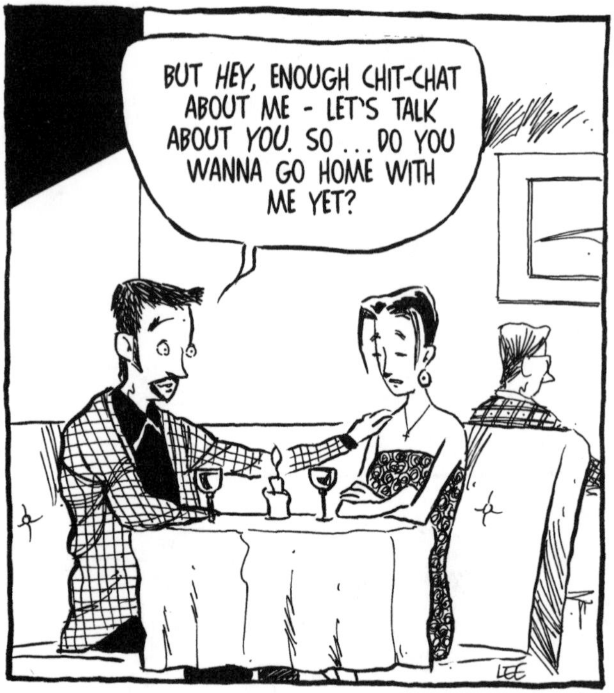
BUT HEY, ENOUGH CHIT-CHAT ABOUT ME - LET'S TALK ABOUT YOU. SO . . . DO YOU WANNA GO HOME WITH ME YET?
LEE

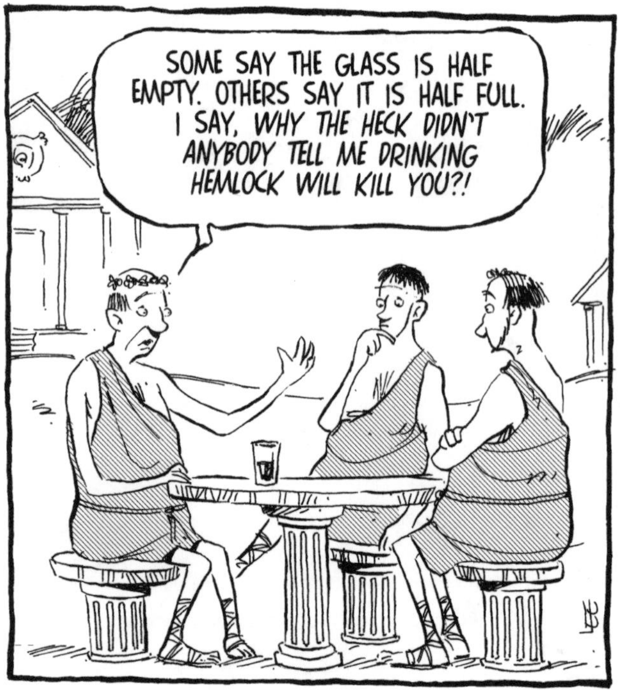
SOME SAY THE GLASS IS HALF EMPTY. OTHERS SAY IT IS HALF FULL. I SAY, WHY THE HECK DIDN'T ANYBODY TELL ME DRINKING HEMLOCK WILL KILL YOU?!

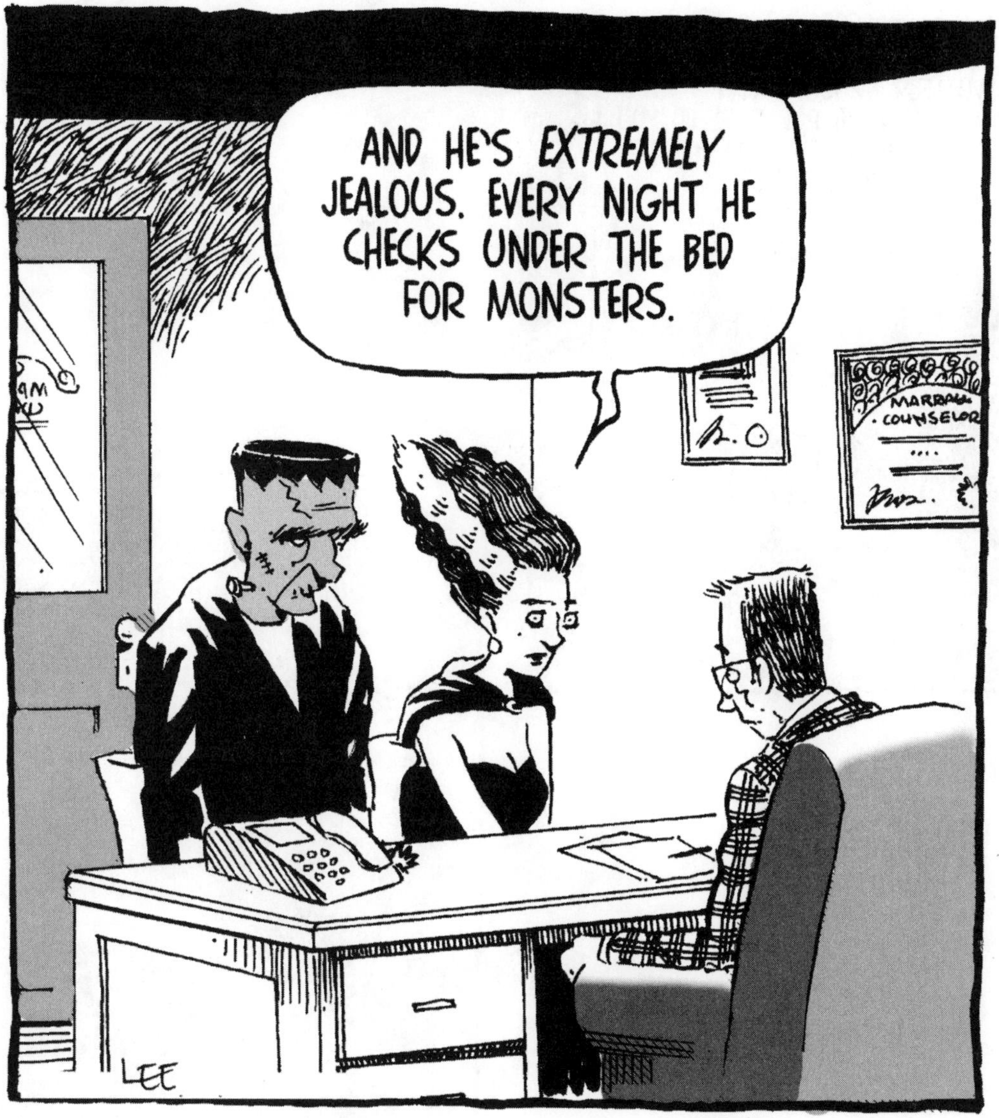
AND HE'S *EXTREMELY* JEALOUS. EVERY NIGHT HE CHECKS UNDER THE BED FOR MONSTERS.
COUNSELOR
LEE

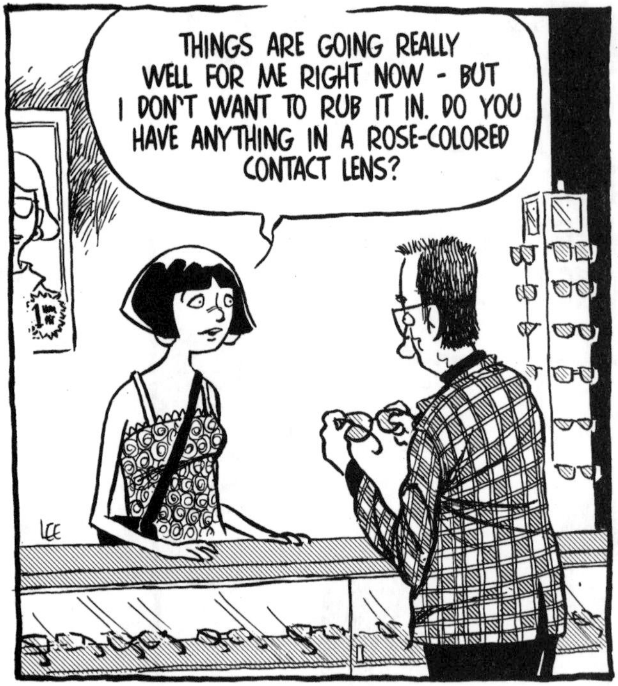
THINGS ARE GOING REALLY WELL FOR ME RIGHT NOW - BUT I DON'T WANT TO RUB IT IN. DO YOU HAVE ANYTHING IN A ROSE-COLORED CONTACT LENS?
LEE

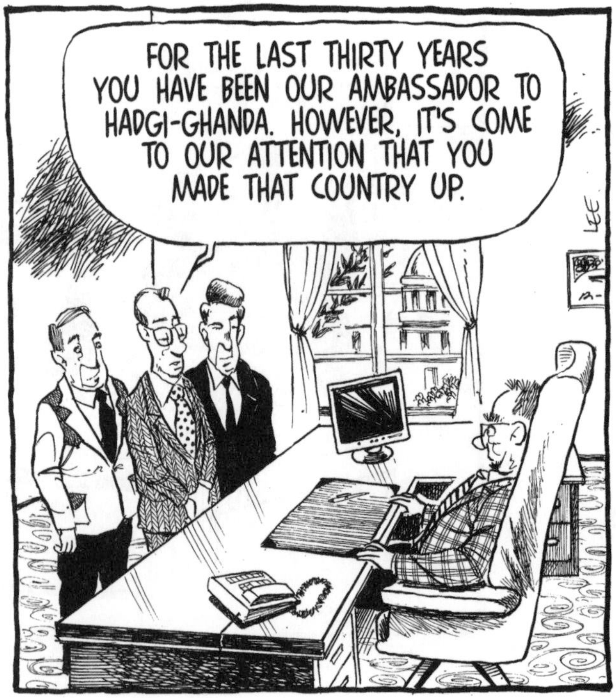
FOR THE LAST THIRTY YEARS YOU HAVE BEEN OUR AMBASSADOR TO HADGI-GHANDA. HOWEVER, IT'S COME TO OUR ATTENTION THAT YOU MADE THAT COUNTRY UP.
LEE

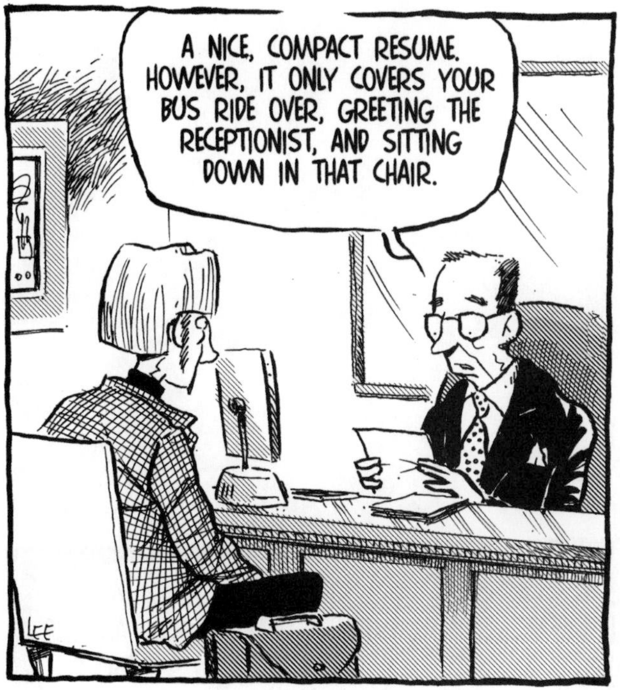
A NICE, COMPACT RESUME. HOWEVER, IT ONLY COVERS YOUR BUS RIDE OVER, GREETING THE RECEPTIONIST, AND SITTING DOWN IN THAT CHAIR.
LEE

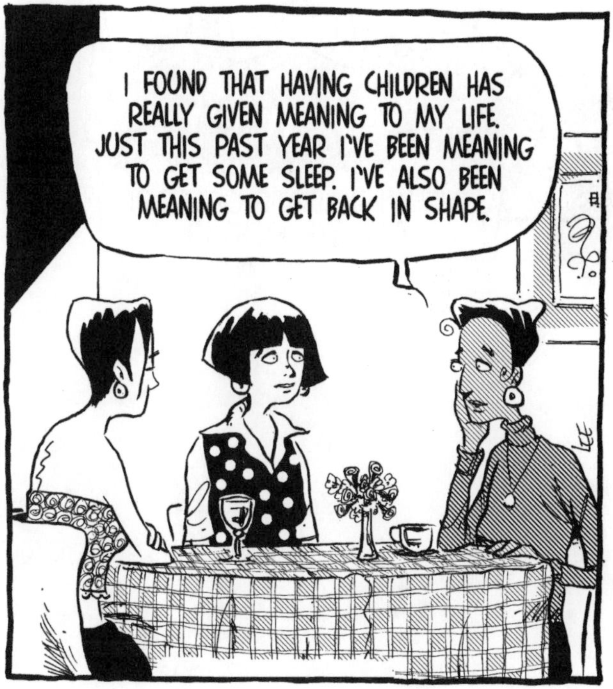
I FOUND THAT HAVING CHILDREN HAS REALLY GIVEN MEANING TO MY LIFE. JUST THIS PAST YEAR I'VE BEEN MEANING TO GET SOME SLEEP. I'VE ALSO BEEN MEANING TO GET BACK IN SHAPE.
LEE

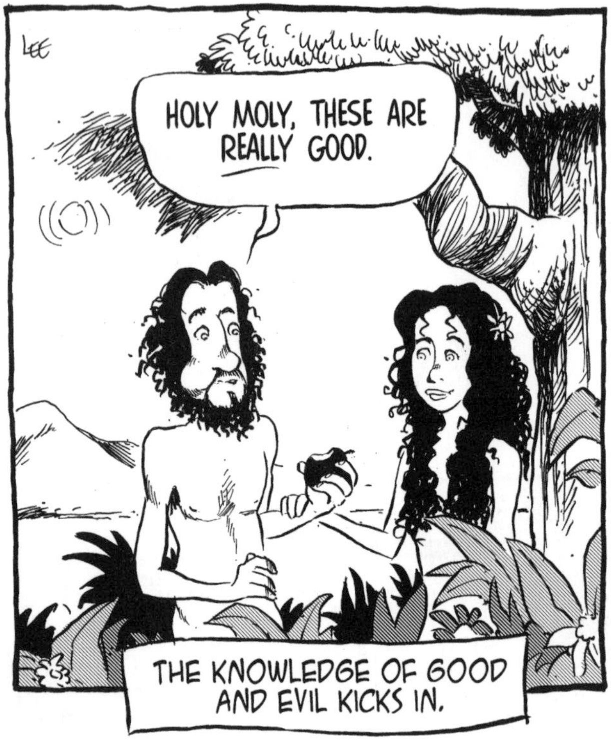
LEE
HOLY MOLY, THESE ARE REALLY GOOD.
THE KNOWLEDGE OF GOOD AND EVIL KICKS IN.

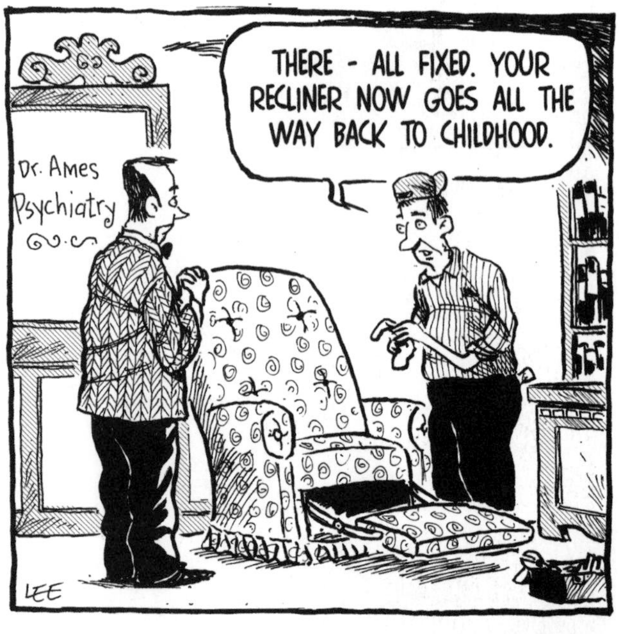
THERE - ALL FIXED. YOUR RECLINER NOW GOES ALL THE WAY BACK TO CHILDHOOD.
Dr. Ames
Psychiatry
LEE

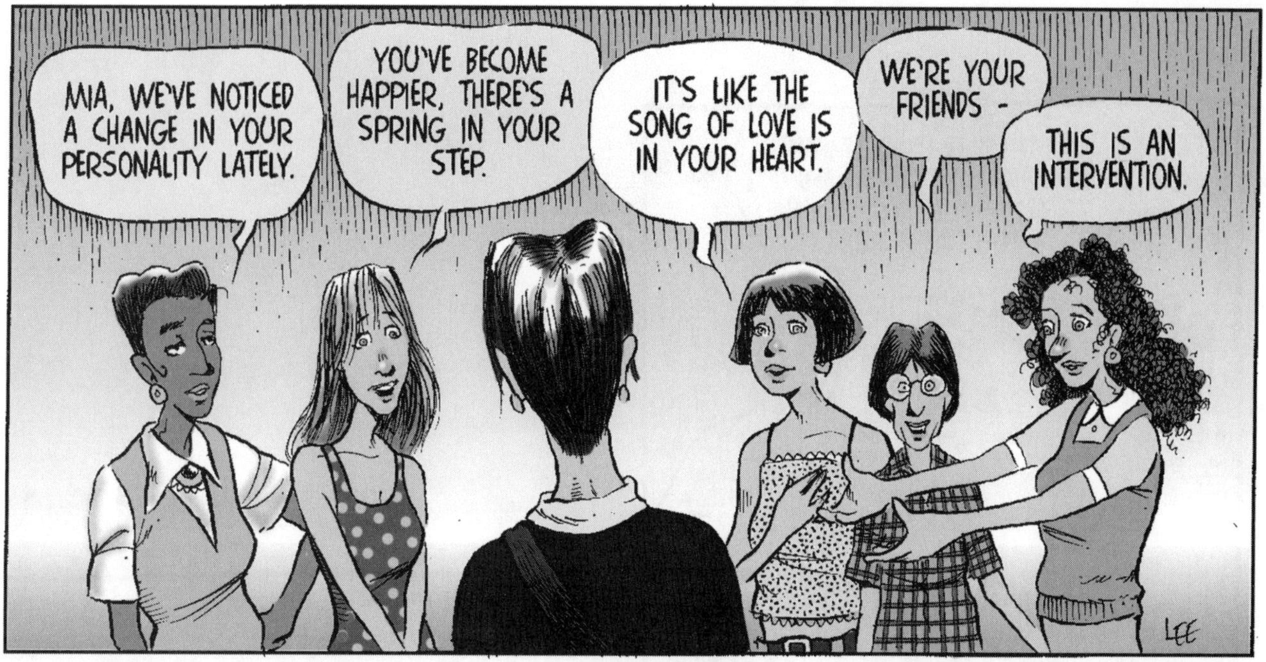
MIA, WE'VE NOTICED A CHANGE IN YOUR PERSONALITY LATELY.
YOU'VE BECOME HAPPIER, THERE'S A SPRING IN YOUR STEP.
IT'S LIKE THE SONG OF LOVE IS IN YOUR HEART.
WE'RE YOUR FRIENDS -
THIS IS AN INTERVENTION.
LEE

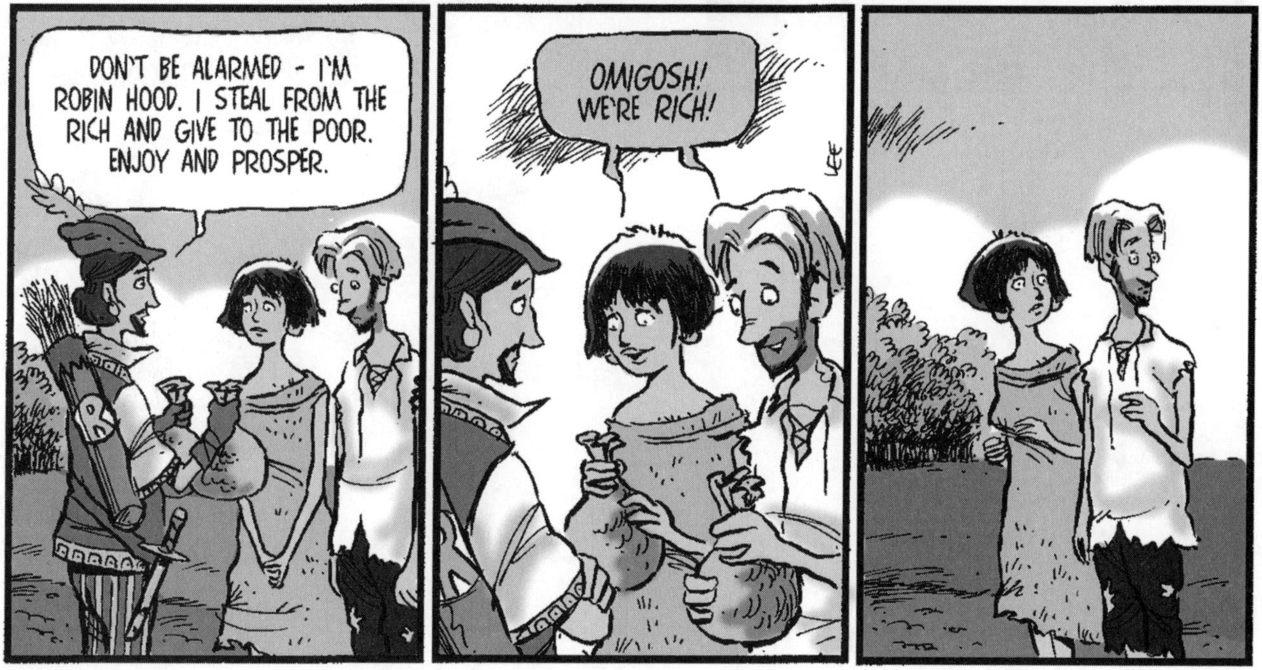
DON'T BE ALARMED - I'M ROBIN HOOD. I STEAL FROM THE RICH AND GIVE TO THE POOR. ENJOY AND PROSPER.
OMIGOSH! WE'RE RICH!
LEE

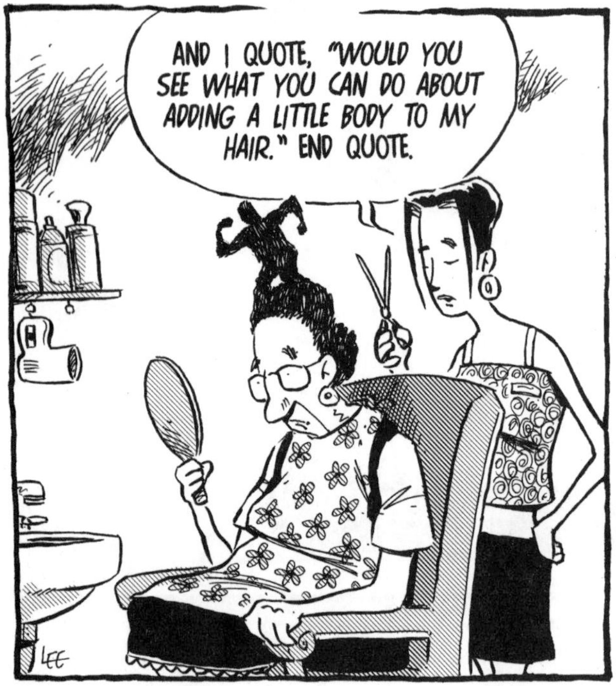
AND I QUOTE, "WOULD YOU SEE WHAT YOU CAN DO ABOUT ADDING A LITTLE BODY TO MY HAIR." END QUOTE.
LEE

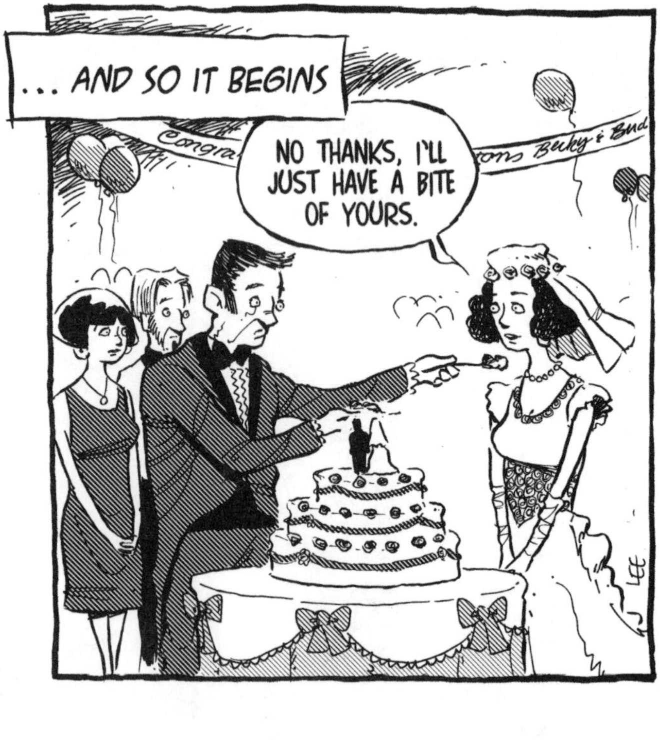
... AND SO IT BEGINS
NO THANKS, I'LL JUST HAVE A BITE OF YOURS.
LEE

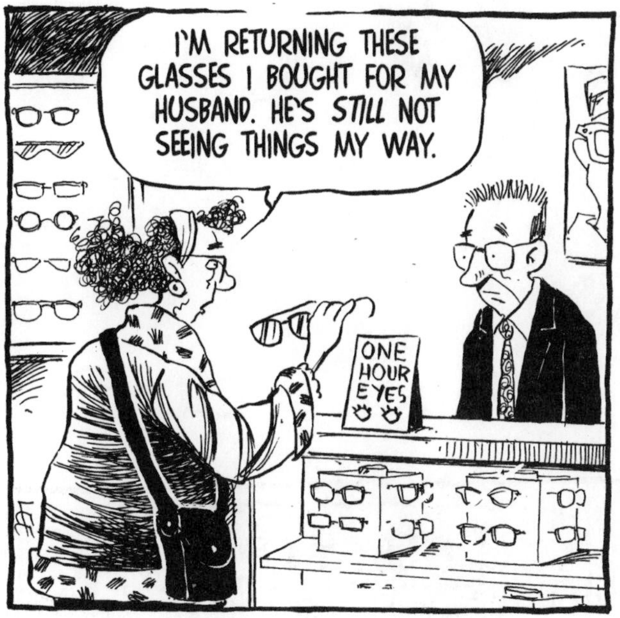
I'M RETURNING THESE GLASSES I BOUGHT FOR MY HUSBAND. HE'S *STILL* NOT SEEING THINGS MY WAY.
ONE HOUR EYES
LEE

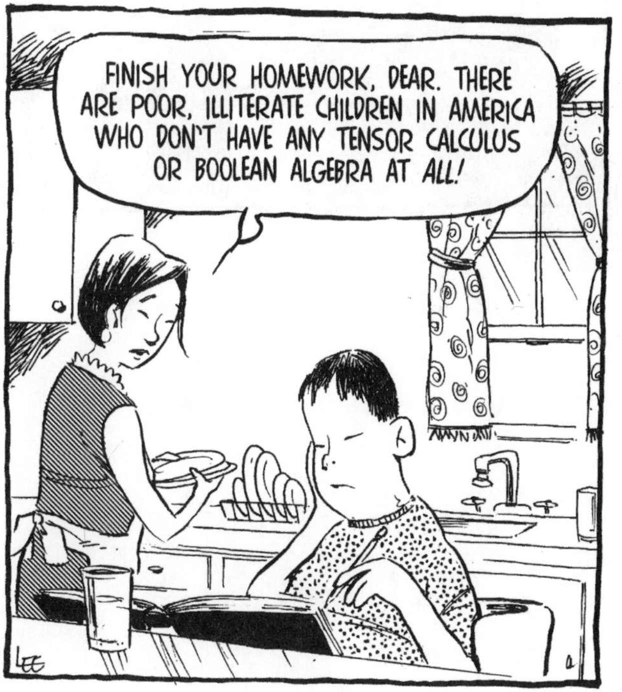
FINISH YOUR HOMEWORK, DEAR. THERE ARE POOR, ILLITERATE CHILDREN IN AMERICA WHO DON'T HAVE ANY TENSOR CALCULUS OR BOOLEAN ALGEBRA AT *ALL!*
LEE

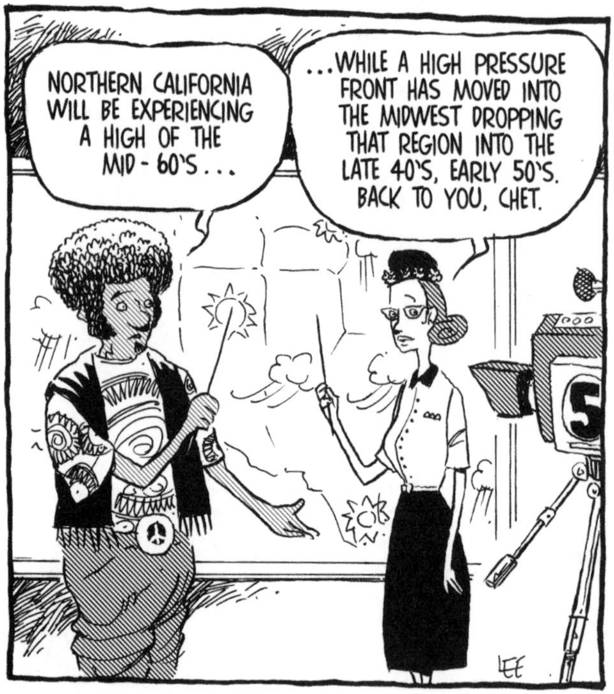
NORTHERN CALIFORNIA WILL BE EXPERIENCING A HIGH OF THE MID - 60'S...
...WHILE A HIGH PRESSURE FRONT HAS MOVED INTO THE MIDWEST DROPPING THAT REGION INTO THE LATE 40'S, EARLY 50'S. BACK TO YOU, CHET.
5
LEE

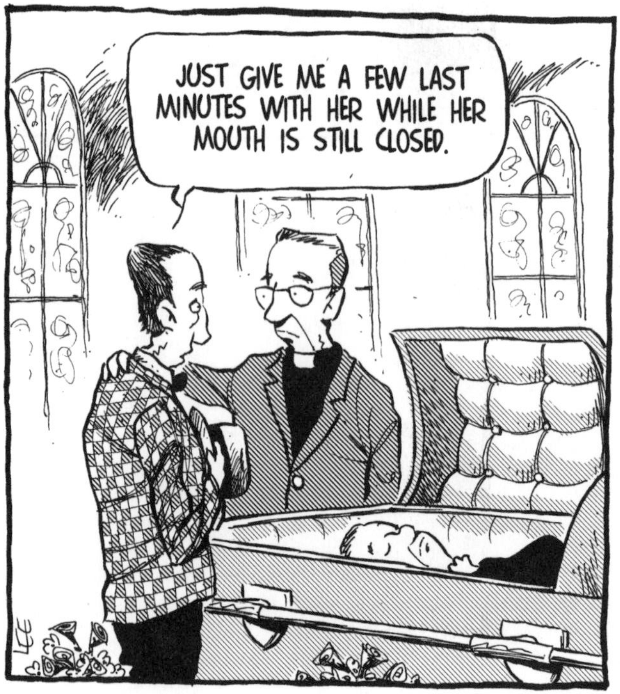
JUST GIVE ME A FEW LAST MINUTES WITH HER WHILE HER MOUTH IS STILL CLOSED.
LEE

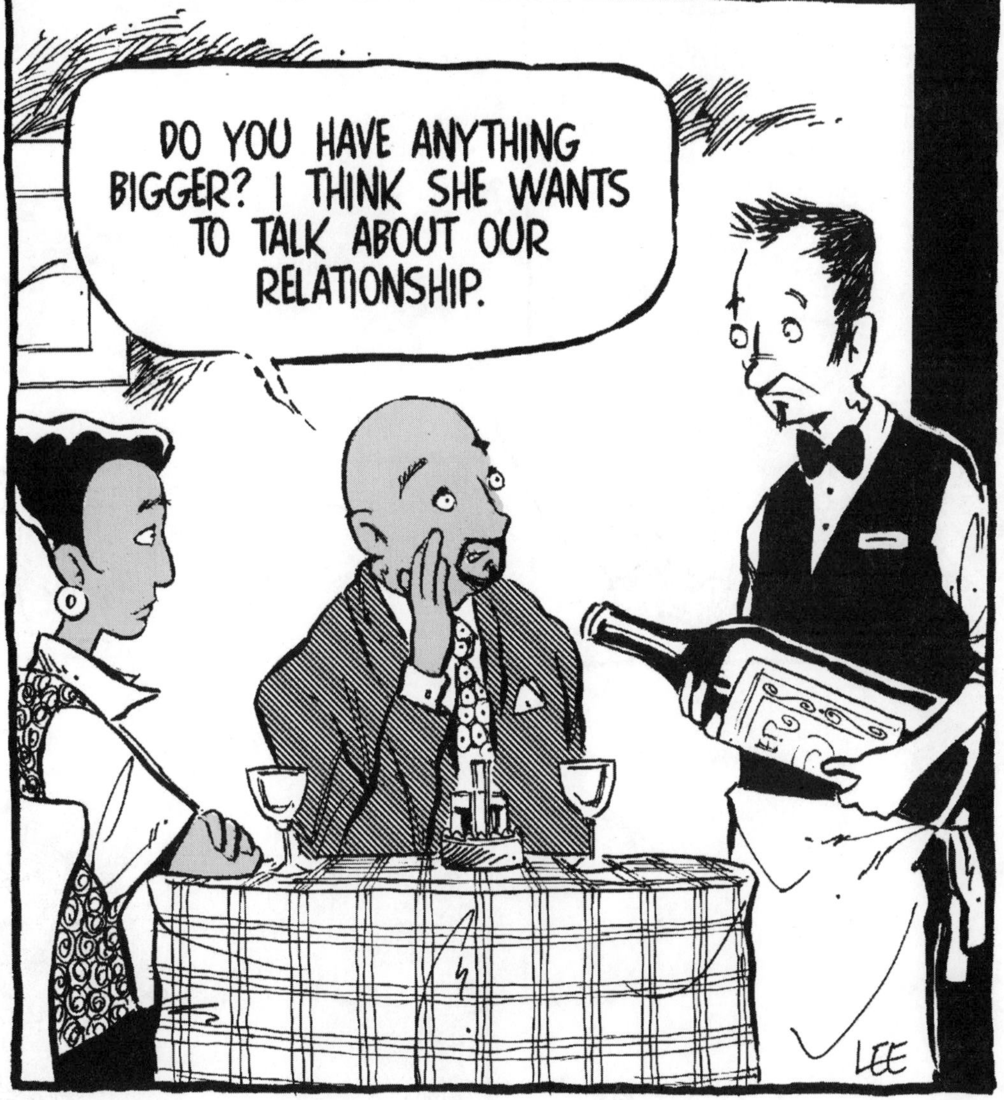
DO YOU HAVE ANYTHING BIGGER? I THINK SHE WANTS TO TALK ABOUT OUR RELATIONSHIP.
LEE

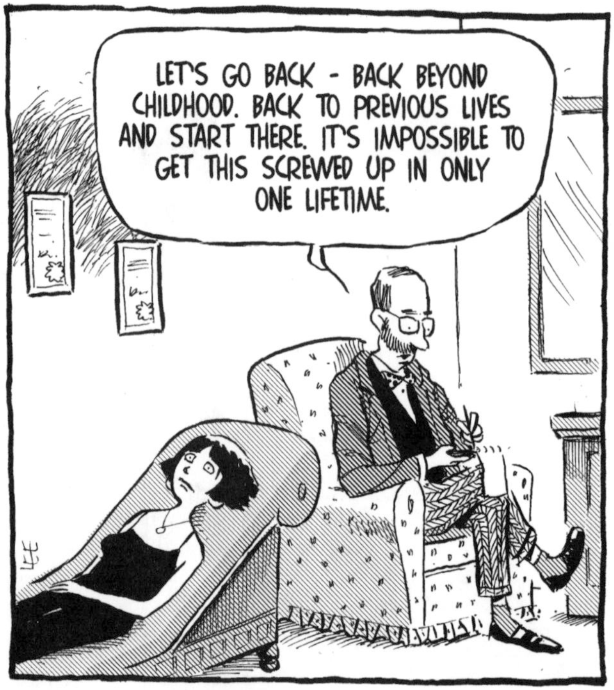
LET'S GO BACK - BACK BEYOND CHILDHOOD. BACK TO PREVIOUS LIVES AND START THERE. IT'S IMPOSSIBLE TO GET THIS SCREWED UP IN ONLY ONE LIFETIME.

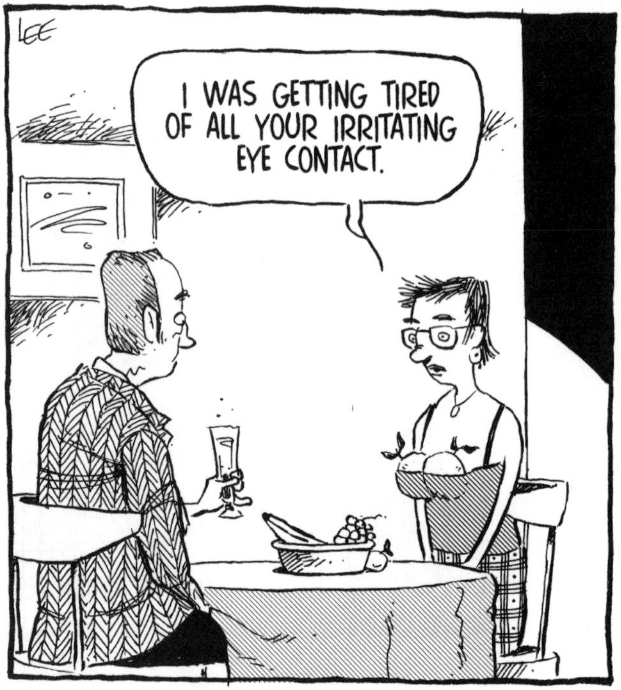
LEE
I WAS GETTING TIRED OF ALL YOUR IRRITATING EYE CONTACT.

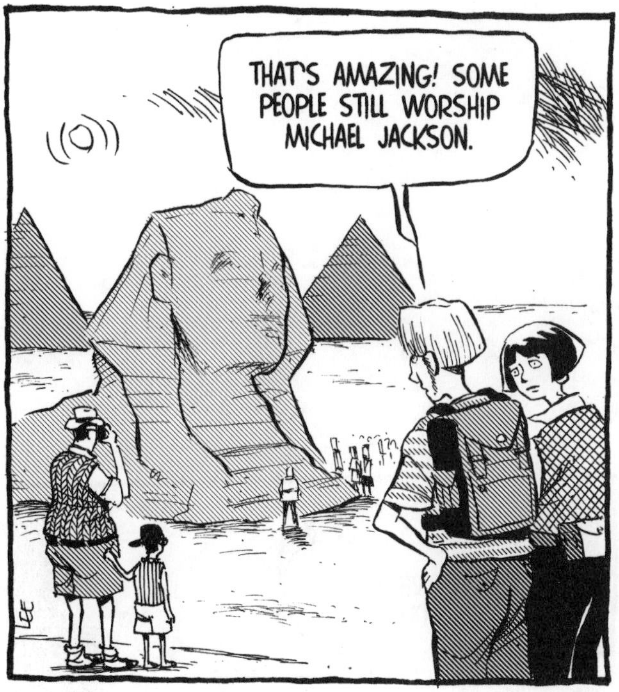
THAT'S AMAZING! SOME PEOPLE STILL WORSHIP MICHAEL JACKSON.
LEE

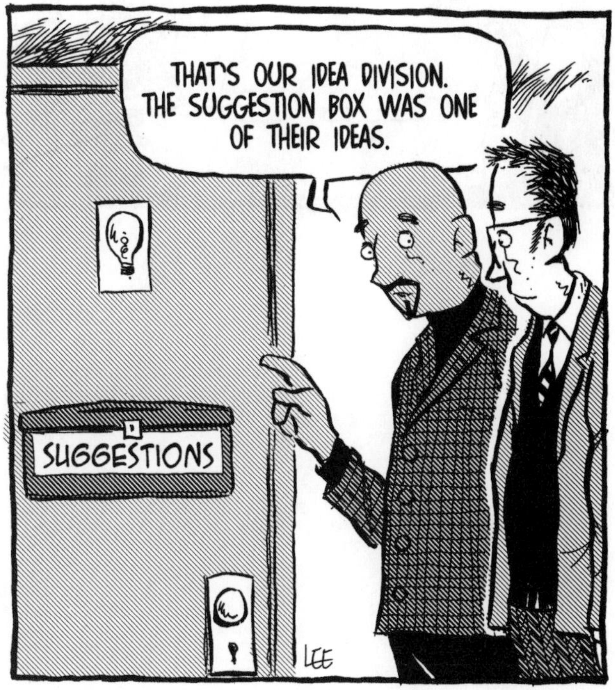
THAT'S OUR IDEA DIVISION. THE SUGGESTION BOX WAS ONE OF THEIR IDEAS.
SUGGESTIONS
LEE

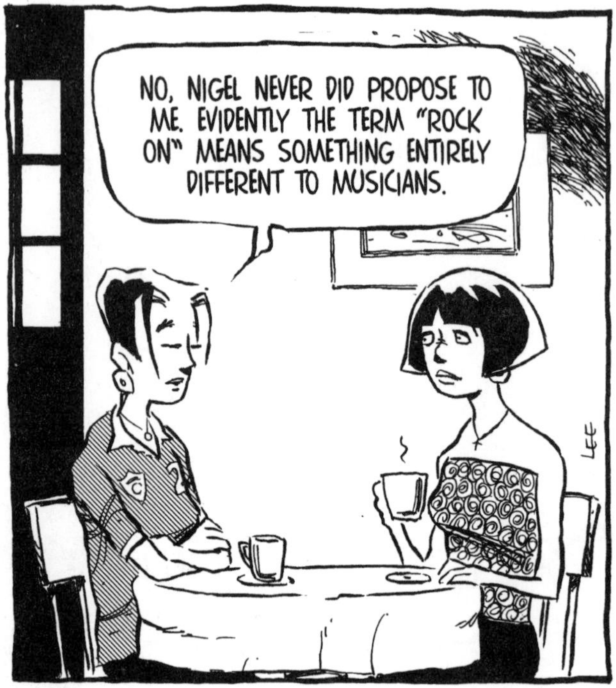
NO, NIGEL NEVER DID PROPOSE TO ME. EVIDENTLY THE TERM "ROCK ON" MEANS SOMETHING ENTIRELY DIFFERENT TO MUSICIANS.

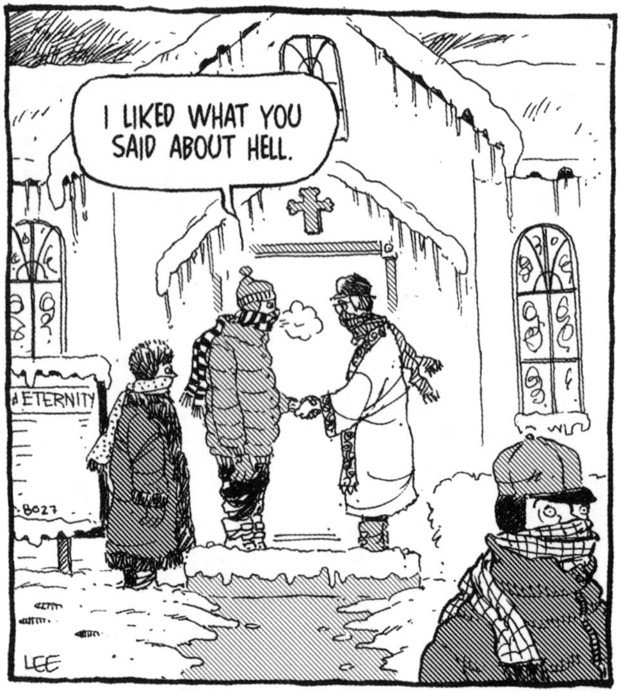
I LIKED WHAT YOU SAID ABOUT HELL.
ETERNITY

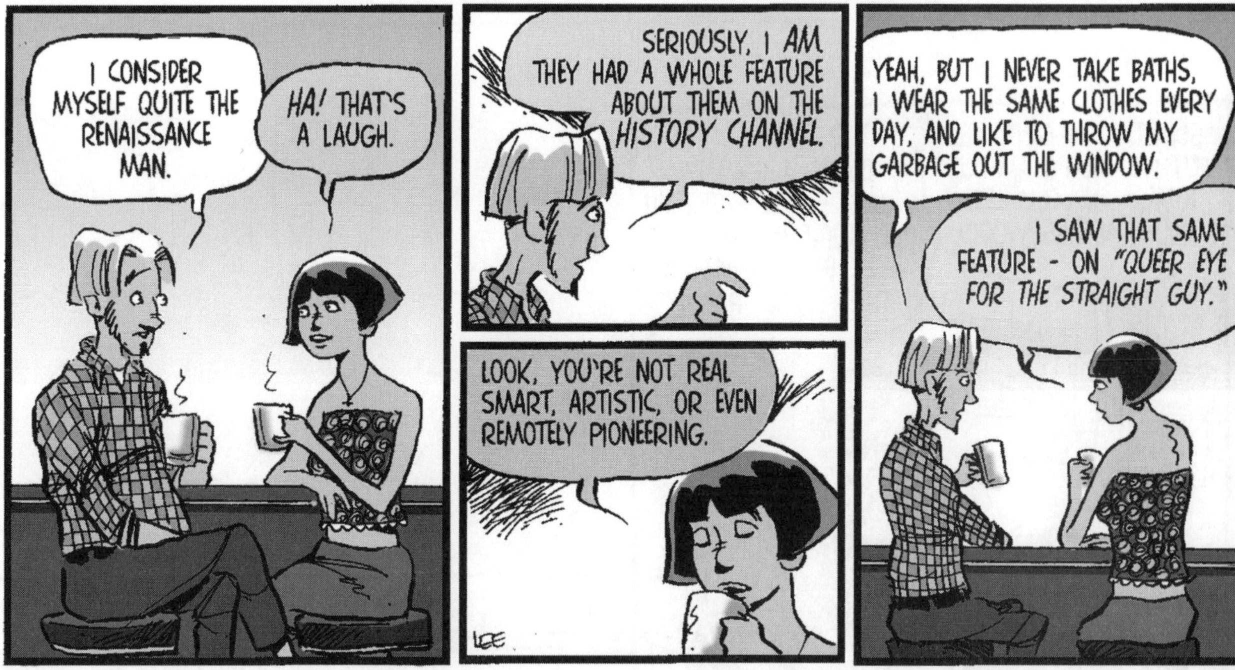
I CONSIDER MYSELF QUITE THE RENAISSANCE MAN.
HA! THAT'S A LAUGH.
SERIOUSLY, I AM. THEY HAD A WHOLE FEATURE ABOUT THEM ON THE HISTORY CHANNEL.
LOOK, YOU'RE NOT REAL SMART, ARTISTIC, OR EVEN REMOTELY PIONEERING.
LEE
YEAH, BUT I NEVER TAKE BATHS, I WEAR THE SAME CLOTHES EVERY DAY, AND LIKE TO THROW MY GARBAGE OUT THE WINDOW.
I SAW THAT SAME FEATURE - ON "QUEER EYE FOR THE STRAIGHT GUY."

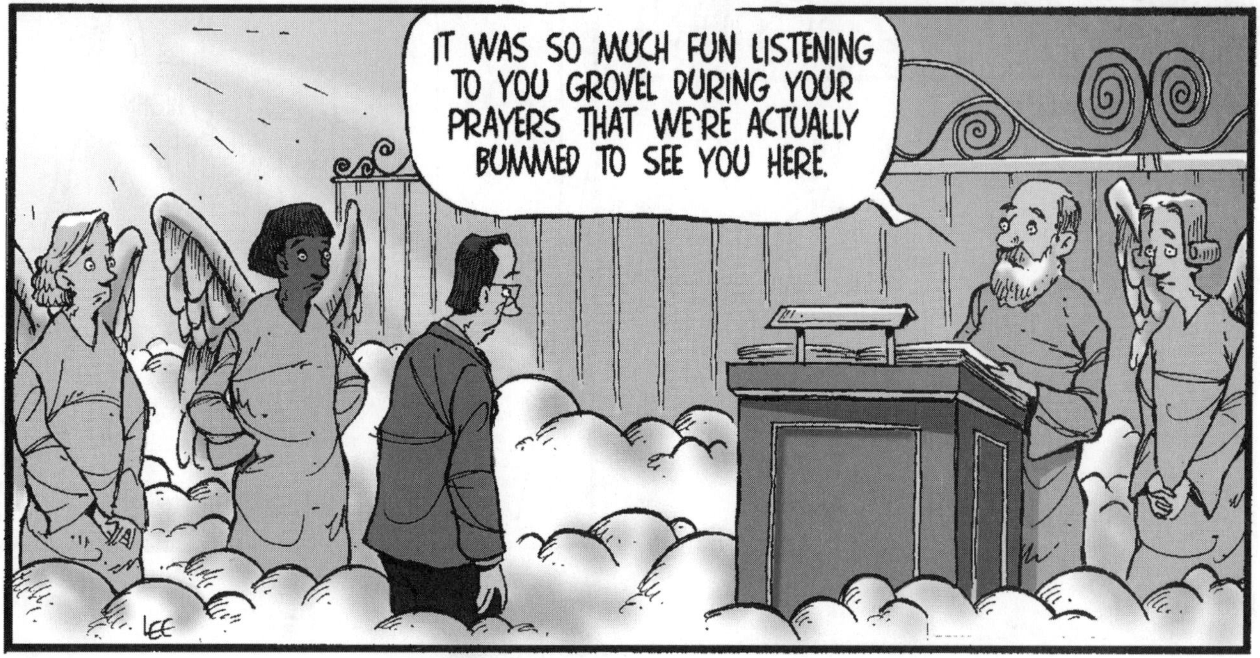
IT WAS SO MUCH FUN LISTENING TO YOU GROVEL DURING YOUR PRAYERS THAT WE'RE ACTUALLY BUMMED TO SEE YOU HERE.
LEE

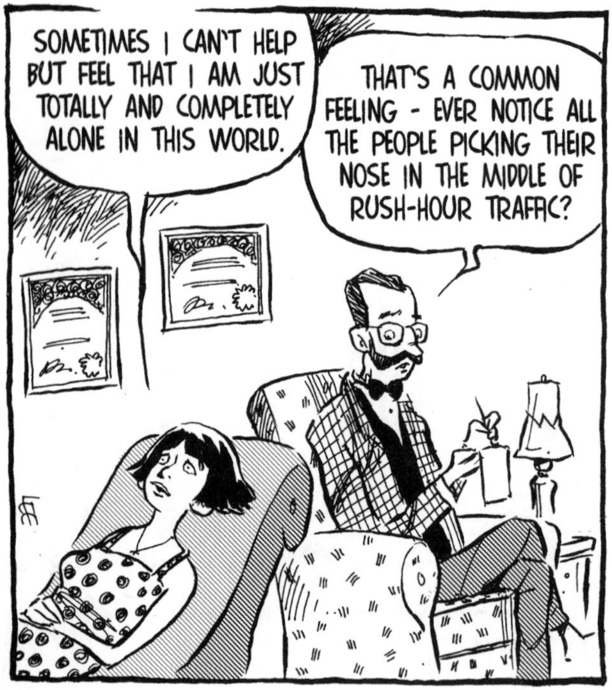
SOMETIMES I CAN'T HELP BUT FEEL THAT I AM JUST TOTALLY AND COMPLETELY ALONE IN THIS WORLD.
THAT'S A COMMON FEELING - EVER NOTICE ALL THE PEOPLE PICKING THEIR NOSE IN THE MIDDLE OF RUSH-HOUR TRAFFIC?
LEE

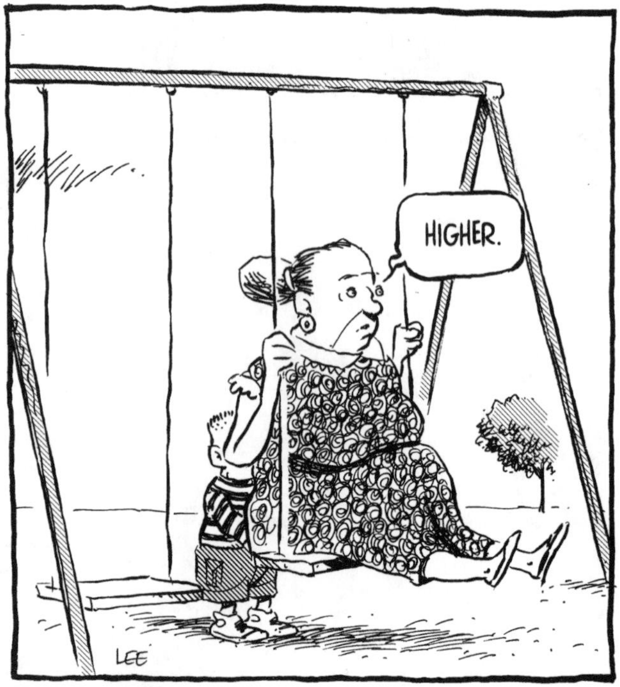
HIGHER.
LEE

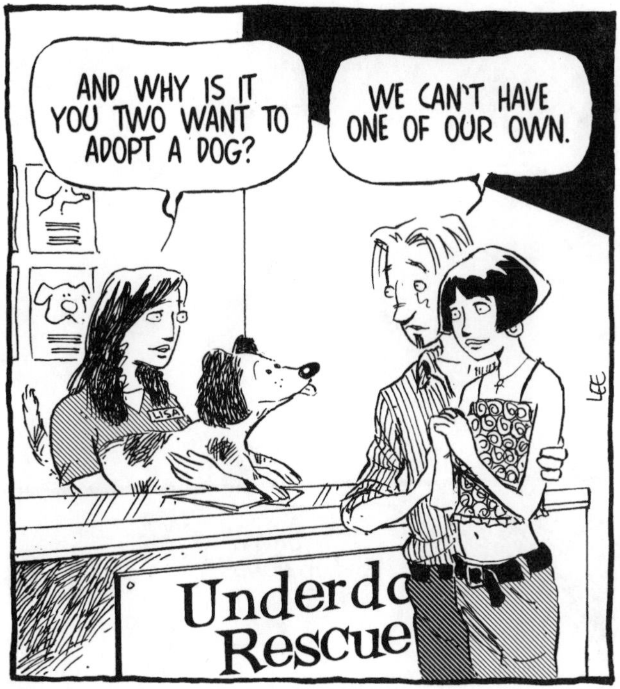
AND WHY IS IT YOU TWO WANT TO ADOPT A DOG?
WE CAN'T HAVE ONE OF OUR OWN.
LISA
Underdo
Rescue
LEE

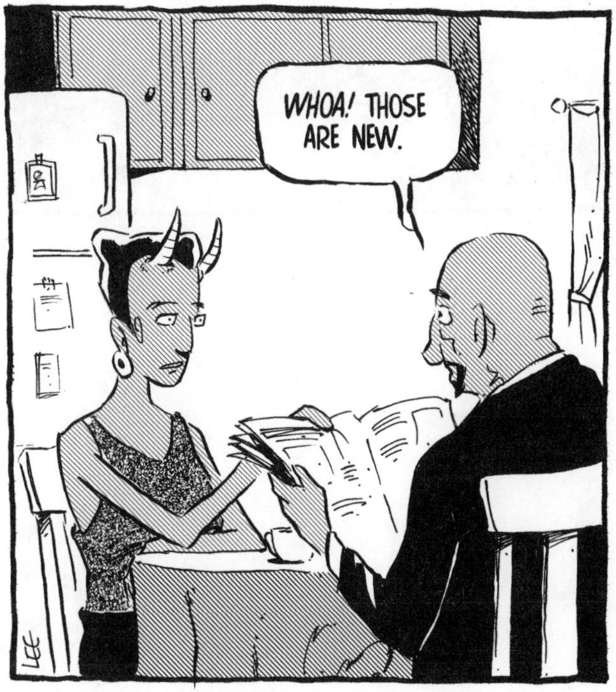
WHOA! THOSE ARE NEW.
LEE

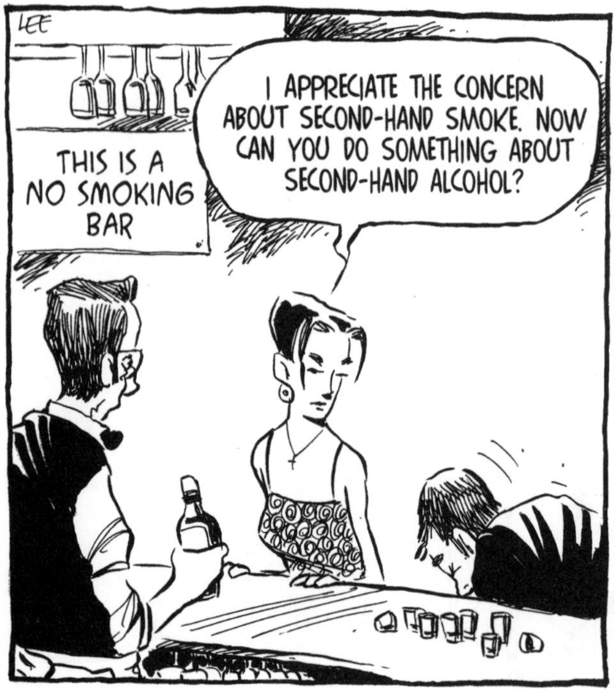
LEE
THIS IS A NO SMOKING BAR
I APPRECIATE THE CONCERN ABOUT SECOND-HAND SMOKE. NOW CAN YOU DO SOMETHING ABOUT SECOND-HAND ALCOHOL?

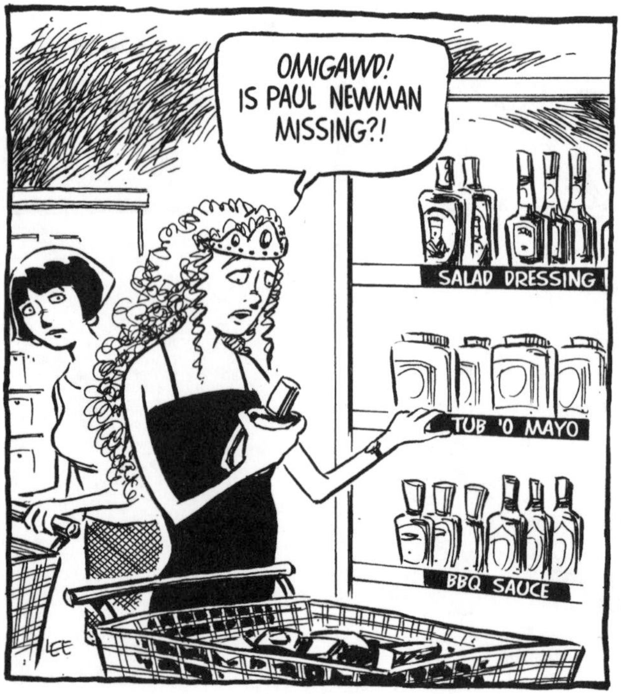
OMIGAWD! IS PAUL NEWMAN MISSING?!
SALAD DRESSING
TUB 'O MAYO
BBQ SAUCE
LEE

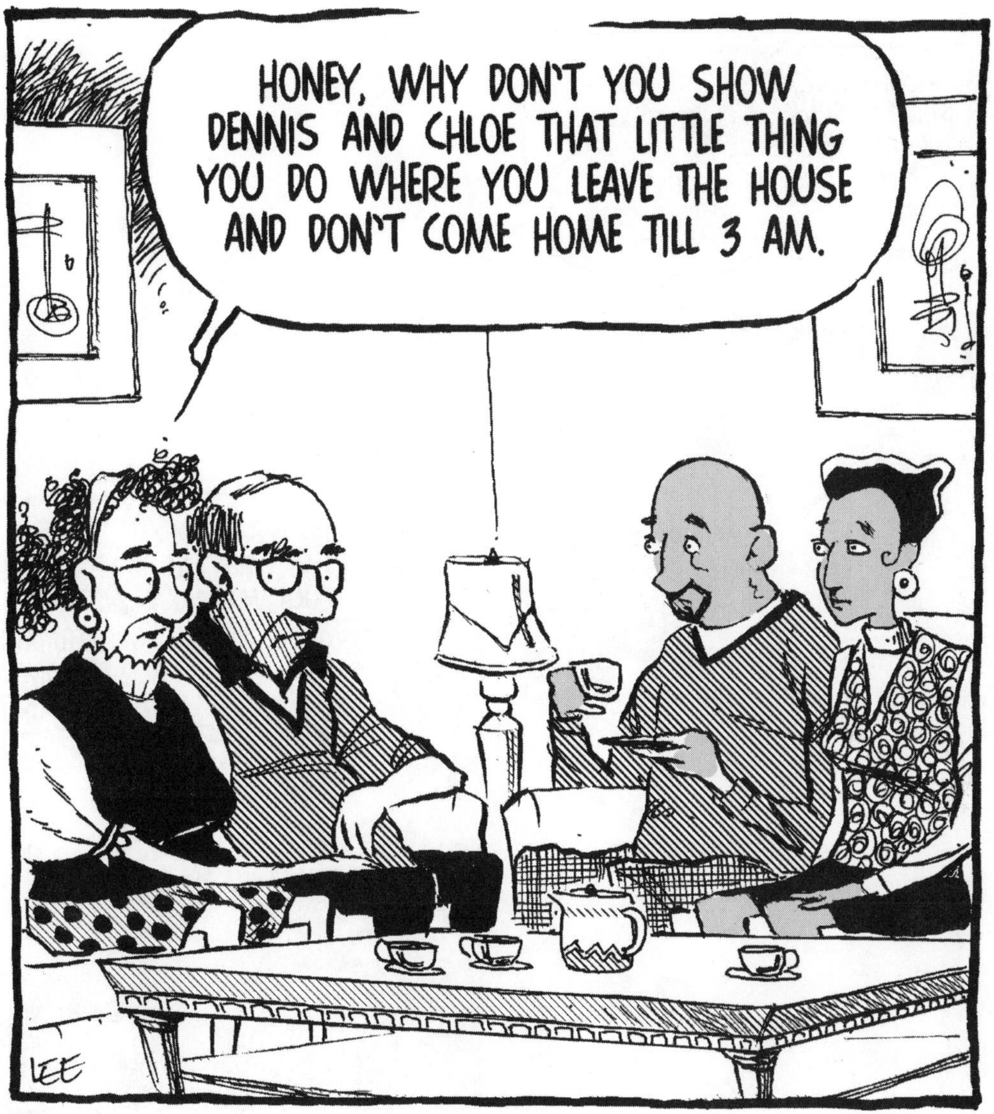
HONEY, WHY DON'T YOU SHOW DENNIS AND CHLOE THAT LITTLE THING YOU DO WHERE YOU LEAVE THE HOUSE AND DON'T COME HOME TILL 3 AM.
LEE

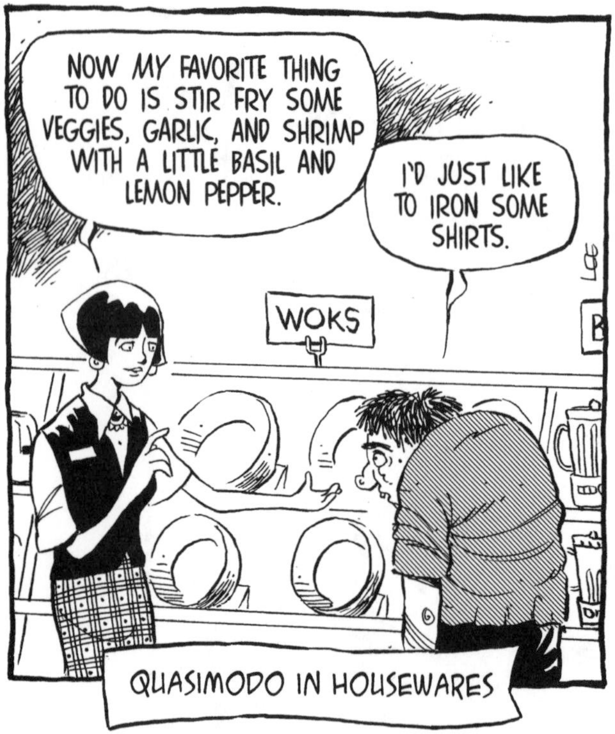
NOW MY FAVORITE THING TO DO IS STIR FRY SOME VEGGIES, GARLIC, AND SHRIMP WITH A LITTLE BASIL AND LEMON PEPPER.
I'D JUST LIKE TO IRON SOME SHIRTS.
WOKS
LEE
QUASIMODO IN HOUSEWARES

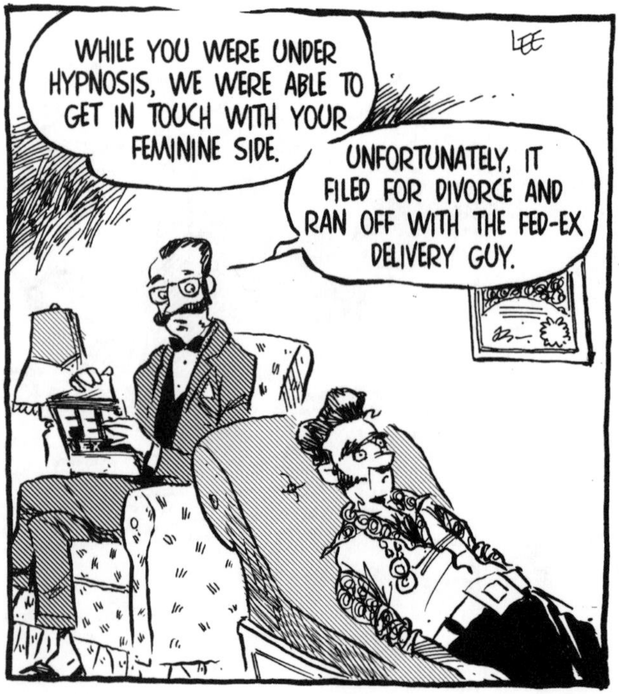
WHILE YOU WERE UNDER HYPNOSIS, WE WERE ABLE TO GET IN TOUCH WITH YOUR FEMININE SIDE.
UNFORTUNATELY, IT FILED FOR DIVORCE AND RAN OFF WITH THE FED-EX DELIVERY GUY.
LEE

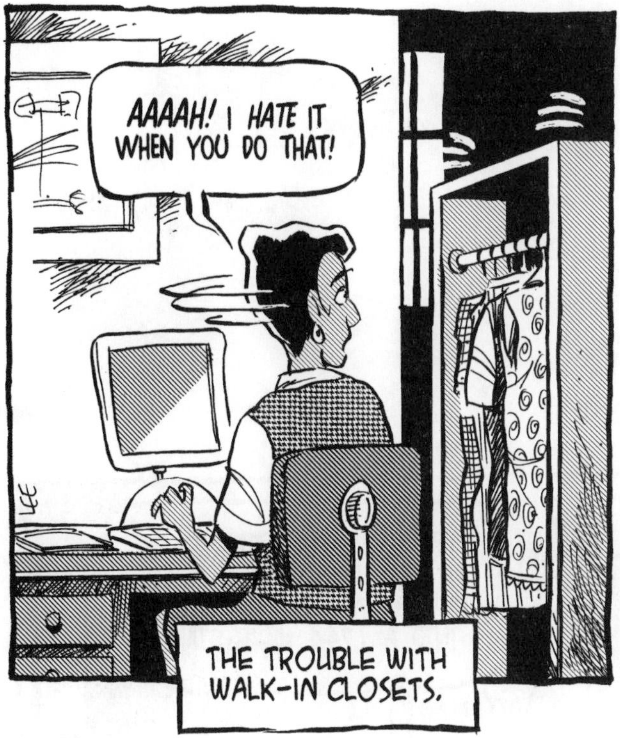
AAAAH! I HATE IT WHEN YOU DO THAT!
LEE
THE TROUBLE WITH WALK-IN CLOSETS.

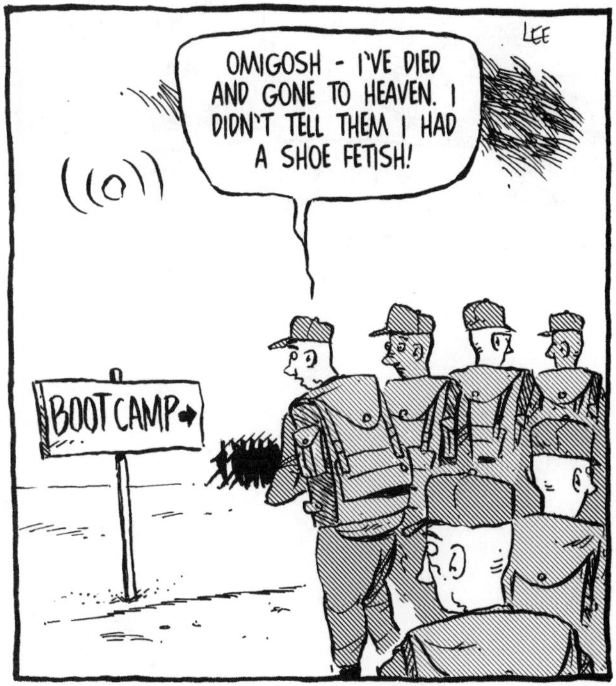
LEE
OMIGOSH - I'VE DIED AND GONE TO HEAVEN. I DIDN'T TELL THEM I HAD A SHOE FETISH!
BOOT CAMP

LEE
I WOULDN'T GET TOO CLOSE, THEY LOOK PRETTY MEAN. WHY DON'T YOU STEP BACK OVER HERE JUST A LITTLE . . .
THE WITNESS RELOCATION PROGRAM: THE EARLY YEARS.

I FEEL LIKE SUCH A TRAMP. THE BAR WAS DARK, I WAS LONELY, AND I LET A STRANGER TALK ME INTO A 9,744 NIGHT-STAND.
Marriage Counselor
DR DEIDER
LEE

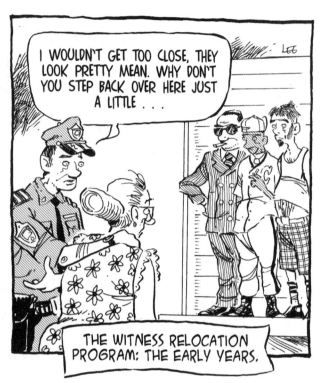

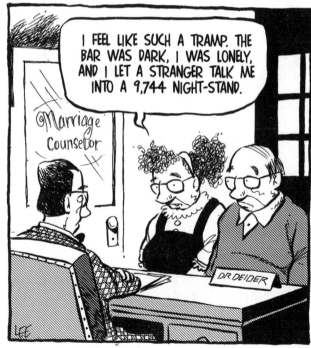

'ELLO LUVS - WANNA HELP ME AND MY BANDMATES CELEBRATE? WE JUST SIGNED OUR FIRST RECORD DEAL.
'YO EAGAN - SHOULD WE TAKE THE 5 FREE CD'S OR GET 12 FOR 99 CENTS?
SWEET! - THE "FROM JUSTIN TO KELLY" SOUNDTRACK!
LEE
AAAHHH
WOOSH
WAS THAT NICO THAT JUST RAN BY HERE SCREAMING?
I'M AFRAID SO. DENNIS THREATENED TO PUNISH HIM IF HE DIDN'T FINISH HIS HOMEWORK.
WOW. HE REALLY RESPONDS - WHAT'S YOUR SECRET?
A PSYCHOLOGIST TOLD US TO TRY PUTTING HIM SOMEWHERE CONFINED FOR A TIME-OUT.
AT FIRST WE TRIED PUTTING HIM IN THE CORNER. THAT DIDN'T WORK. NEXT WE TRIED PUTTING HIM IN HIS ROOM. - THAT DIDN'T WORK.
THEN WE TRIED PUTTING HIM STRAIGHT INTO BED AND THAT DIDN'T EVEN WORK. WE STARTED TO RUN OUT OF PLACES TO PUT HIM.
LEE
SO WE DECIDED TO SHOW HIM HIS BIRTHING VIDEO - ON REWIND.

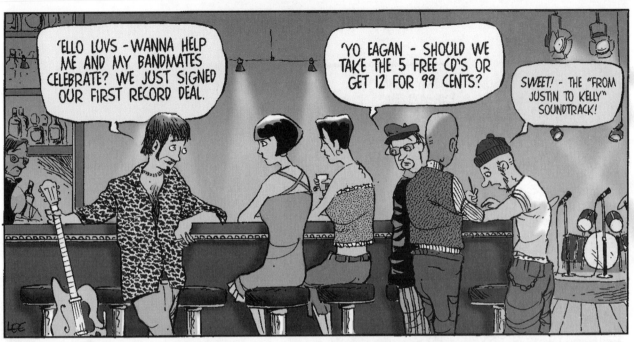

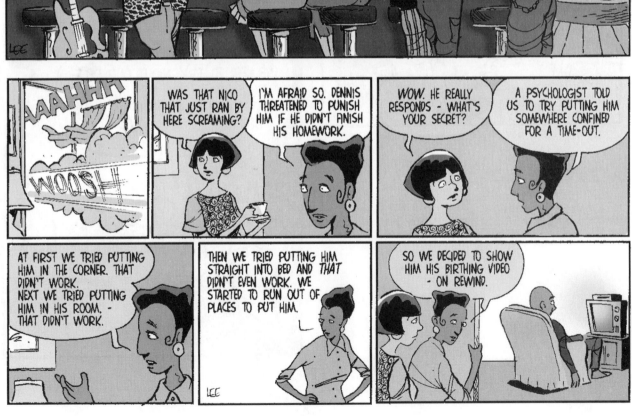

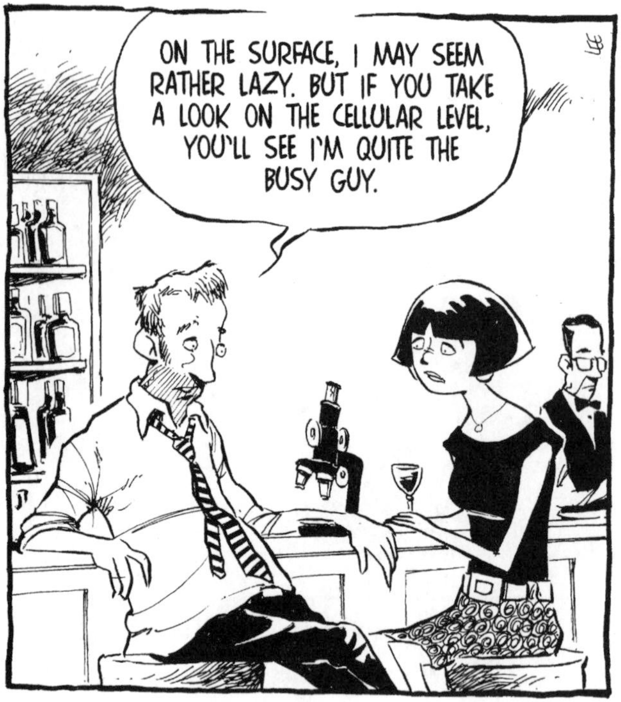
ON THE SURFACE, I MAY SEEM RATHER LAZY. BUT IF YOU TAKE A LOOK ON THE CELLULAR LEVEL, YOU'LL SEE I'M QUITE THE BUSY GUY.
LEE

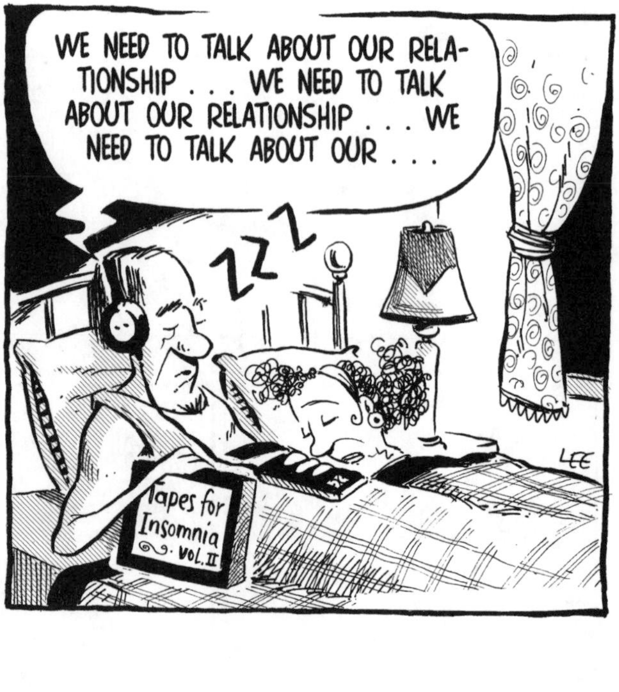
WE NEED TO TALK ABOUT OUR RELATIONSHIP . . . WE NEED TO TALK ABOUT OUR RELATIONSHIP . . . WE NEED TO TALK ABOUT OUR . . .
ZZZ
Tapes for Insomnia VOL. II
LEE

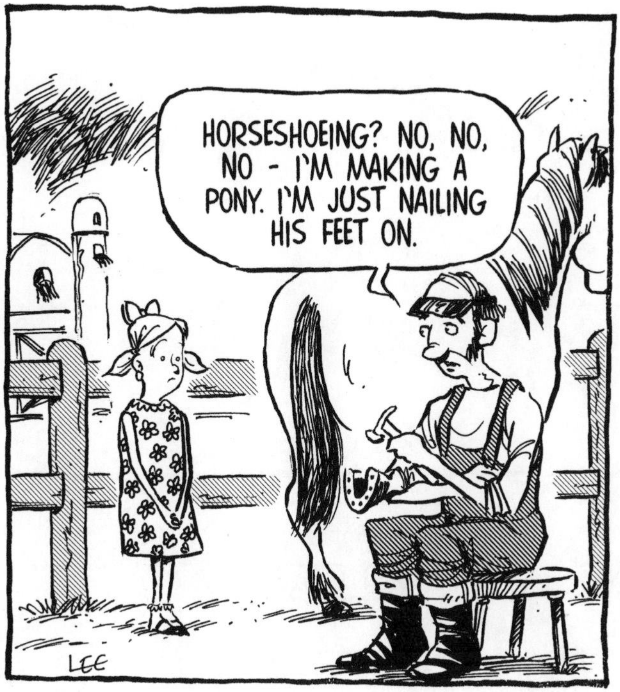
HORSESHOEING? NO, NO, NO - I'M MAKING A PONY. I'M JUST NAILING HIS FEET ON.
LEE

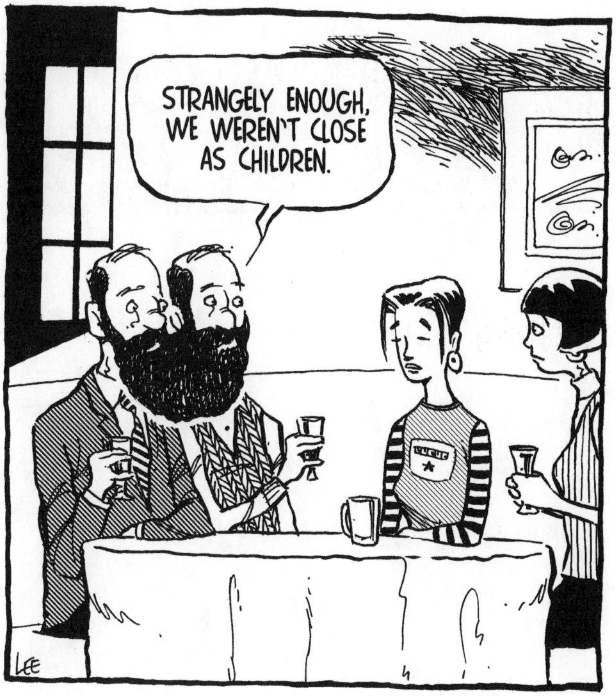
STRANGELY ENOUGH, WE WEREN'T CLOSE AS CHILDREN.
LEE

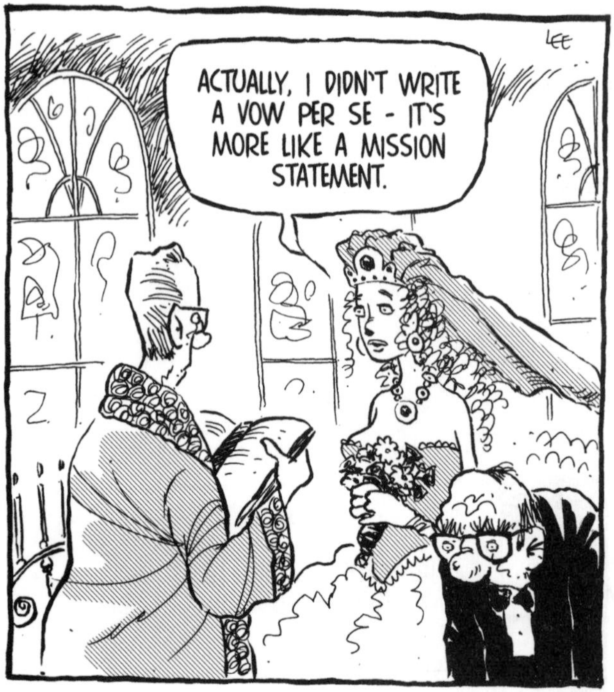
ACTUALLY, I DIDN'T WRITE A VOW PER SE - IT'S MORE LIKE A MISSION STATEMENT.
LEE

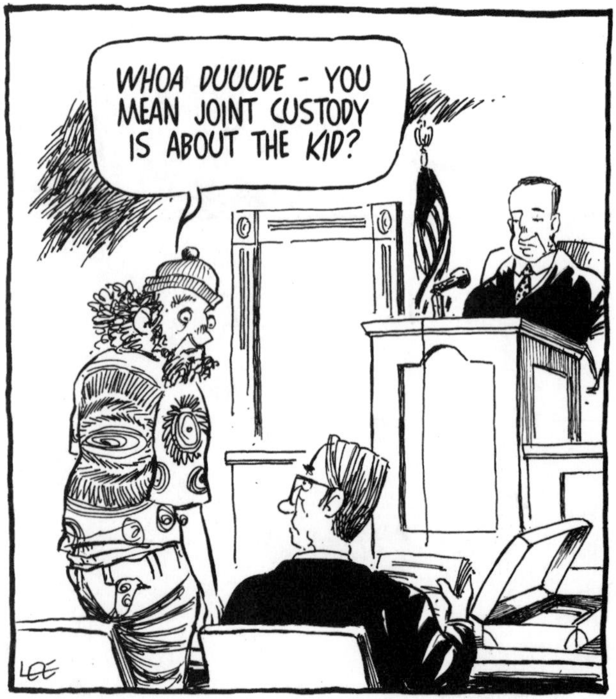
WHOA DUUUDE - YOU MEAN JOINT CUSTODY IS ABOUT THE *KID*?
LEE

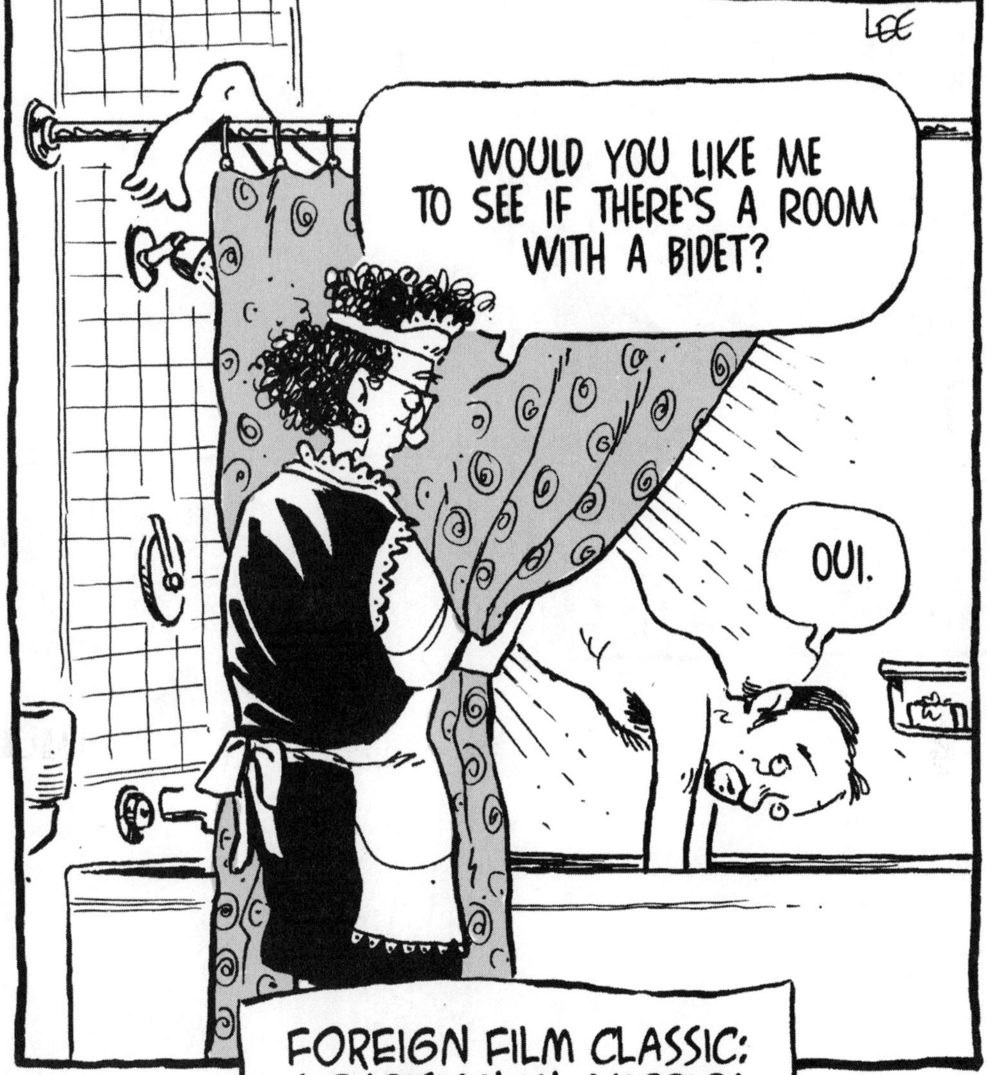
LEE
WOULD YOU LIKE ME TO SEE IF THERE'S A ROOM WITH A BIDET?
OUI.
FOREIGN FILM CLASSIC:
A PARISIAN IN AMERICA

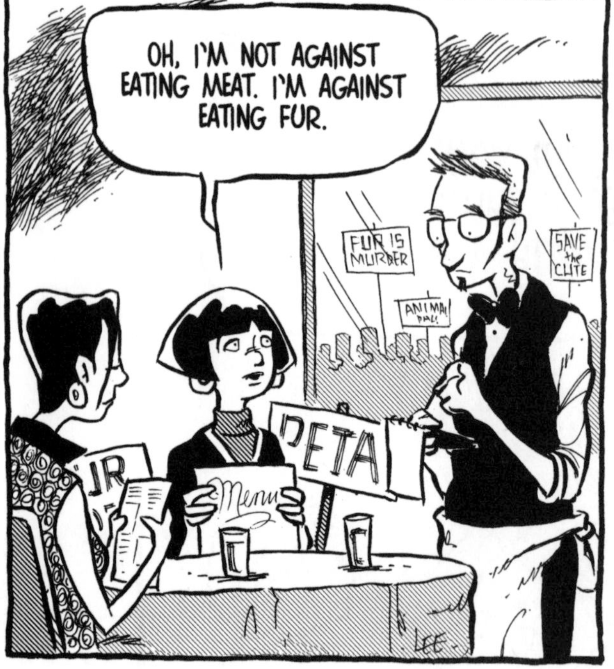
OH, I'M NOT AGAINST EATING MEAT. I'M AGAINST EATING FUR.
FUR IS MURDER
SAVE the CUTE
PETA
Menu
LEE

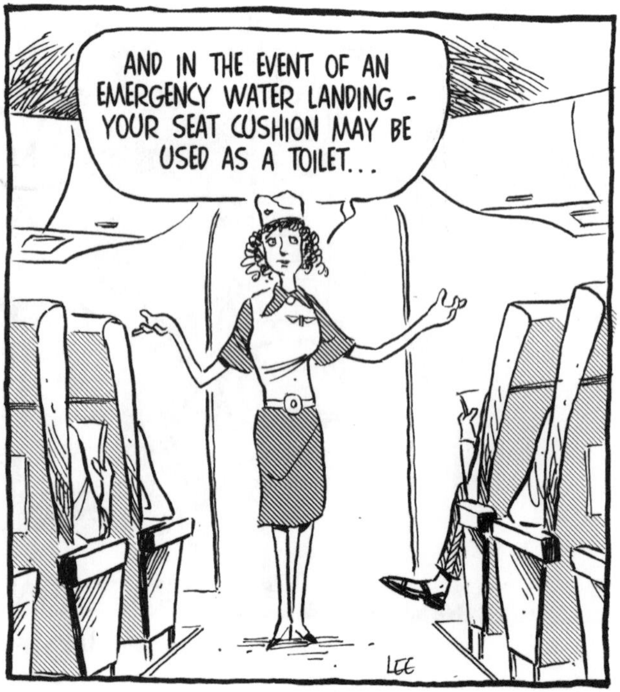
AND IN THE EVENT OF AN EMERGENCY WATER LANDING - YOUR SEAT CUSHION MAY BE USED AS A TOILET...
LEE

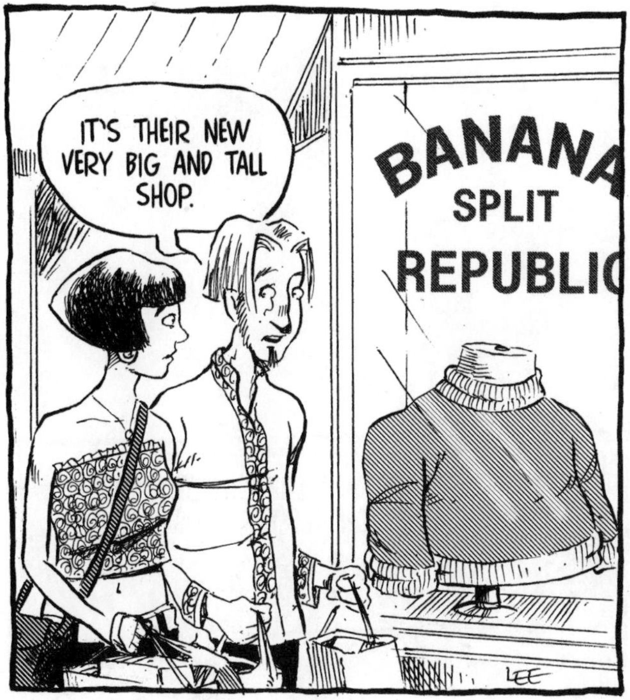
IT'S THEIR NEW VERY BIG AND TALL SHOP.
BANANA SPLIT REPUBLIC
LEE

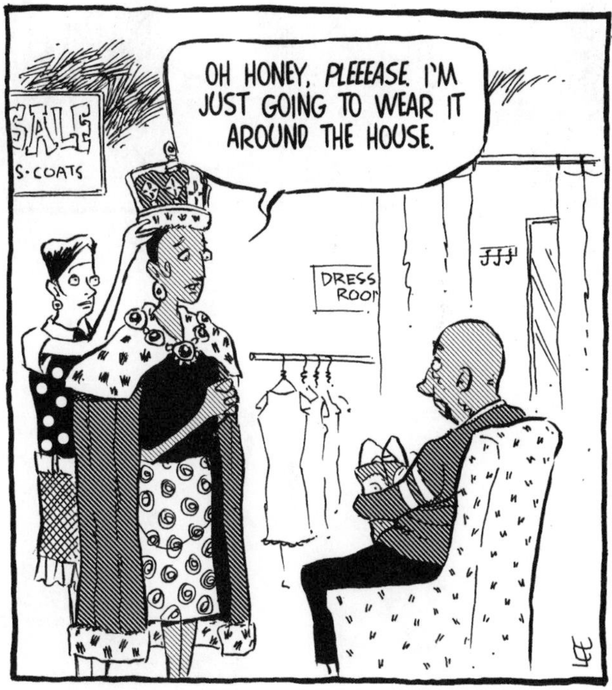
OH HONEY, PLEEEASE. I'M JUST GOING TO WEAR IT AROUND THE HOUSE.
SALE
S·COATS
DRESS ROO
LEE

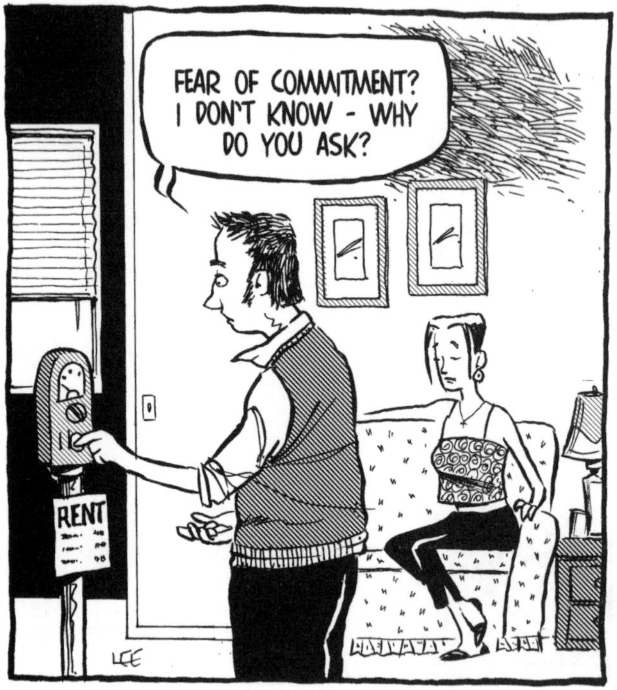
FEAR OF COMMITMENT? I DON'T KNOW - WHY DO YOU ASK?
RENT
LEE

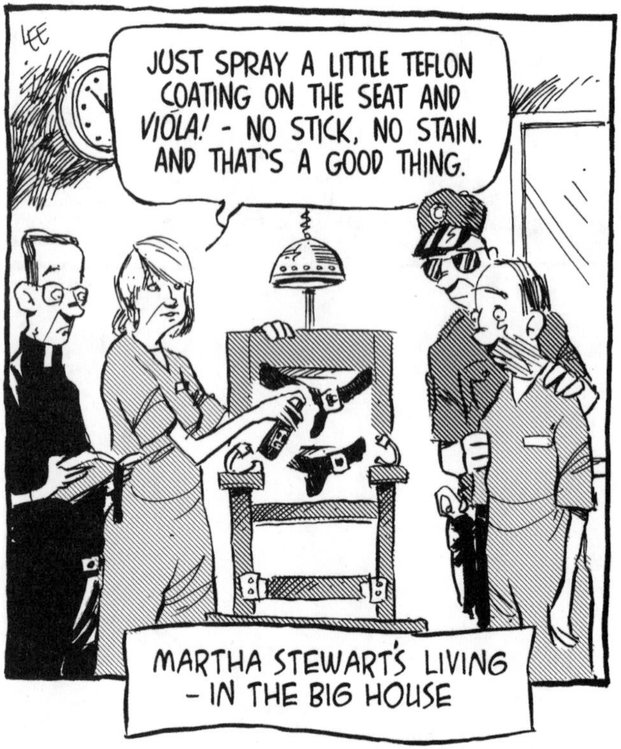
LEE
JUST SPRAY A LITTLE TEFLON COATING ON THE SEAT AND *VIOLA!* - NO STICK, NO STAIN. AND THAT'S A GOOD THING.
MARTHA STEWART'S LIVING - IN THE BIG HOUSE

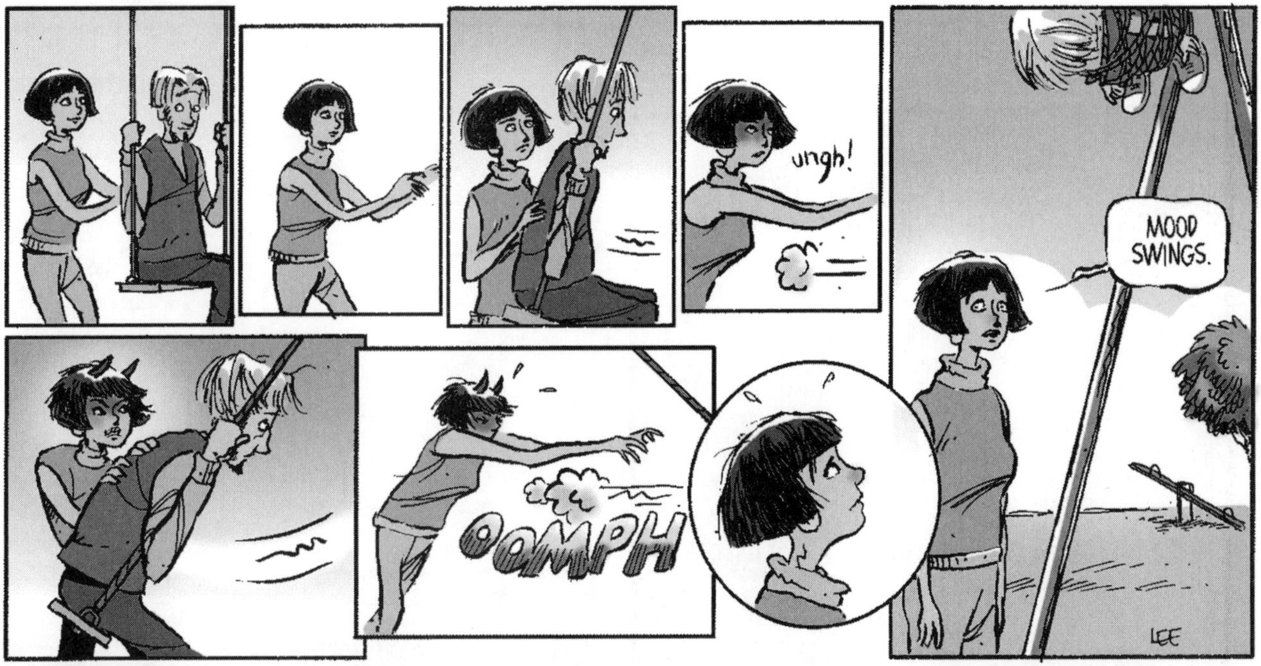
ungh!
OOMPH
MOOD SWINGS.
LEE

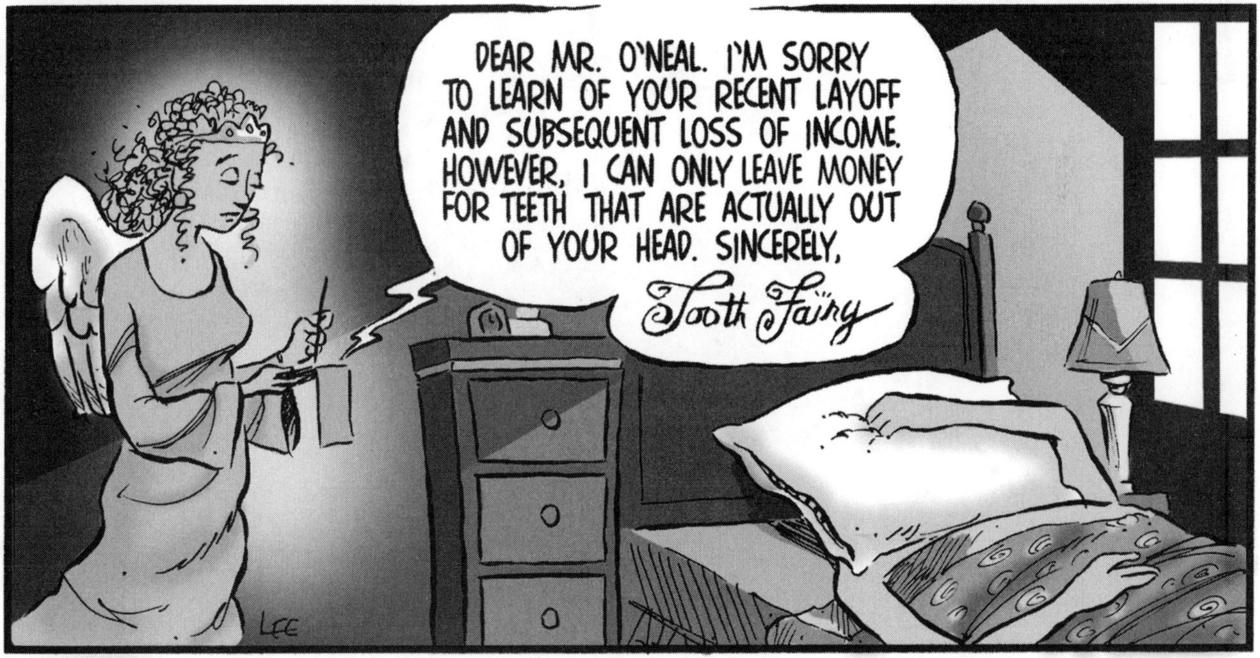
DEAR MR. O'NEAL. I'M SORRY TO LEARN OF YOUR RECENT LAYOFF AND SUBSEQUENT LOSS OF INCOME. HOWEVER, I CAN ONLY LEAVE MONEY FOR TEETH THAT ARE ACTUALLY OUT OF YOUR HEAD. SINCERELY,
Tooth Fairy
LEE

No thanks. I'm on the Atkins diet and it Looks Like you're sportin' dual carbs.
Dear Readers: Sorry, I'm not a cartoonist - my husband is. But it's his birthday and I gave him the day off.

DAMMIT MAN, I'M A DOCTOR NOT A ROLLER-COASTER OPERATOR. IS YOUR CHEST GOING TO BE BREATHING UP AND DOWN LIKE THAT THE ENTIRE TIME?
LEE

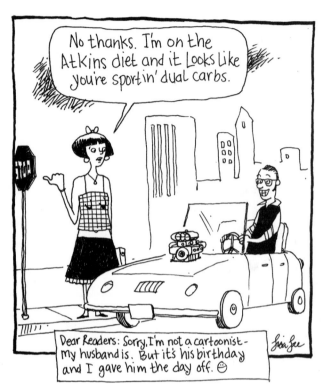

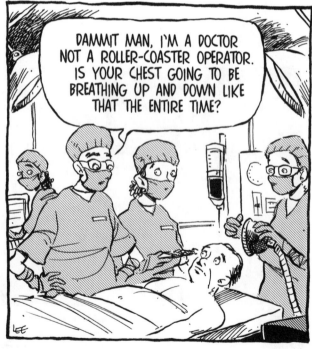

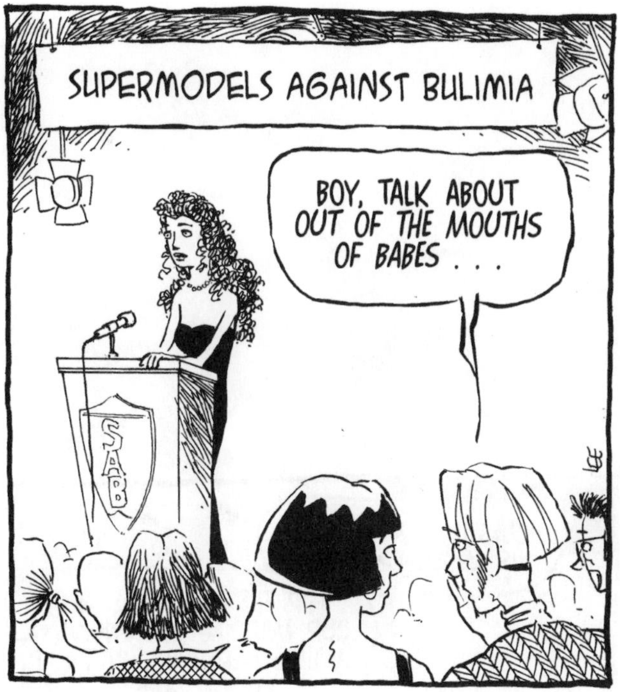
SUPERMODELS AGAINST BULIMIA
BOY, TALK ABOUT OUT OF THE MOUTHS OF BABES . . .
SAB

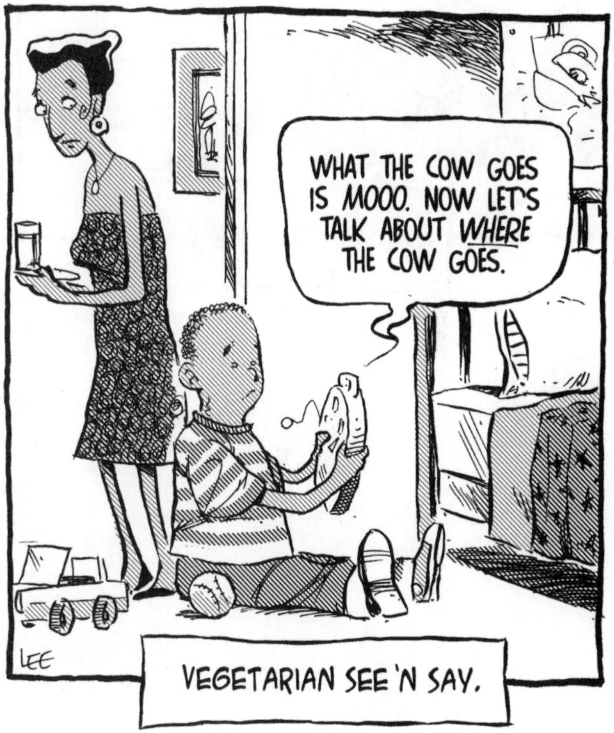
WHAT THE COW GOES IS MOOO. NOW LET'S TALK ABOUT WHERE THE COW GOES.

VEGETARIAN SEE 'N SAY.

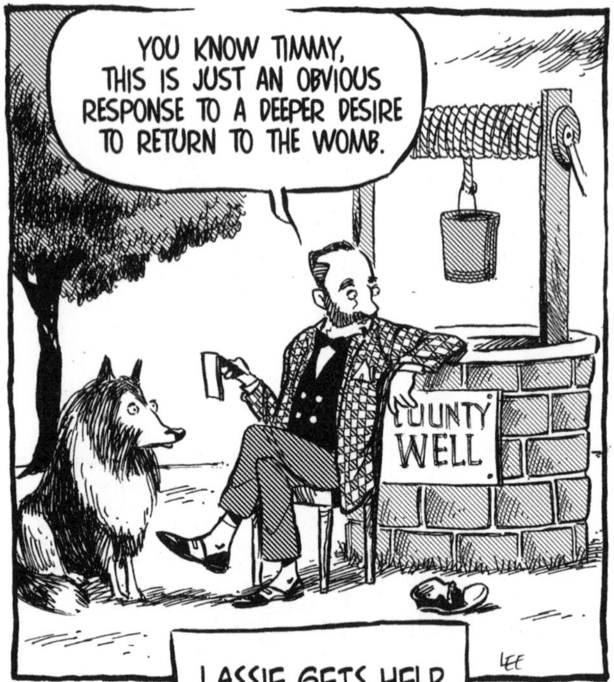
YOU KNOW TIMMY, THIS IS JUST AN OBVIOUS RESPONSE TO A DEEPER DESIRE TO RETURN TO THE WOMB.
COUNTY WELL
LEE

LASSIE GETS HELP

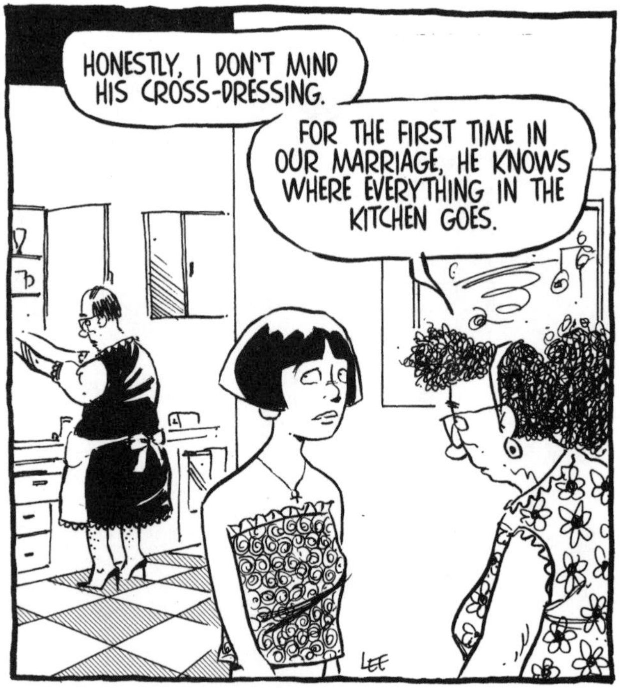
HONESTLY, I DON'T MIND HIS CROSS-DRESSING.
FOR THE FIRST TIME IN OUR MARRIAGE, HE KNOWS WHERE EVERYTHING IN THE KITCHEN GOES.
LEE

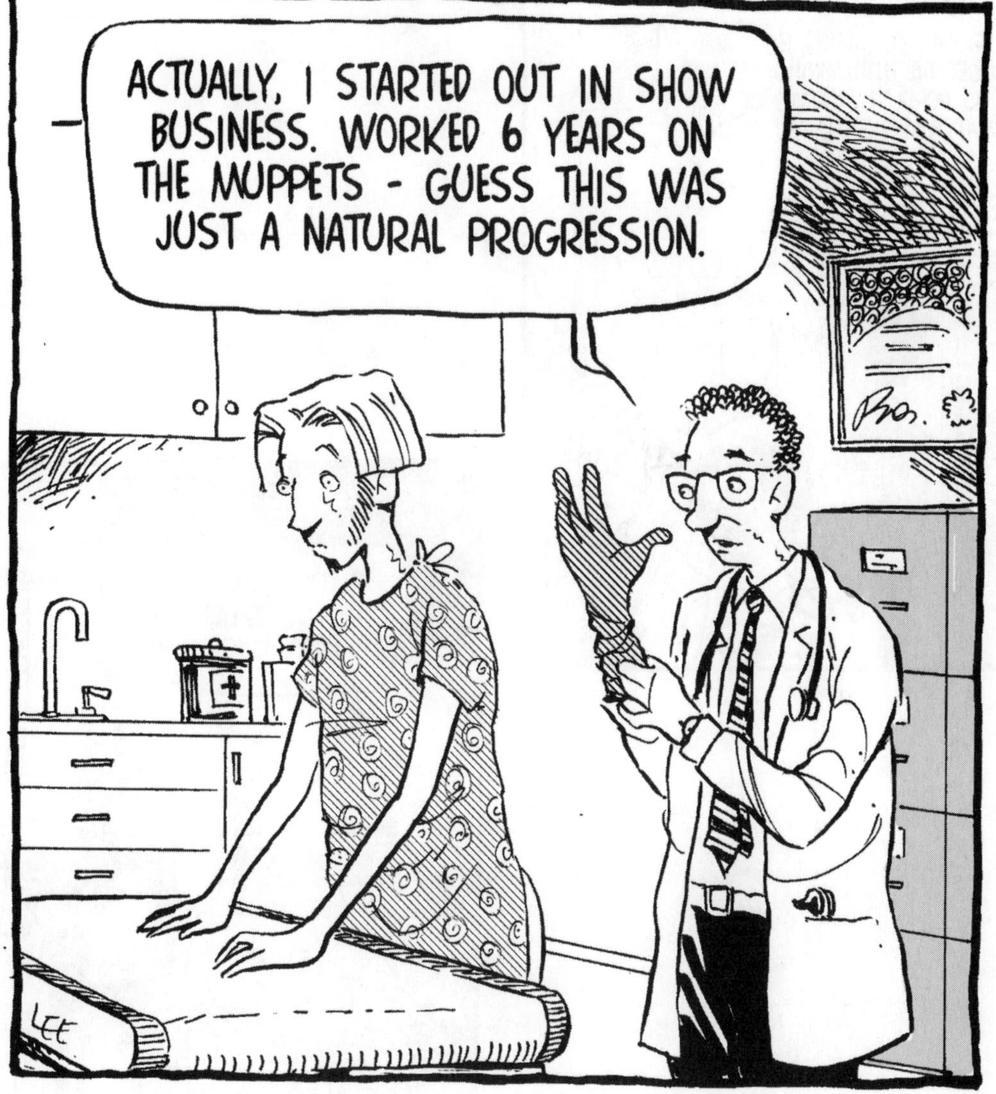
ACTUALLY, I STARTED OUT IN SHOW BUSINESS. WORKED 6 YEARS ON THE MUPPETS - GUESS THIS WAS JUST A NATURAL PROGRESSION.
LEE

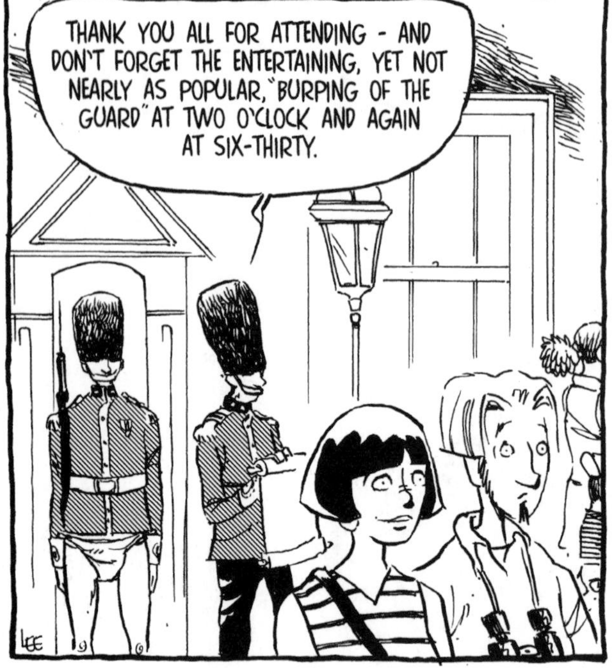
THANK YOU ALL FOR ATTENDING - AND DON'T FORGET THE ENTERTAINING, YET NOT NEARLY AS POPULAR, "BURPING OF THE GUARD" AT TWO O'CLOCK AND AGAIN AT SIX-THIRTY.
LEE

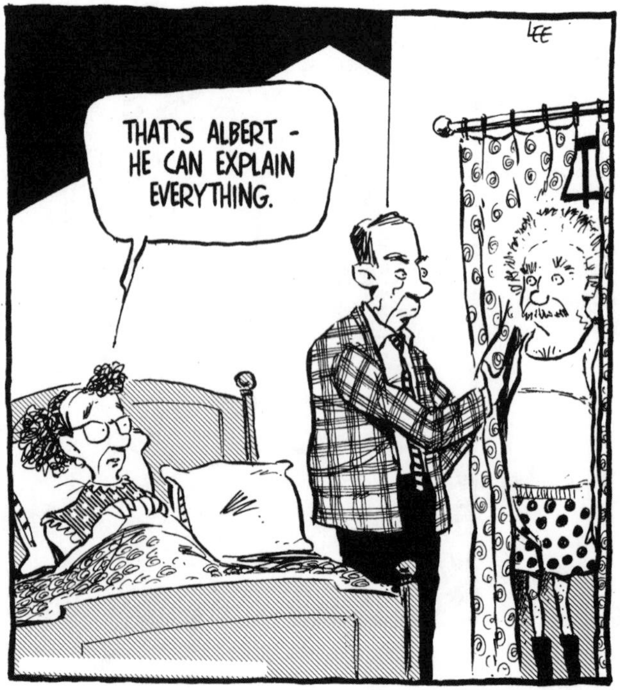
LEE
THAT'S ALBERT - HE CAN EXPLAIN EVERYTHING.

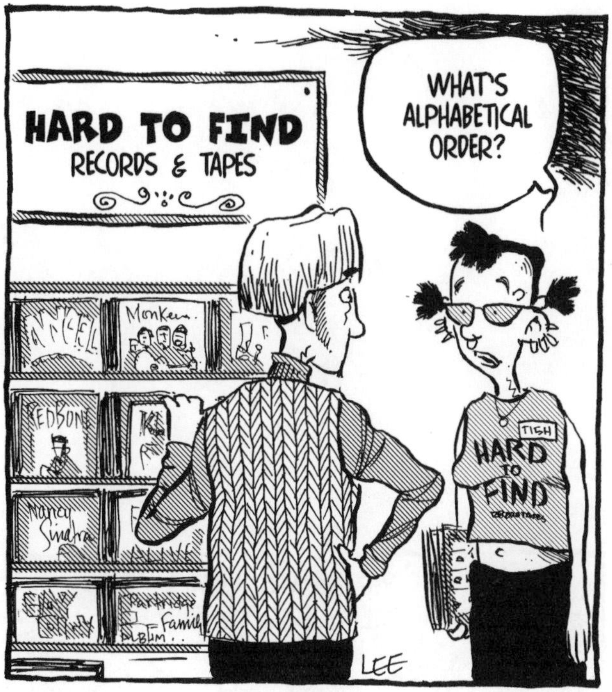
HARD TO FIND
RECORDS & TAPES
WHAT'S ALPHABETICAL ORDER?
TISH
HARD TO FIND
LEE

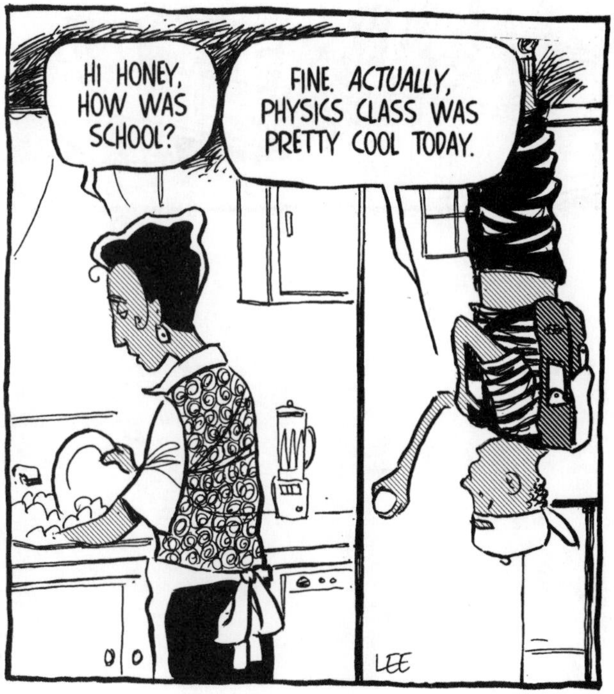
HI HONEY, HOW WAS SCHOOL?
FINE. *ACTUALLY,* PHYSICS CLASS WAS PRETTY COOL TODAY.
LEE

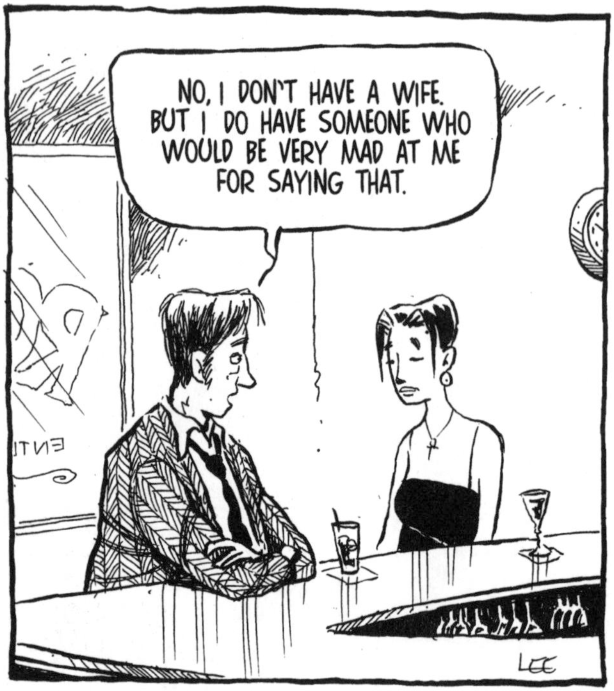
NO, I DON'T HAVE A WIFE. BUT I DO HAVE SOMEONE WHO WOULD BE VERY MAD AT ME FOR SAYING THAT.
LEE

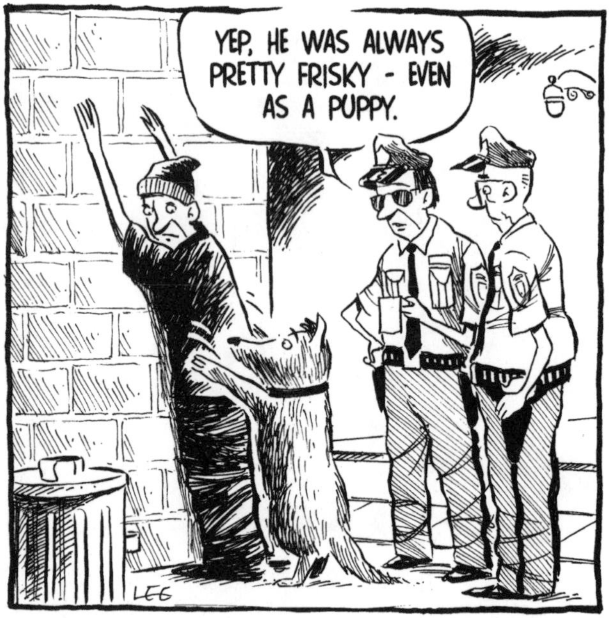
YEP, HE WAS ALWAYS PRETTY FRISKY - EVEN AS A PUPPY.
LEE

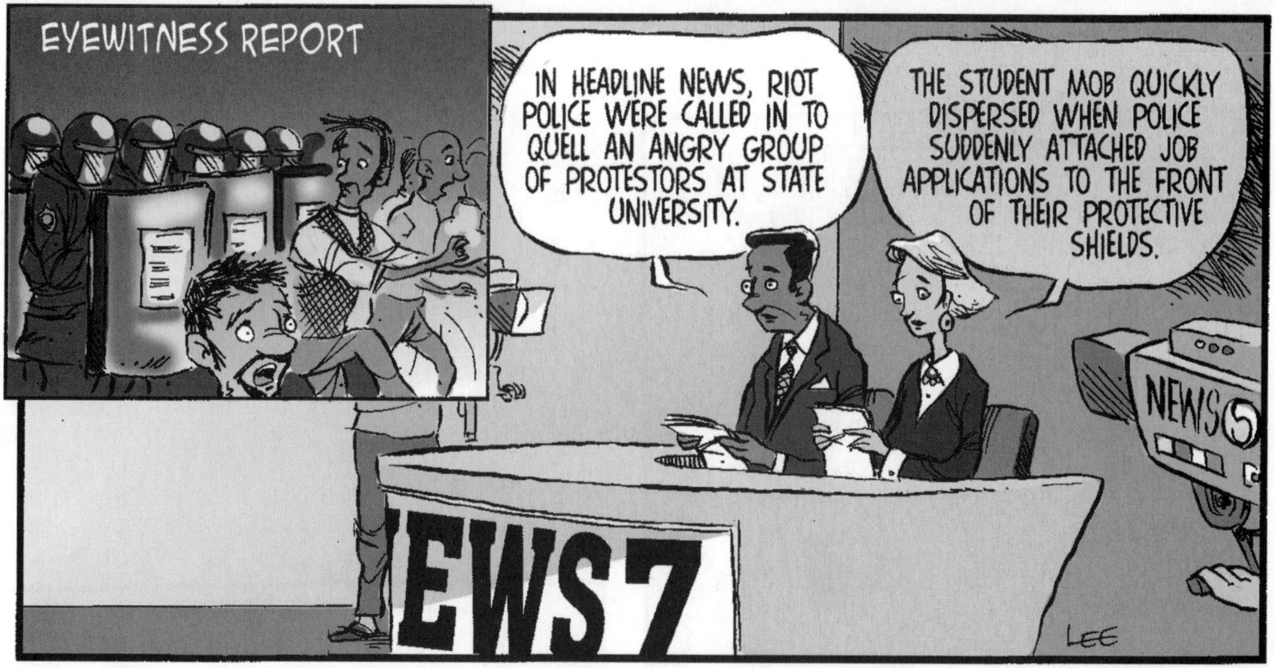
EYEWITNESS REPORT
IN HEADLINE NEWS, RIOT POLICE WERE CALLED IN TO QUELL AN ANGRY GROUP OF PROTESTORS AT STATE UNIVERSITY.
THE STUDENT MOB QUICKLY DISPERSED WHEN POLICE SUDDENLY ATTACHED JOB APPLICATIONS TO THE FRONT OF THEIR PROTECTIVE SHIELDS.
NEWS 5
NEWS 7
LEE

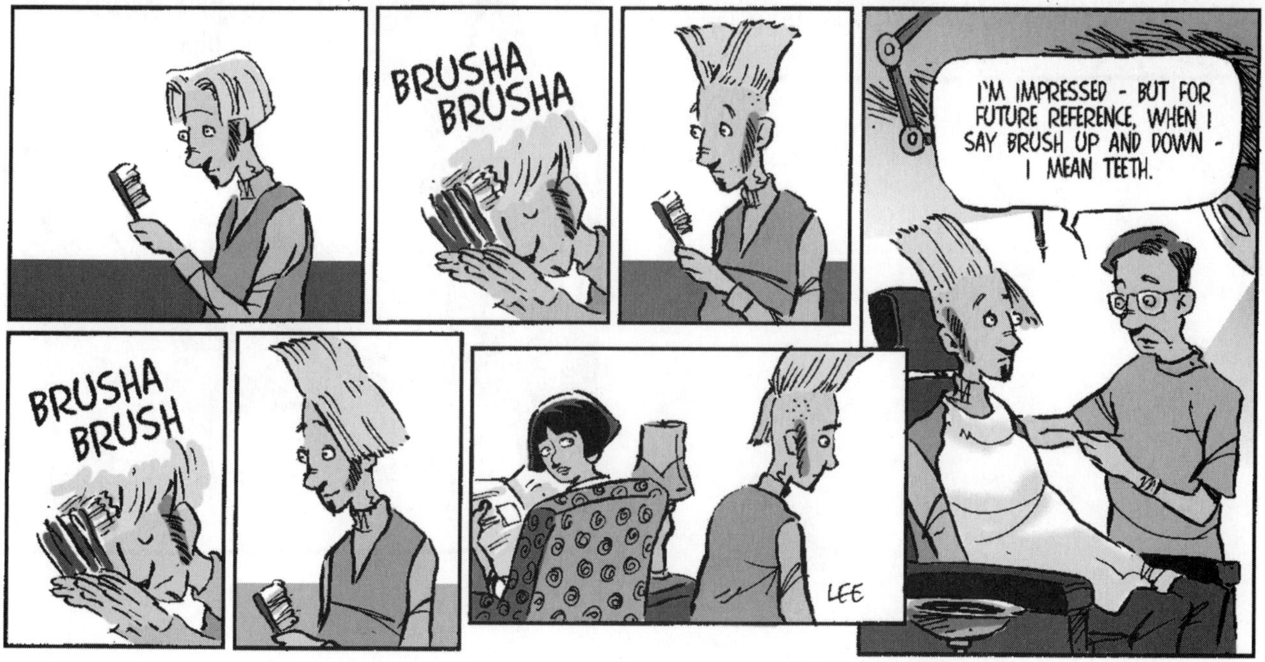
BRUSHA BRUSHA
BRUSHA BRUSH
LEE
I'M IMPRESSED - BUT FOR FUTURE REFERENCE, WHEN I SAY BRUSH UP AND DOWN - I MEAN TEETH.

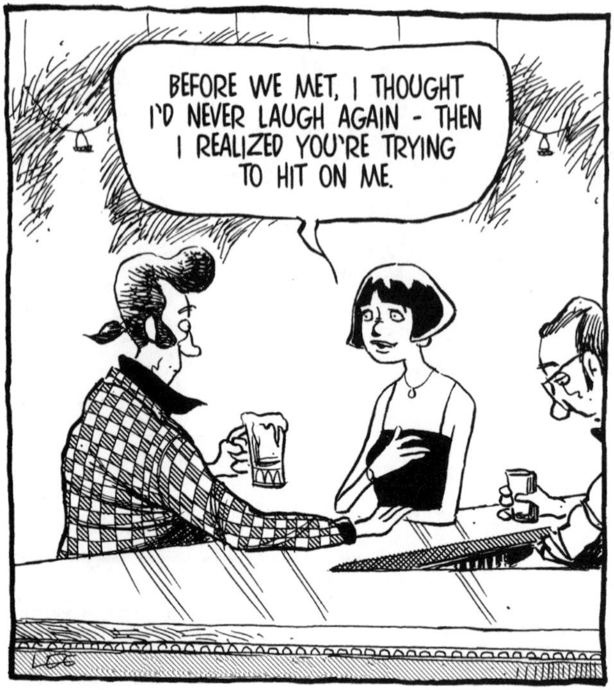
BEFORE WE MET, I THOUGHT I'D NEVER LAUGH AGAIN - THEN I REALIZED YOU'RE TRYING TO HIT ON ME.
LEE

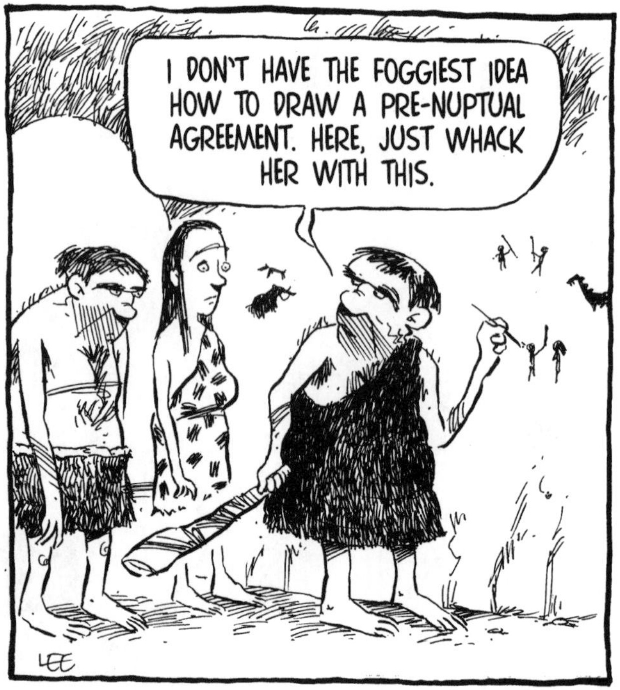
I DON'T HAVE THE FOGGIEST IDEA HOW TO DRAW A PRE-NUPTUAL AGREEMENT. HERE, JUST WHACK HER WITH THIS.
LEE

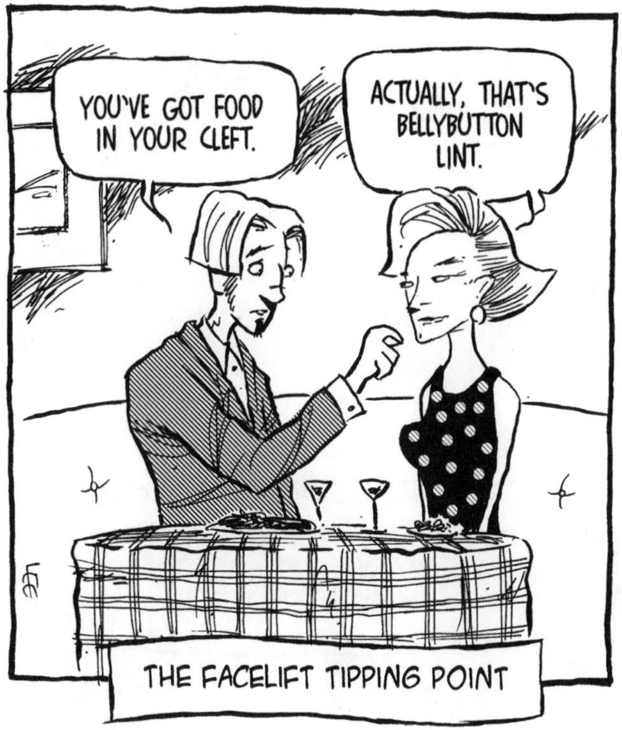
YOU'VE GOT FOOD IN YOUR CLEFT.
ACTUALLY, THAT'S BELLYBUTTON LINT.
THE FACELIFT TIPPING POINT

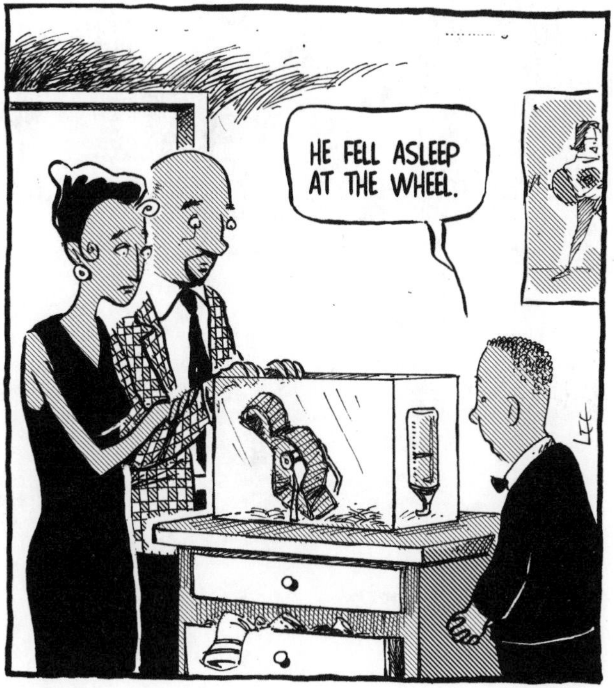
HE FELL ASLEEP AT THE WHEEL.

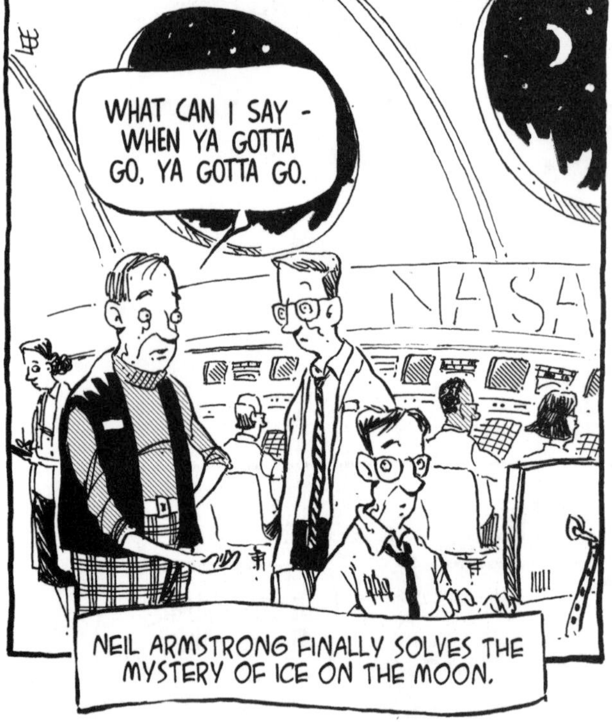
WHAT CAN I SAY - WHEN YA GOTTA GO, YA GOTTA GO.
NASA
NEIL ARMSTRONG FINALLY SOLVES THE MYSTERY OF ICE ON THE MOON.

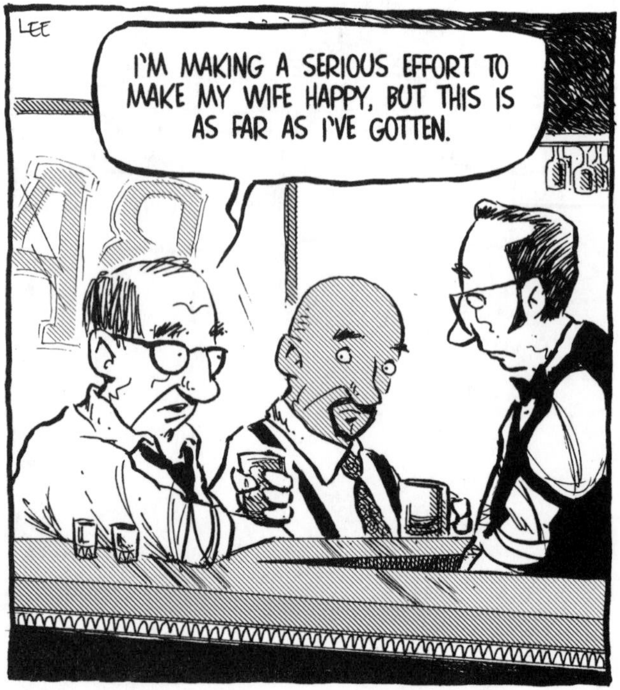
I'M MAKING A SERIOUS EFFORT TO MAKE MY WIFE HAPPY, BUT THIS IS AS FAR AS I'VE GOTTEN.

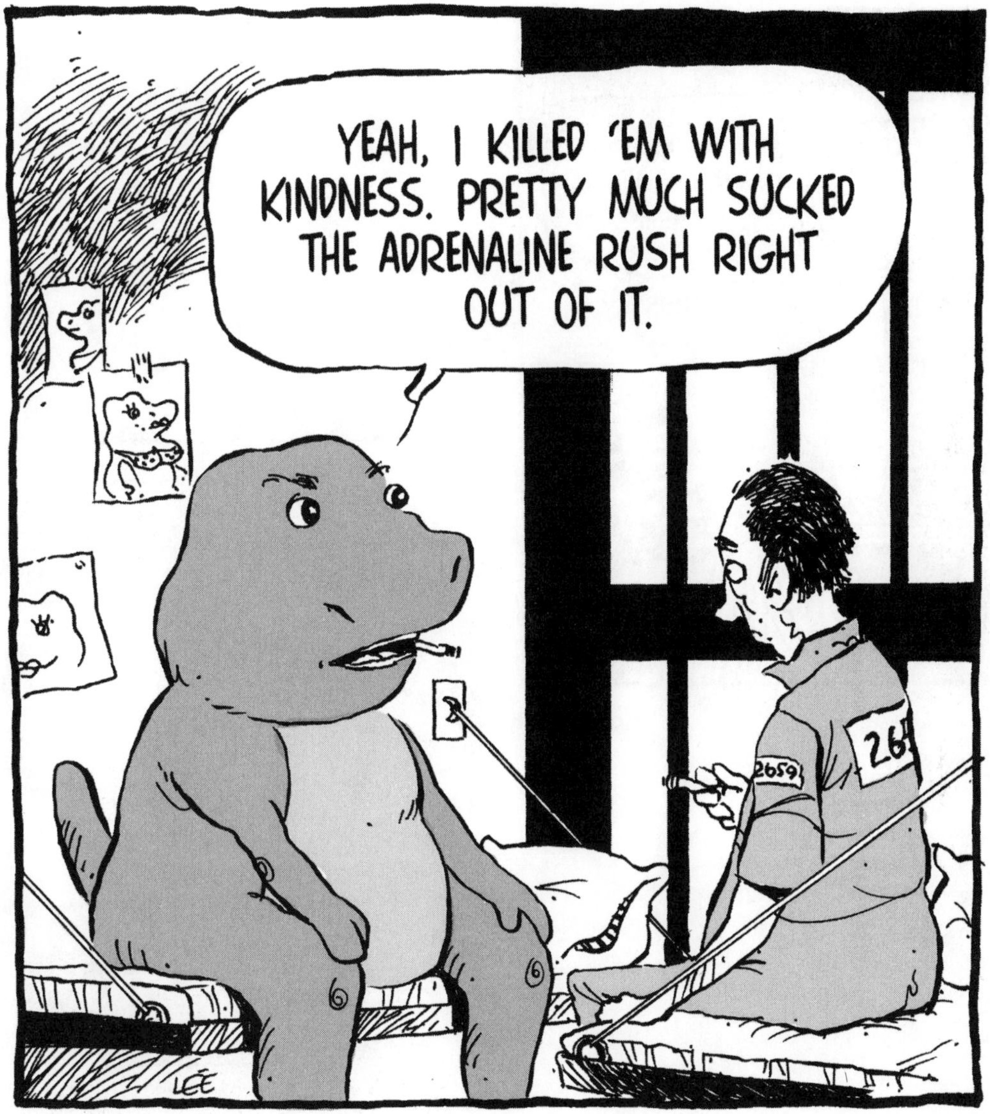
YEAH, I KILLED 'EM WITH KINDNESS. PRETTY MUCH SUCKED THE ADRENALINE RUSH RIGHT OUT OF IT.
2659
LEE

MODERN PROVERBS
I CRIED BECAUSE I HAD NO SHOES. THEN I MET A MAN WHO HAD NO PROBLEM INCREASING MY VISA CARD LIMIT.
LEE

3'X8', CLOSE TO FREEWAY...
LOTS OF PRIVACY...
WONDER IF HE'LL SUBLET...
LEE
APARTMENT HUNTING IN MANHATTAN

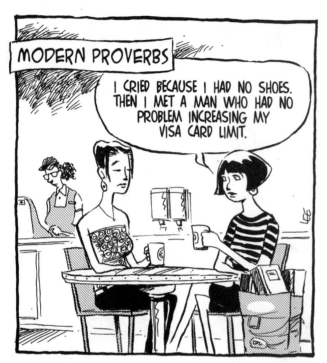

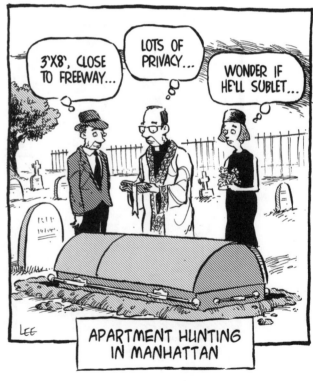

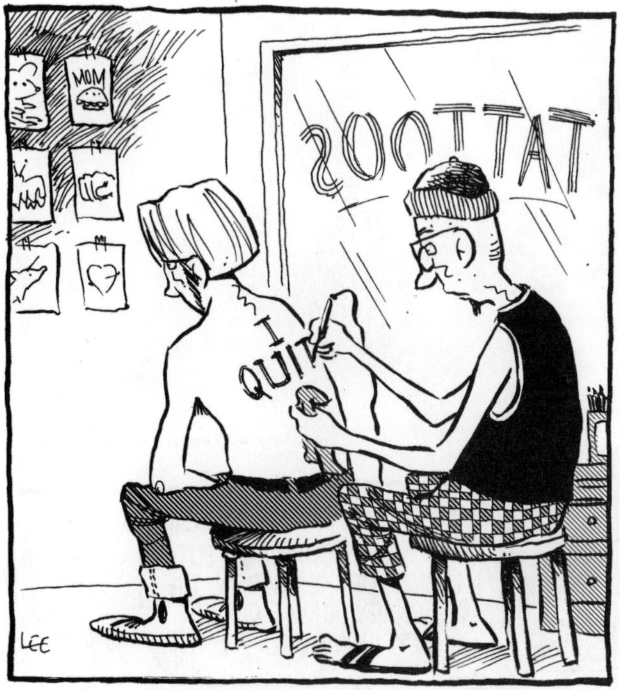

MOM
TATTOOS
I QUIT
LEE

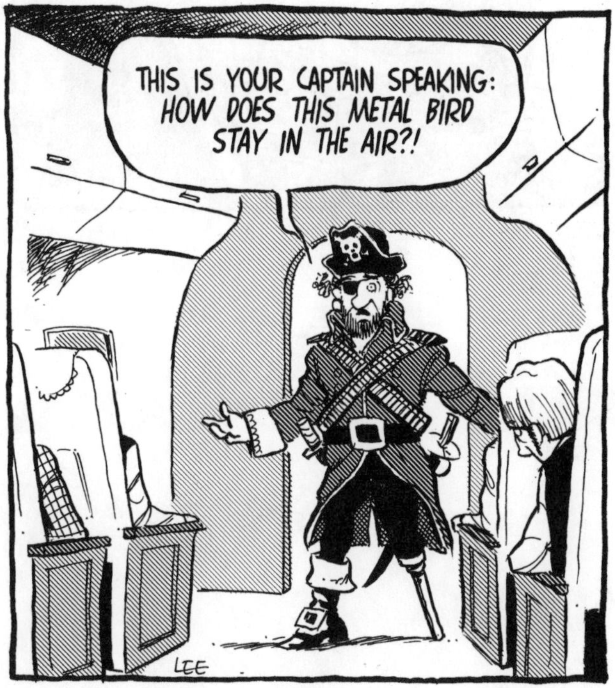

THIS IS YOUR CAPTAIN SPEAKING: HOW DOES THIS METAL BIRD STAY IN THE AIR?!
LEE

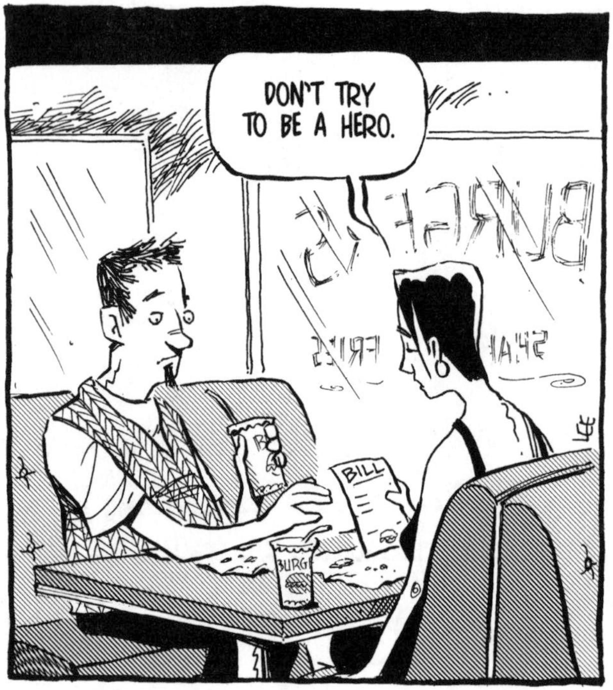
DON'T TRY TO BE A HERO.

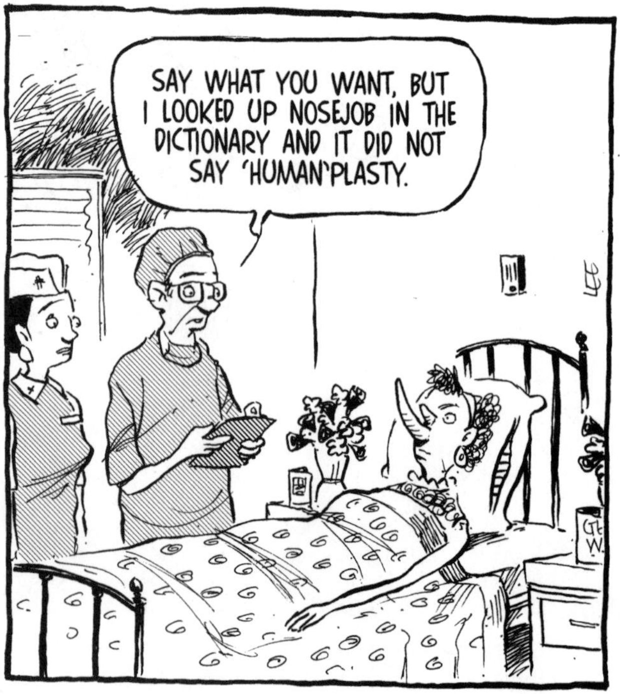
SAY WHAT YOU WANT, BUT I LOOKED UP NOSEJOB IN THE DICTIONARY AND IT DID NOT SAY 'HUMAN'PLASTY.

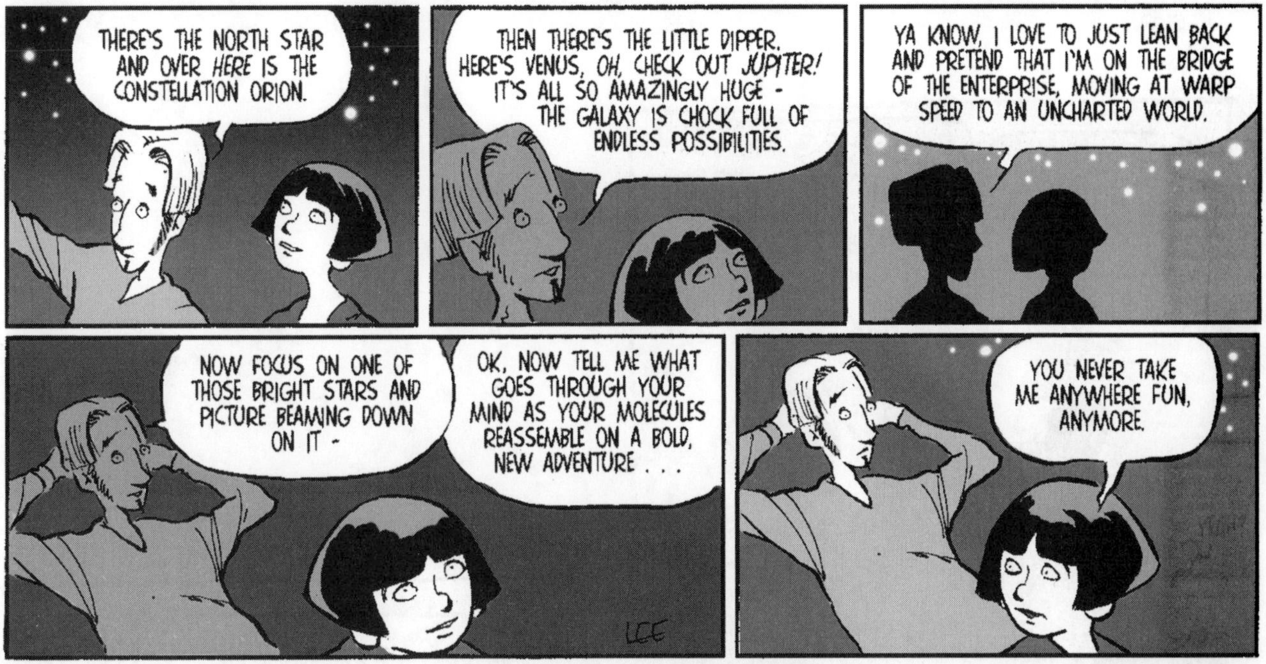
THERE'S THE NORTH STAR AND OVER *HERE* IS THE CONSTELLATION ORION.
THEN THERE'S THE LITTLE DIPPER. HERE'S VENUS, *OH,* CHECK OUT *JUPITER!* IT'S ALL SO AMAZINGLY HUGE - THE GALAXY IS CHOCK FULL OF ENDLESS POSSIBILITIES.
YA KNOW, I LOVE TO JUST LEAN BACK AND PRETEND THAT I'M ON THE BRIDGE OF THE ENTERPRISE, MOVING AT WARP SPEED TO AN UNCHARTED WORLD.
NOW FOCUS ON ONE OF THOSE BRIGHT STARS AND PICTURE BEAMING DOWN ON IT -
OK, NOW TELL ME WHAT GOES THROUGH YOUR MIND AS YOUR MOLECULES REASSEMBLE ON A BOLD, NEW ADVENTURE . . .
YOU NEVER TAKE ME ANYWHERE FUN, ANYMORE.
LEE

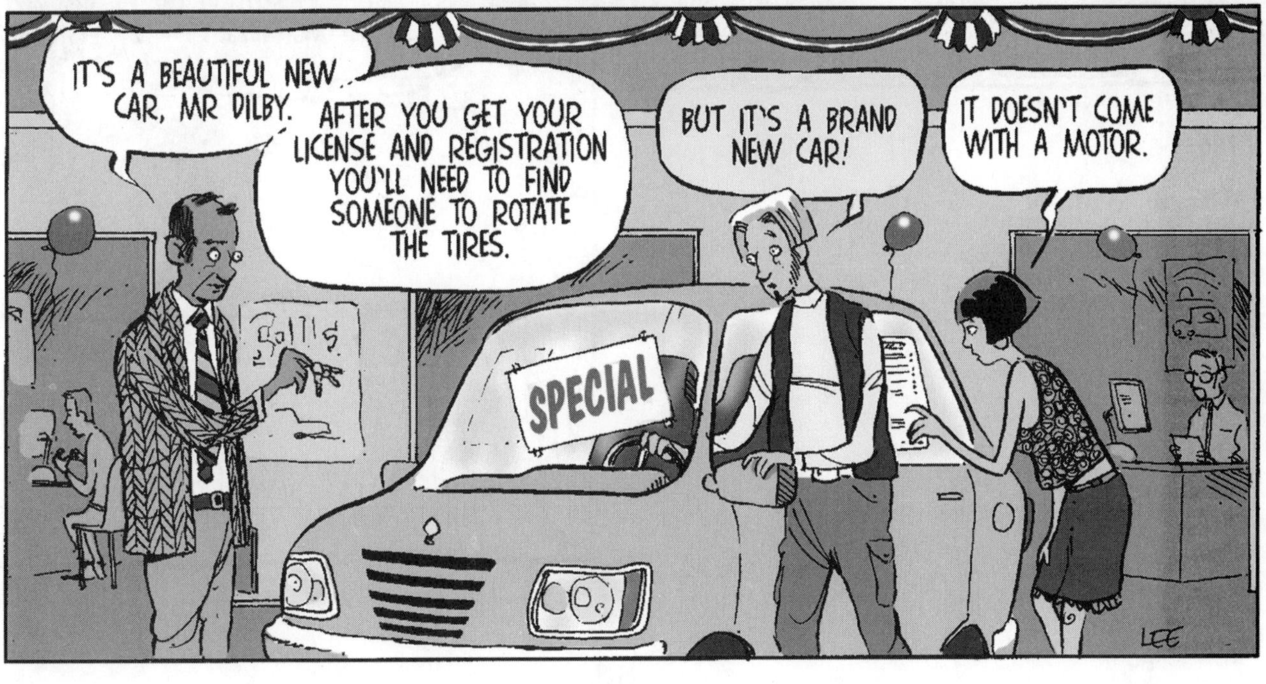
IT'S A BEAUTIFUL NEW CAR, MR DILBY.
AFTER YOU GET YOUR LICENSE AND REGISTRATION YOU'LL NEED TO FIND SOMEONE TO ROTATE THE TIRES.
BUT IT'S A BRAND NEW CAR!
IT DOESN'T COME WITH A MOTOR.
SPECIAL
LEE

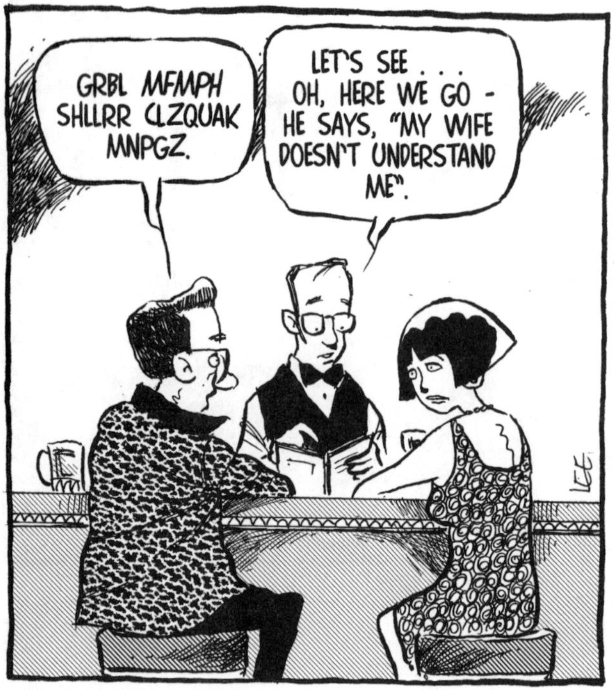
GRBL MFMPH SHLLRR CLZQUAK MNPGZ.
LET'S SEE . . . OH, HERE WE GO - HE SAYS, "MY WIFE DOESN'T UNDERSTAND ME".
LEE

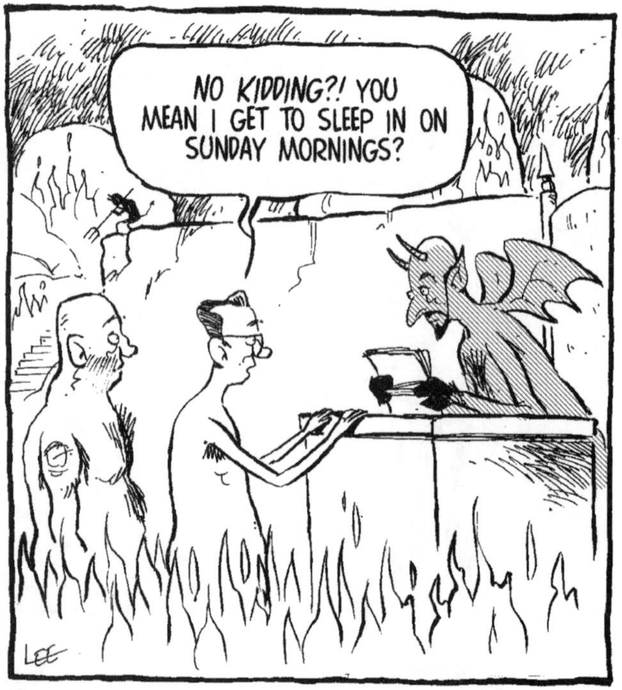
NO KIDDING?! YOU MEAN I GET TO SLEEP IN ON SUNDAY MORNINGS?
LEE

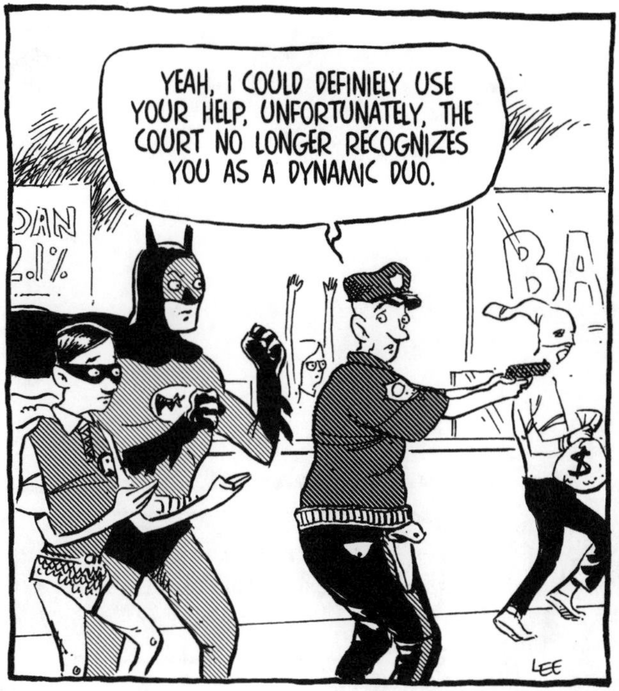
YEAH, I COULD DEFINIELY USE YOUR HELP, UNFORTUNATELY, THE COURT NO LONGER RECOGNIZES YOU AS A DYNAMIC DUO.
LEE

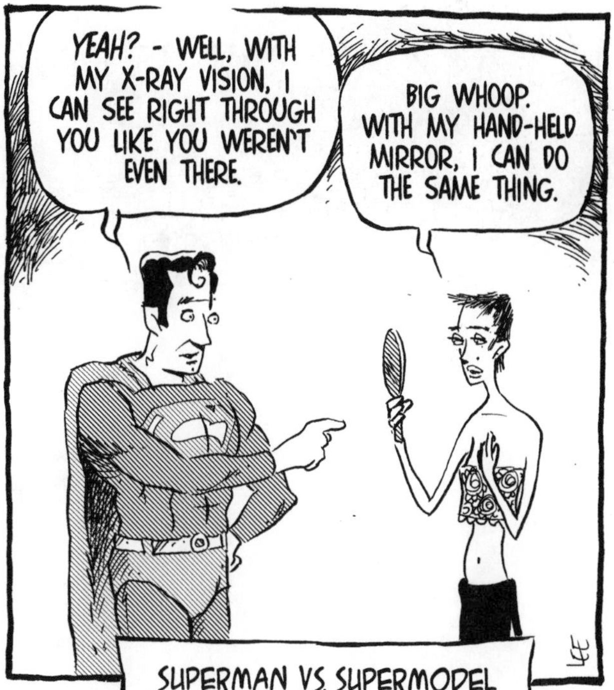
YEAH? - WELL, WITH MY X-RAY VISION, I CAN SEE RIGHT THROUGH YOU LIKE YOU WEREN'T EVEN THERE.
BIG WHOOP. WITH MY HAND-HELD MIRROR, I CAN DO THE SAME THING.
LEE

SUPERMAN VS. SUPERMODEL

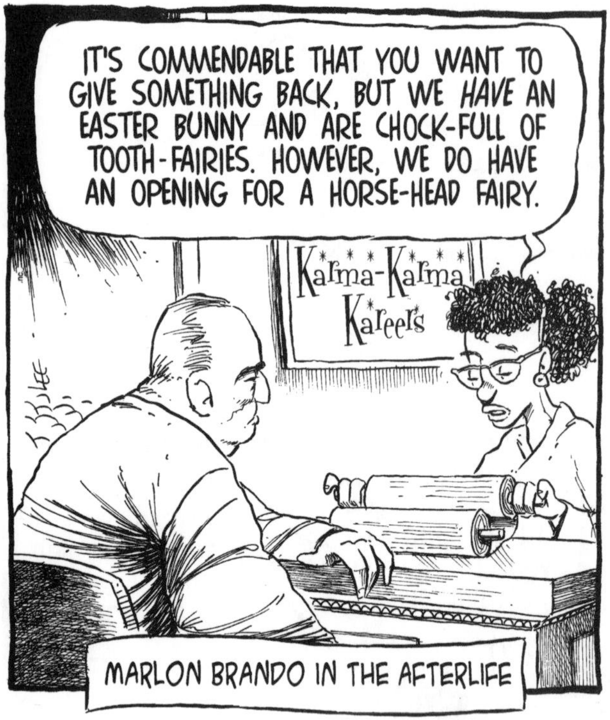
IT'S COMMENDABLE THAT YOU WANT TO GIVE SOMETHING BACK, BUT WE *HAVE* AN EASTER BUNNY AND ARE CHOCK-FULL OF TOOTH-FAIRIES. HOWEVER, WE DO HAVE AN OPENING FOR A HORSE-HEAD FAIRY.
Karma-Karma Kareers
LEE
MARLON BRANDO IN THE AFTERLIFE

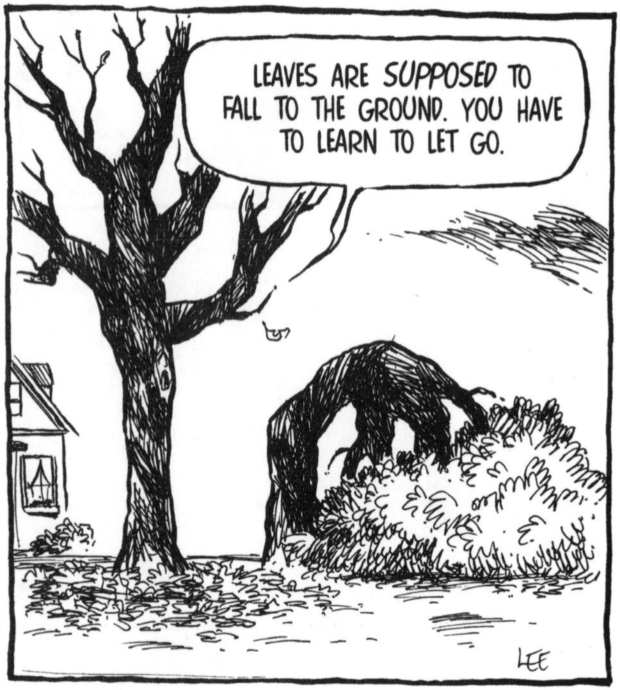
LEAVES ARE *SUPPOSED* TO FALL TO THE GROUND. YOU HAVE TO LEARN TO LET GO.
LEE

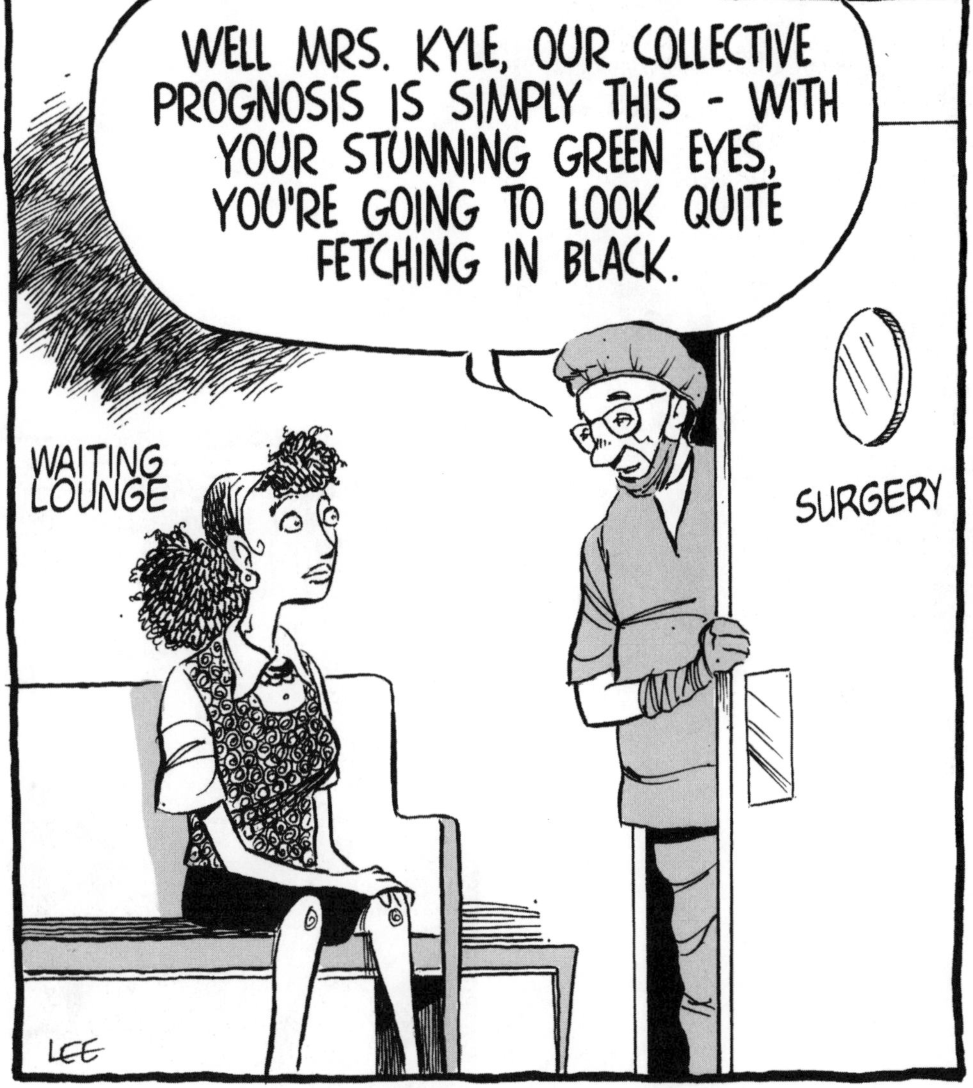
WELL MRS. KYLE, OUR COLLECTIVE PROGNOSIS IS SIMPLY THIS - WITH YOUR STUNNING GREEN EYES, YOU'RE GOING TO LOOK QUITE FETCHING IN BLACK.
WAITING LOUNGE
SURGERY
LEE

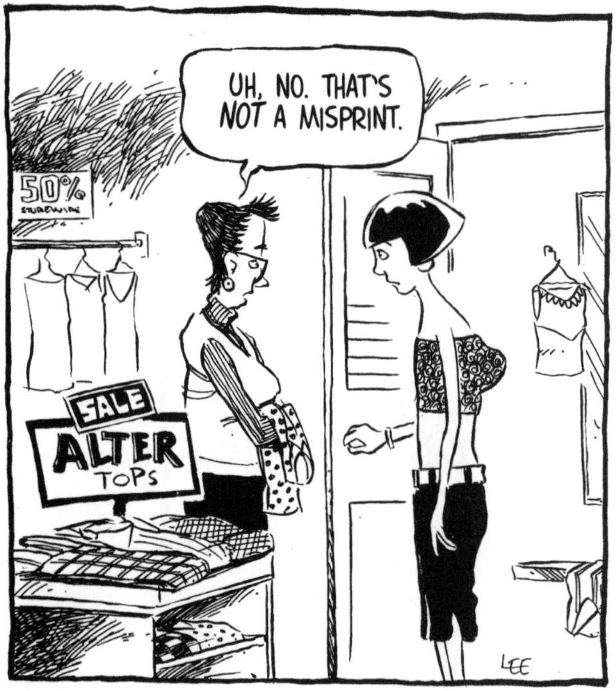
UH, NO. THAT'S NOT A MISPRINT.
50%
SALE
ALTER TOPS
LEE

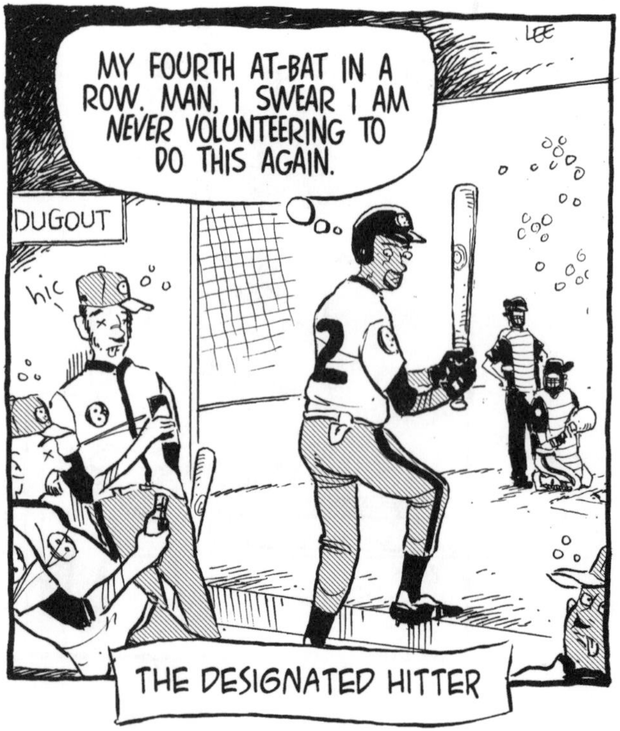
MY FOURTH AT-BAT IN A ROW. MAN, I SWEAR I AM NEVER VOLUNTEERING TO DO THIS AGAIN.
DUGOUT
hic
LEE
THE DESIGNATED HITTER

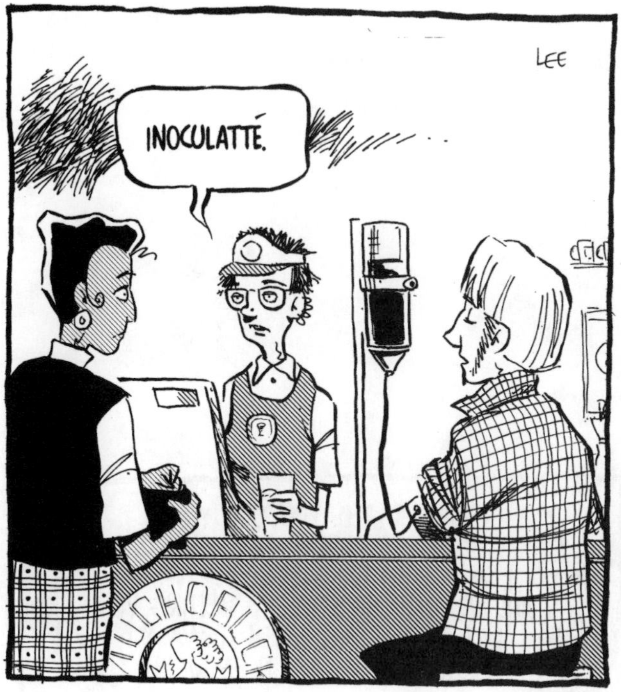
LEE
INOCULATTÉ.
UCHOBUCK

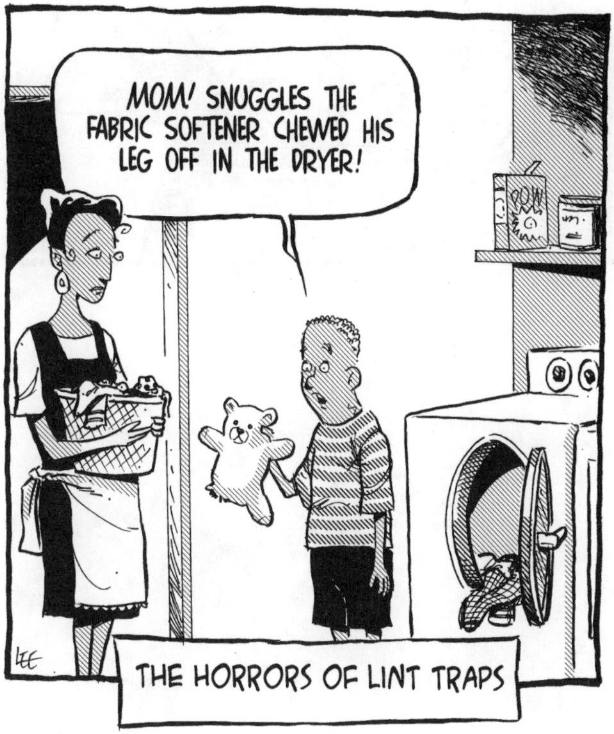
MOM! SNUGGLES THE FABRIC SOFTENER CHEWED HIS LEG OFF IN THE DRYER!
POW
LEE
THE HORRORS OF LINT TRAPS

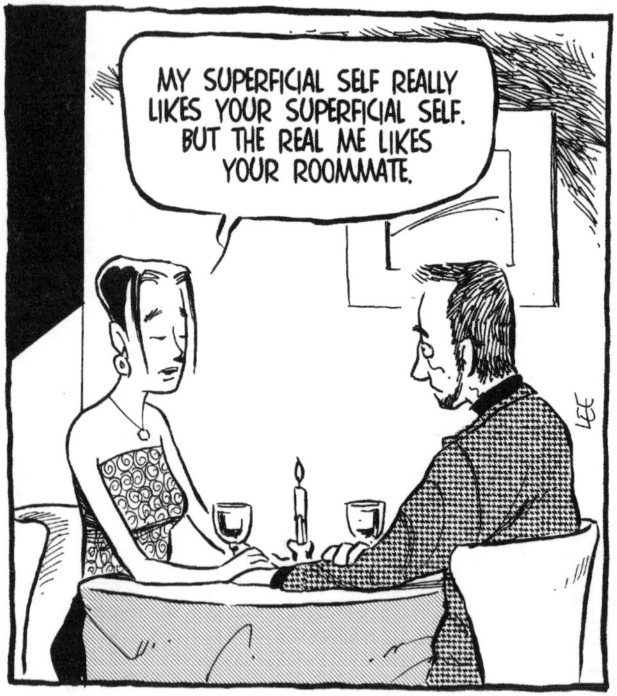
MY SUPERFICIAL SELF REALLY LIKES YOUR SUPERFICIAL SELF. BUT THE REAL ME LIKES YOUR ROOMMATE.
LEE

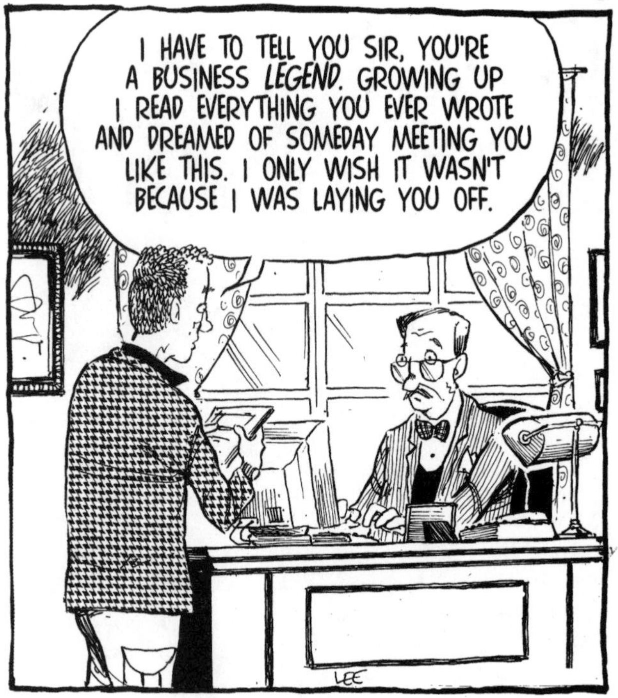
I HAVE TO TELL YOU SIR, YOU'RE A BUSINESS *LEGEND*. GROWING UP I READ EVERYTHING YOU EVER WROTE AND DREAMED OF SOMEDAY MEETING YOU LIKE THIS. I ONLY WISH IT WASN'T BECAUSE I WAS LAYING YOU OFF.
LEE

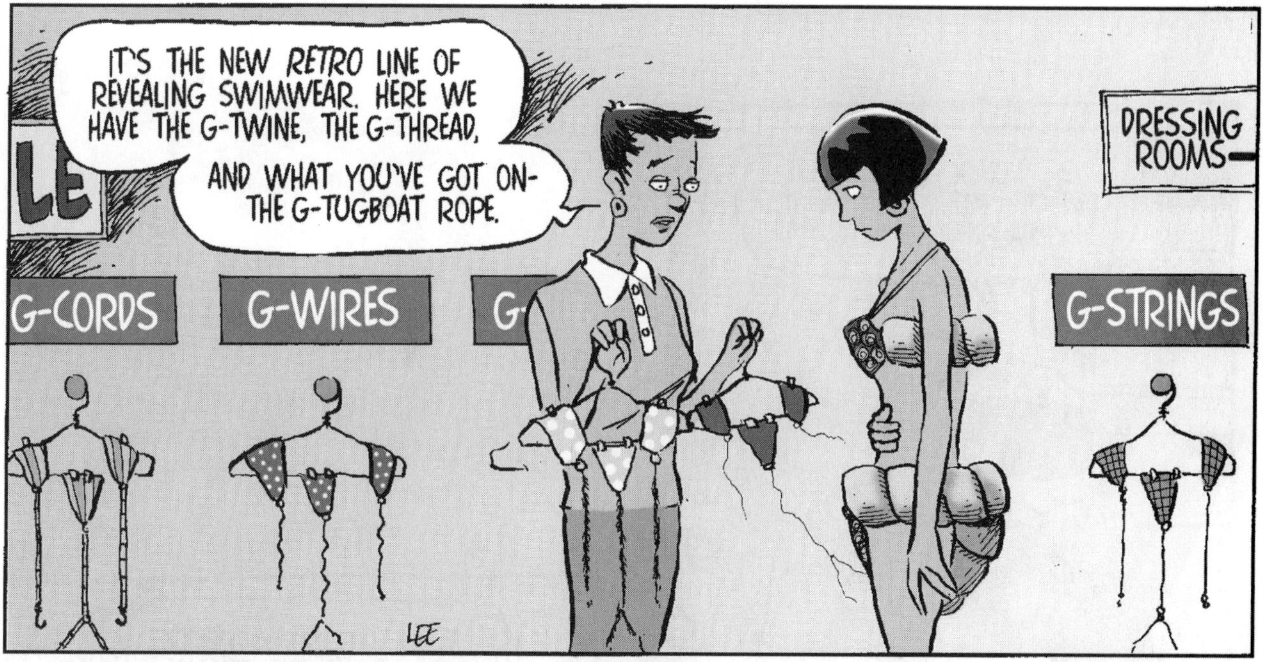
IT'S THE NEW RETRO LINE OF REVEALING SWIMWEAR. HERE WE HAVE THE G-TWINE, THE G-THREAD,
AND WHAT YOU'VE GOT ON- THE G-TUGBOAT ROPE.
DRESSING ROOMS
G-CORDS
G-WIRES
G-STRINGS
LEE

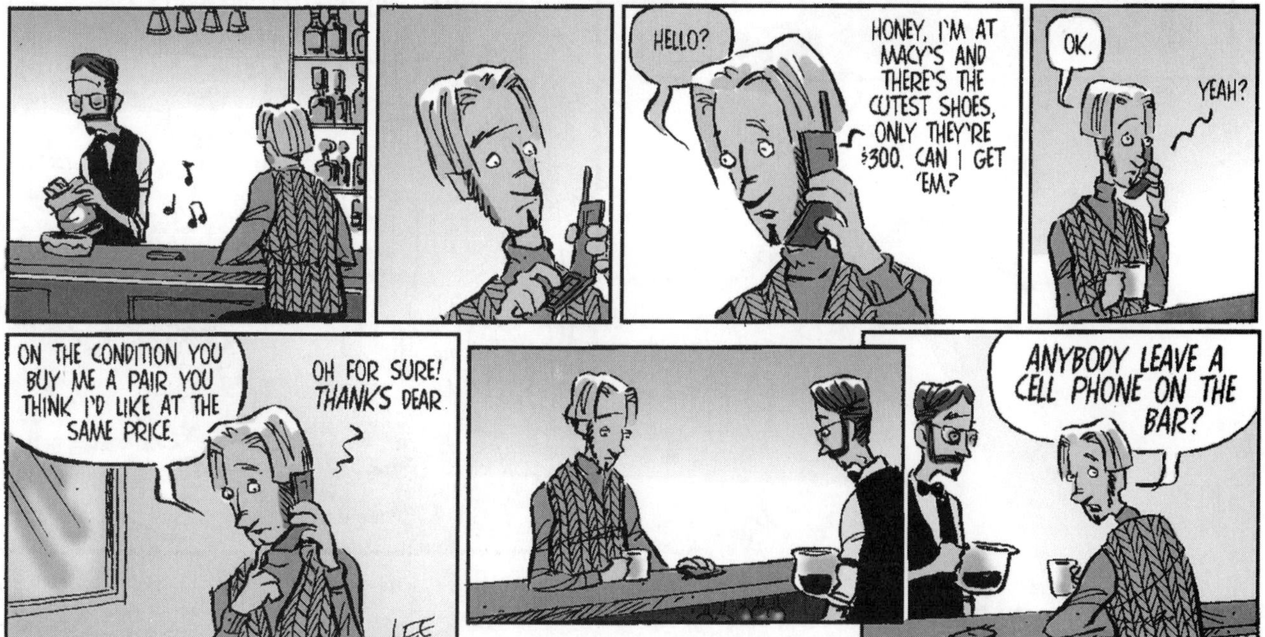
HELLO?
HONEY, I'M AT MACY'S AND THERE'S THE CUTEST SHOES, ONLY THEY'RE $300. CAN I GET 'EM?
OK.
YEAH?
ON THE CONDITION YOU BUY ME A PAIR YOU THINK I'D LIKE AT THE SAME PRICE.
OH FOR SURE! THANKS DEAR.
ANYBODY LEAVE A CELL PHONE ON THE BAR?
LEE

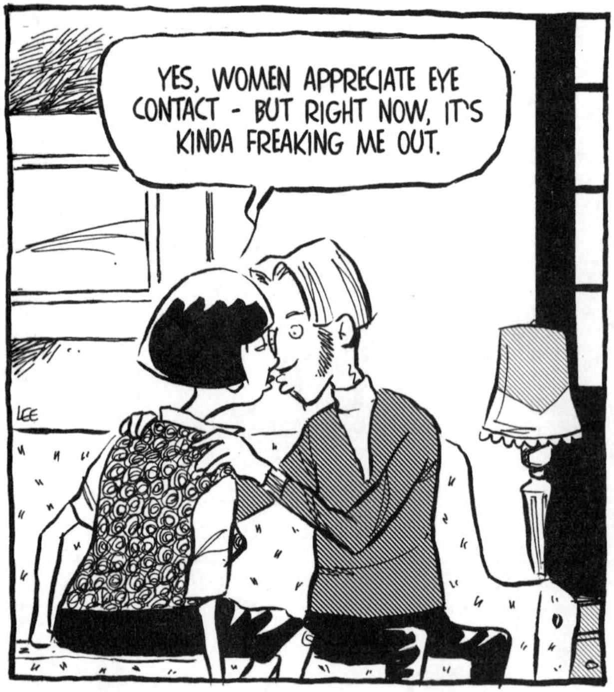
YES, WOMEN APPRECIATE EYE CONTACT - BUT RIGHT NOW, IT'S KINDA FREAKING ME OUT.
LEE

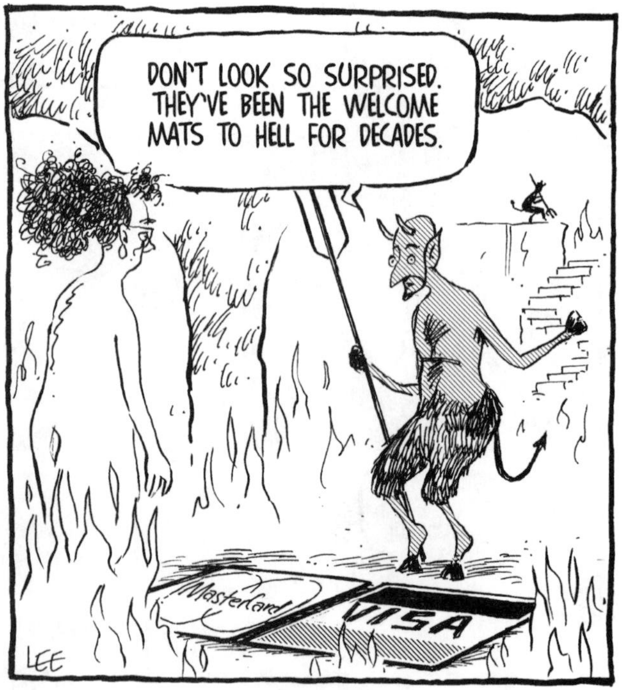
DON'T LOOK SO SURPRISED. THEY'VE BEEN THE WELCOME MATS TO HELL FOR DECADES.
MasterCard
VISA
LEE

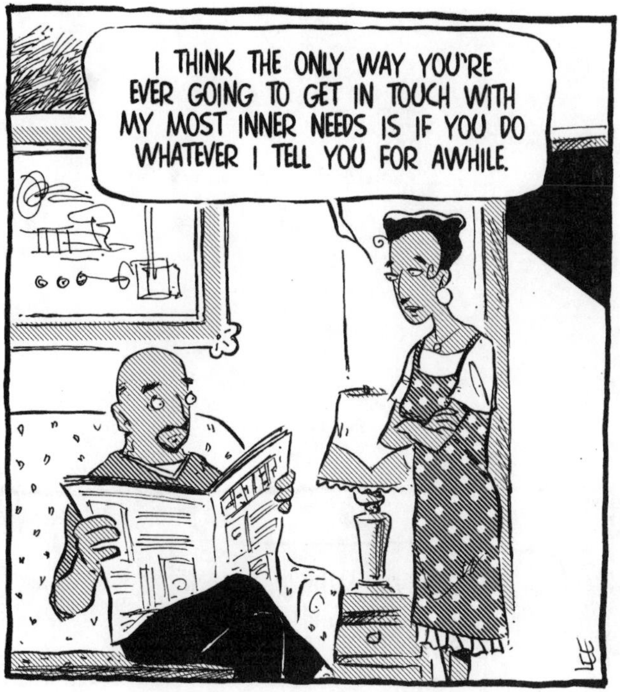
I THINK THE ONLY WAY YOU'RE EVER GOING TO GET IN TOUCH WITH MY MOST INNER NEEDS IS IF YOU DO WHATEVER I TELL YOU FOR AWHILE.
LEE

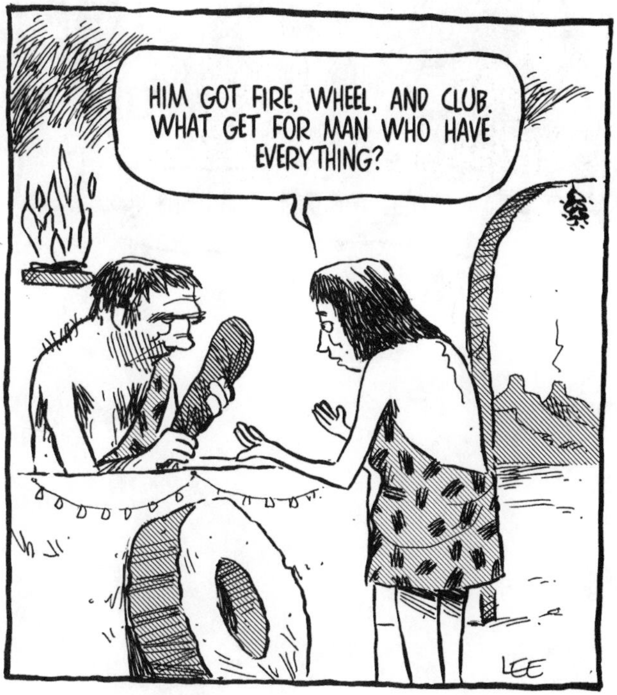
HIM GOT FIRE, WHEEL, AND CLUB. WHAT GET FOR MAN WHO HAVE EVERYTHING?
LEE

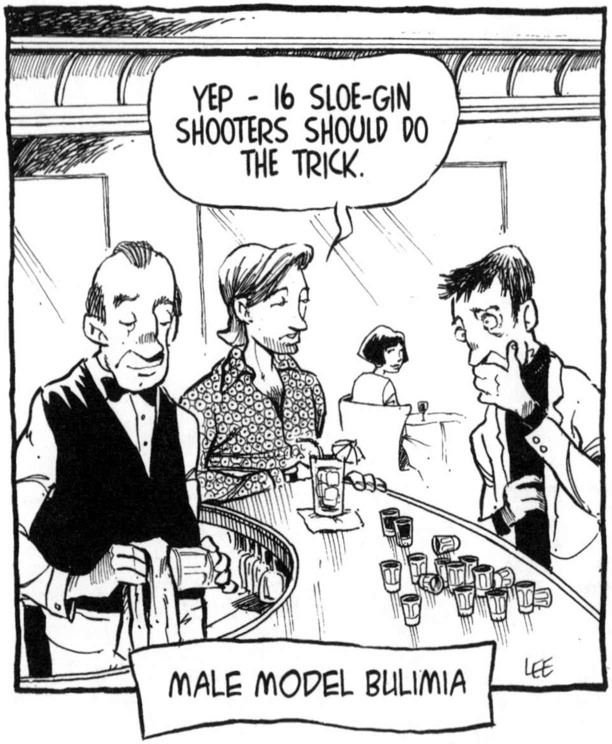
YEP - 16 SLOE-GIN SHOOTERS SHOULD DO THE TRICK.
LEE
MALE MODEL BULIMIA

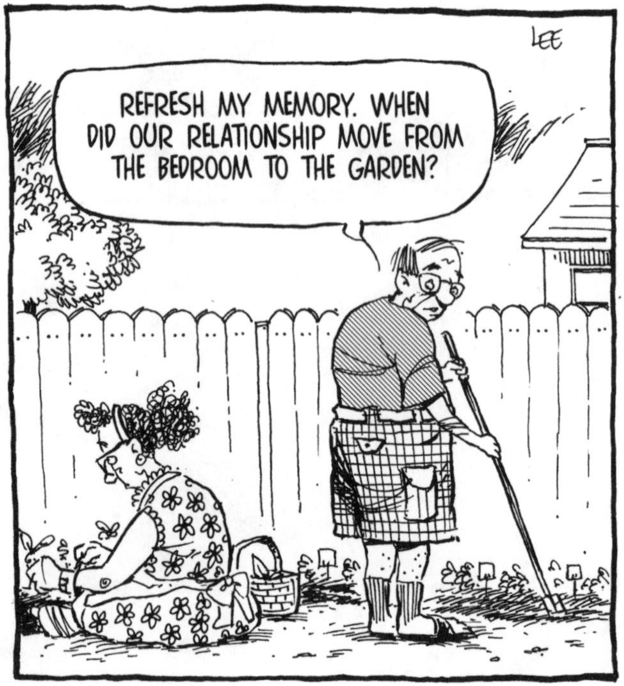
LEE
REFRESH MY MEMORY. WHEN DID OUR RELATIONSHIP MOVE FROM THE BEDROOM TO THE GARDEN?

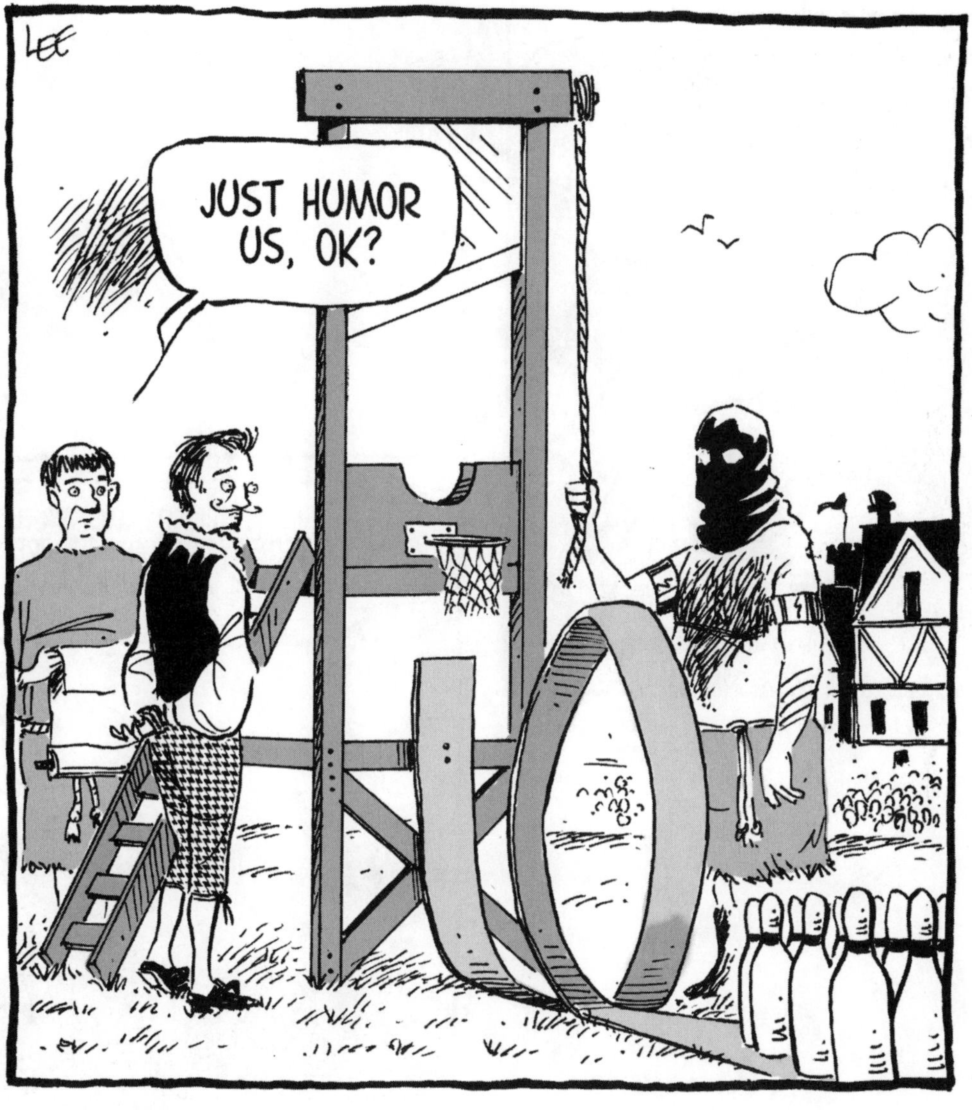
LEE
JUST HUMOR US, OK?

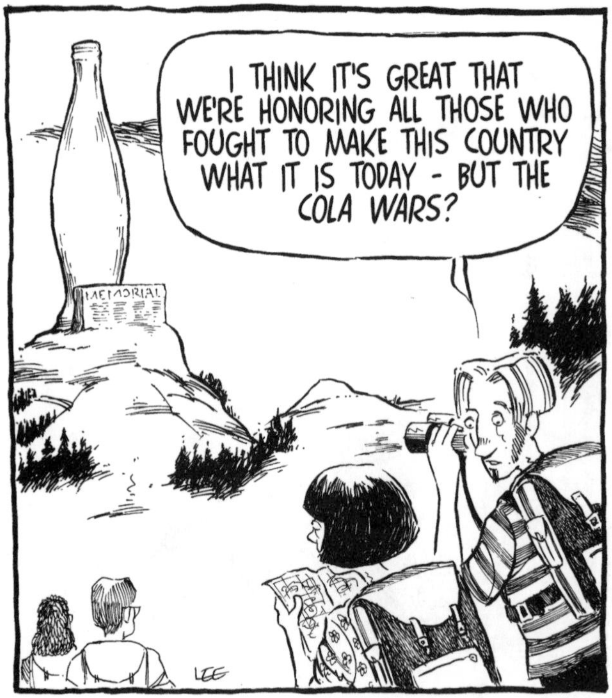
I THINK IT'S GREAT THAT WE'RE HONORING ALL THOSE WHO FOUGHT TO MAKE THIS COUNTRY WHAT IT IS TODAY - BUT THE COLA WARS?
MEMORIAL
LEE

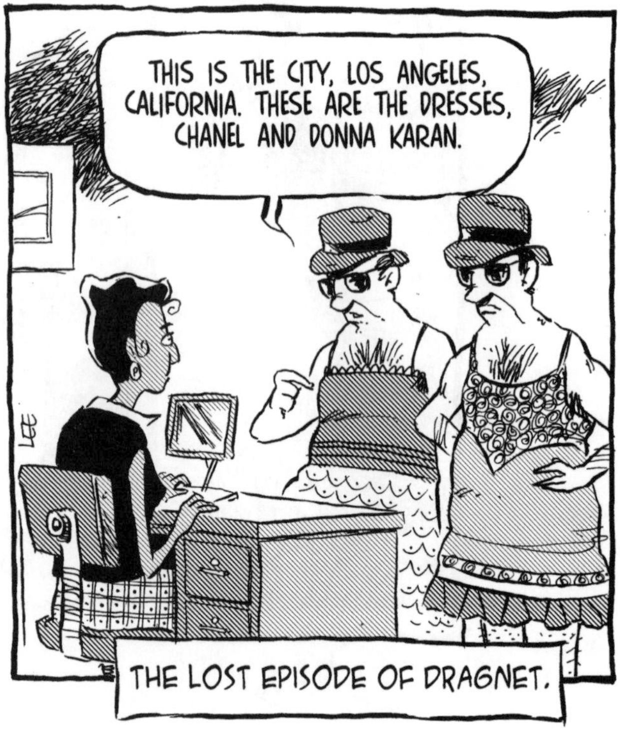
THIS IS THE CITY, LOS ANGELES, CALIFORNIA. THESE ARE THE DRESSES, CHANEL AND DONNA KARAN.
LEE
THE LOST EPISODE OF DRAGNET.

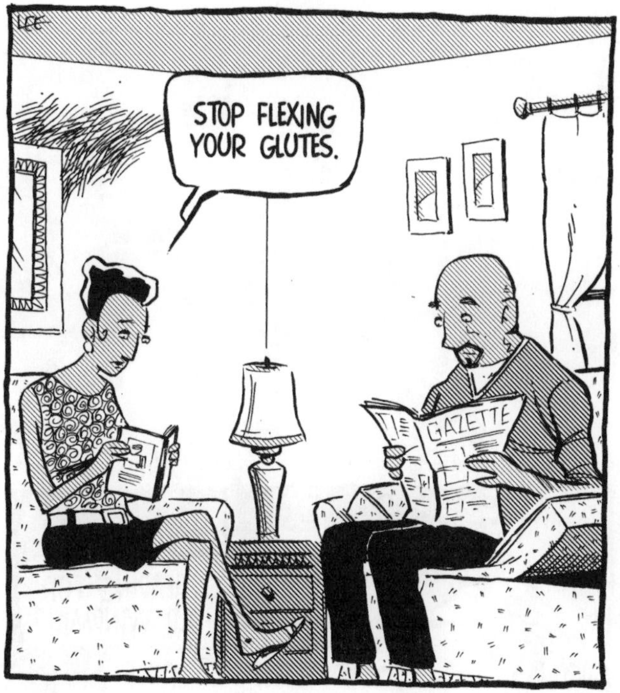
LEE
STOP FLEXING YOUR GLUTES.
GAZETTE

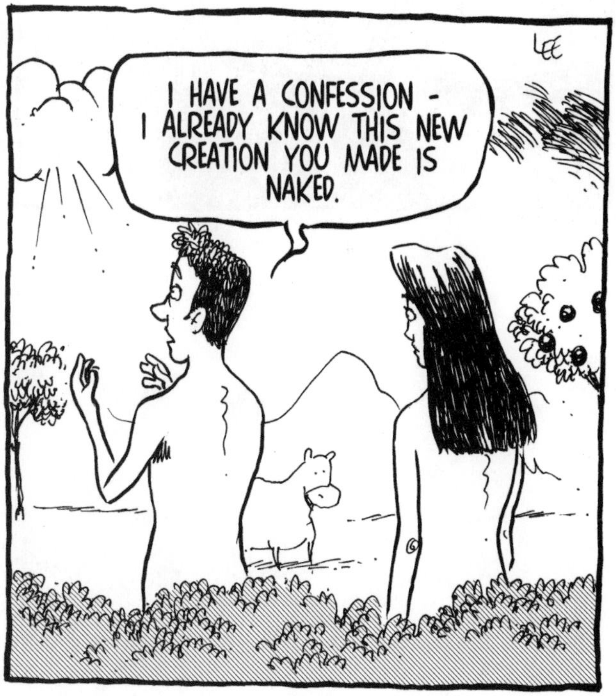
LEE
I HAVE A CONFESSION - I ALREADY KNOW THIS NEW CREATION YOU MADE IS NAKED.

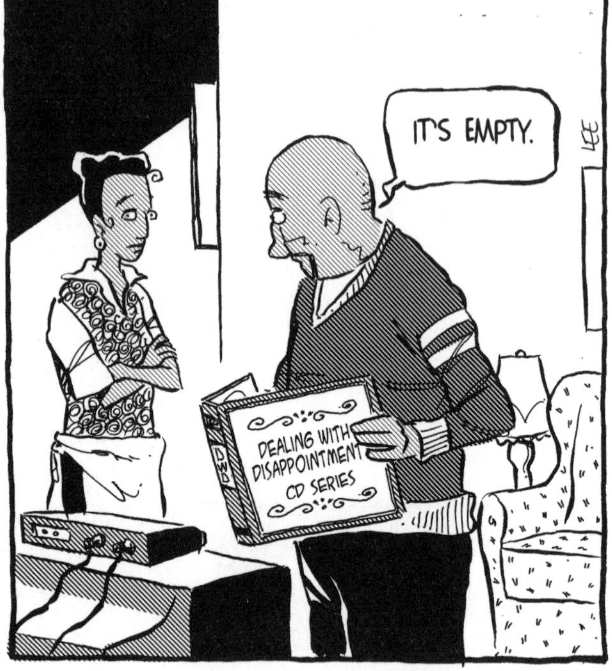
IT'S EMPTY.
DEALING WITH DISAPPOINTMENT CD SERIES
DWD
LEE

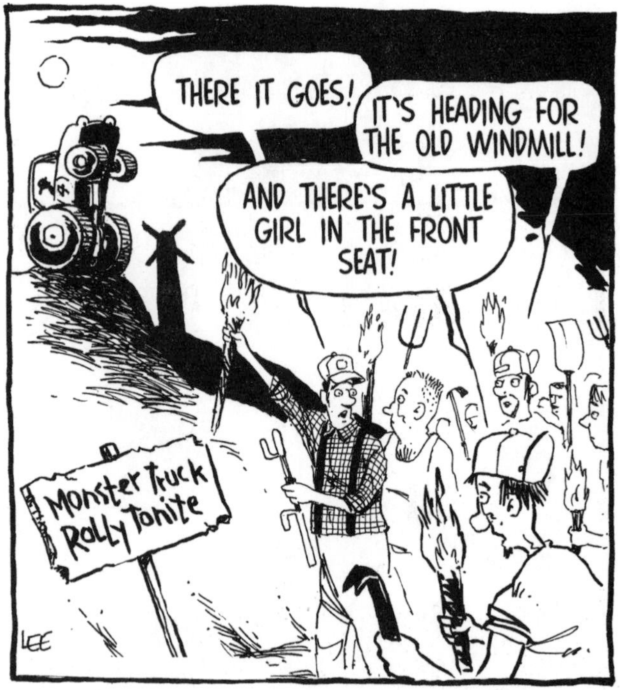
THERE IT GOES!
IT'S HEADING FOR THE OLD WINDMILL!
AND THERE'S A LITTLE GIRL IN THE FRONT SEAT!
Monster Truck Rolly Tonite
LEE

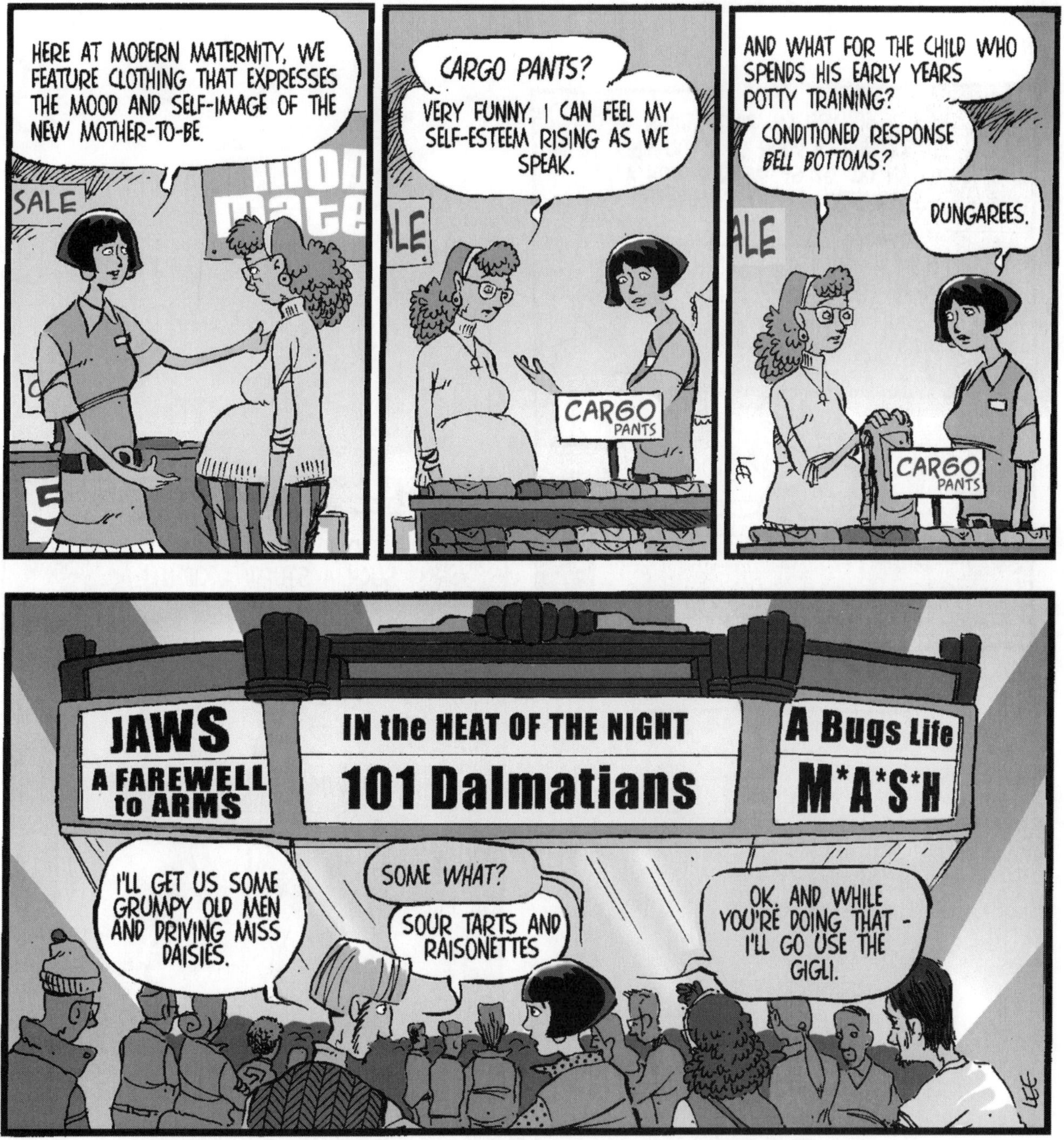
HERE AT MODERN MATERNITY, WE FEATURE CLOTHING THAT EXPRESSES THE MOOD AND SELF-IMAGE OF THE NEW MOTHER-TO-BE.
SALE
CARGO PANTS?
VERY FUNNY. I CAN FEEL MY SELF-ESTEEM RISING AS WE SPEAK.
CARGO PANTS
AND WHAT FOR THE CHILD WHO SPENDS HIS EARLY YEARS POTTY TRAINING?
CONDITIONED RESPONSE BELL BOTTOMS?
DUNGAREES.
CARGO PANTS
JAWS
A FAREWELL to ARMS
IN the HEAT OF THE NIGHT
101 Dalmatians
A Bugs Life
M*A*S*H
I'LL GET US SOME GRUMPY OLD MEN AND DRIVING MISS DAISIES.
SOME WHAT?
SOUR TARTS AND RAISONETTES
OK. AND WHILE YOU'RE DOING THAT - I'LL GO USE THE GIGLI.

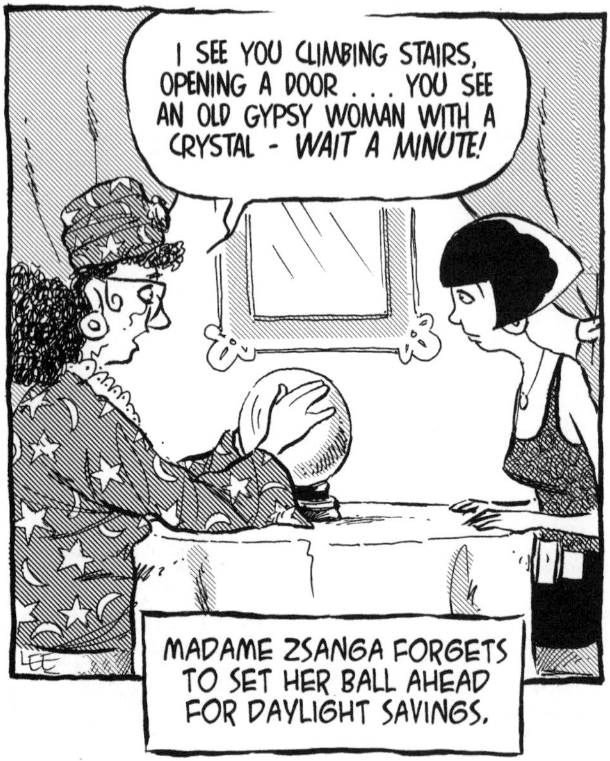
I SEE YOU CLIMBING STAIRS, OPENING A DOOR . . . YOU SEE AN OLD GYPSY WOMAN WITH A CRYSTAL - WAIT A MINUTE!
LEE
MADAME ZSANGA FORGETS TO SET HER BALL AHEAD FOR DAYLIGHT SAVINGS.

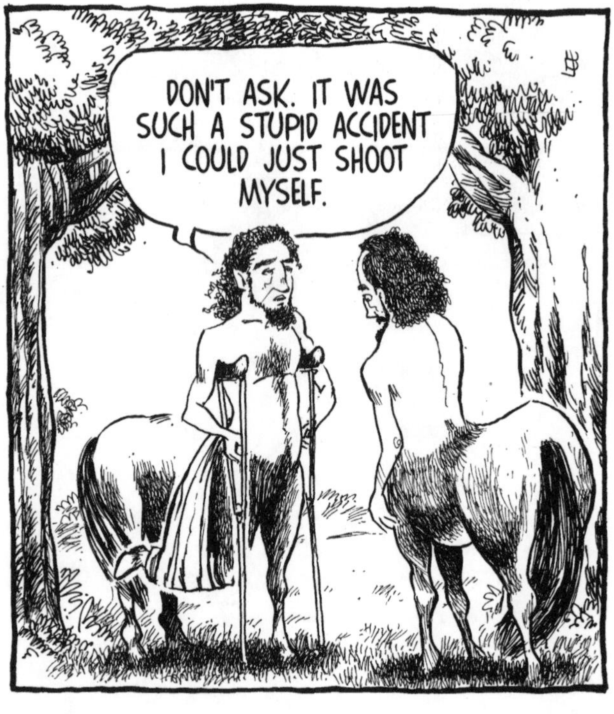
LEE
DON'T ASK. IT WAS SUCH A STUPID ACCIDENT I COULD JUST SHOOT MYSELF.

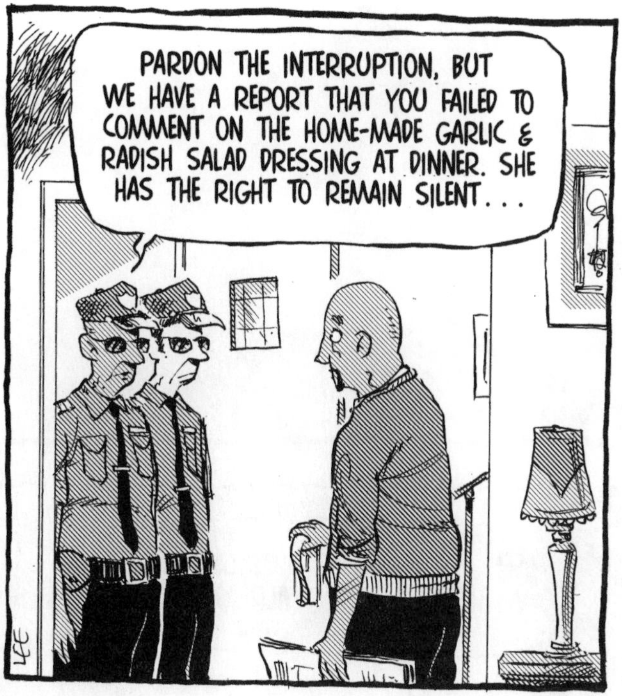
PARDON THE INTERRUPTION, BUT WE HAVE A REPORT THAT YOU FAILED TO COMMENT ON THE HOME-MADE GARLIC & RADISH SALAD DRESSING AT DINNER. SHE HAS THE RIGHT TO REMAIN SILENT...
LEE

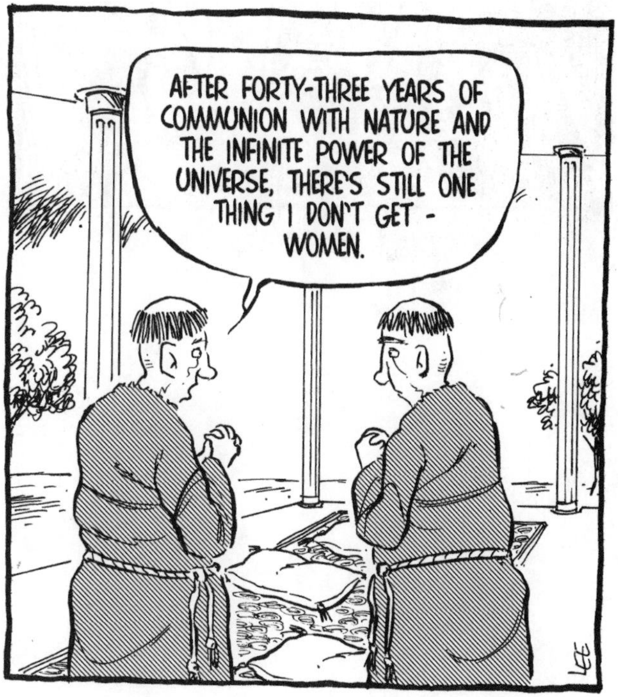
AFTER FORTY-THREE YEARS OF COMMUNION WITH NATURE AND THE INFINITE POWER OF THE UNIVERSE, THERE'S STILL ONE THING I DON'T GET - WOMEN.
LEE

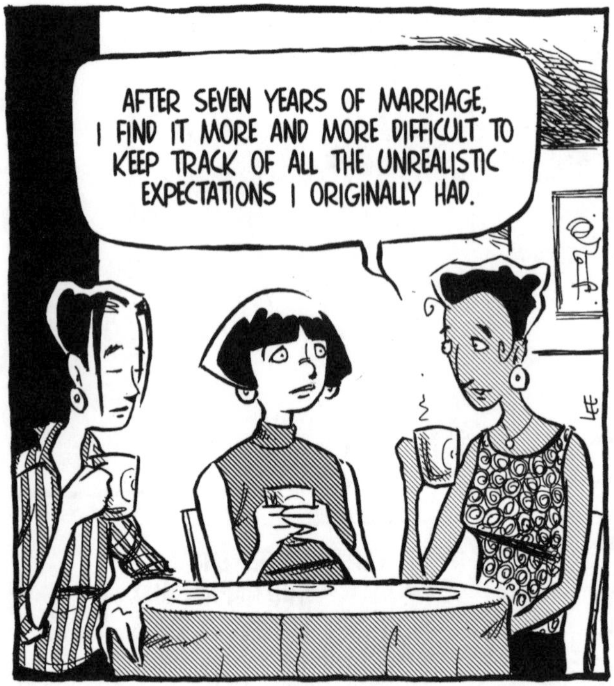
AFTER SEVEN YEARS OF MARRIAGE, I FIND IT MORE AND MORE DIFFICULT TO KEEP TRACK OF ALL THE UNREALISTIC EXPECTATIONS I ORIGINALLY HAD.
LEE

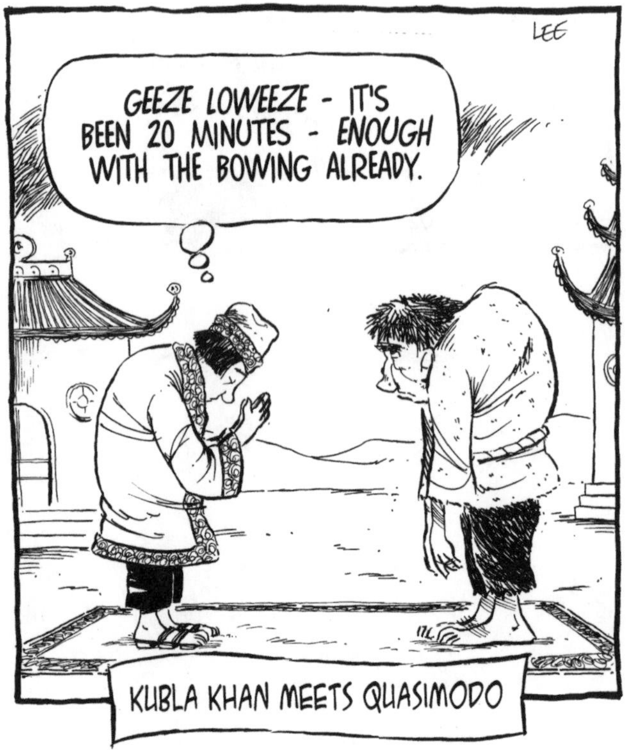
LEE
GEEZE LOWEEZE - IT'S BEEN 20 MINUTES - ENOUGH WITH THE BOWING ALREADY.
KUBLA KHAN MEETS QUASIMODO

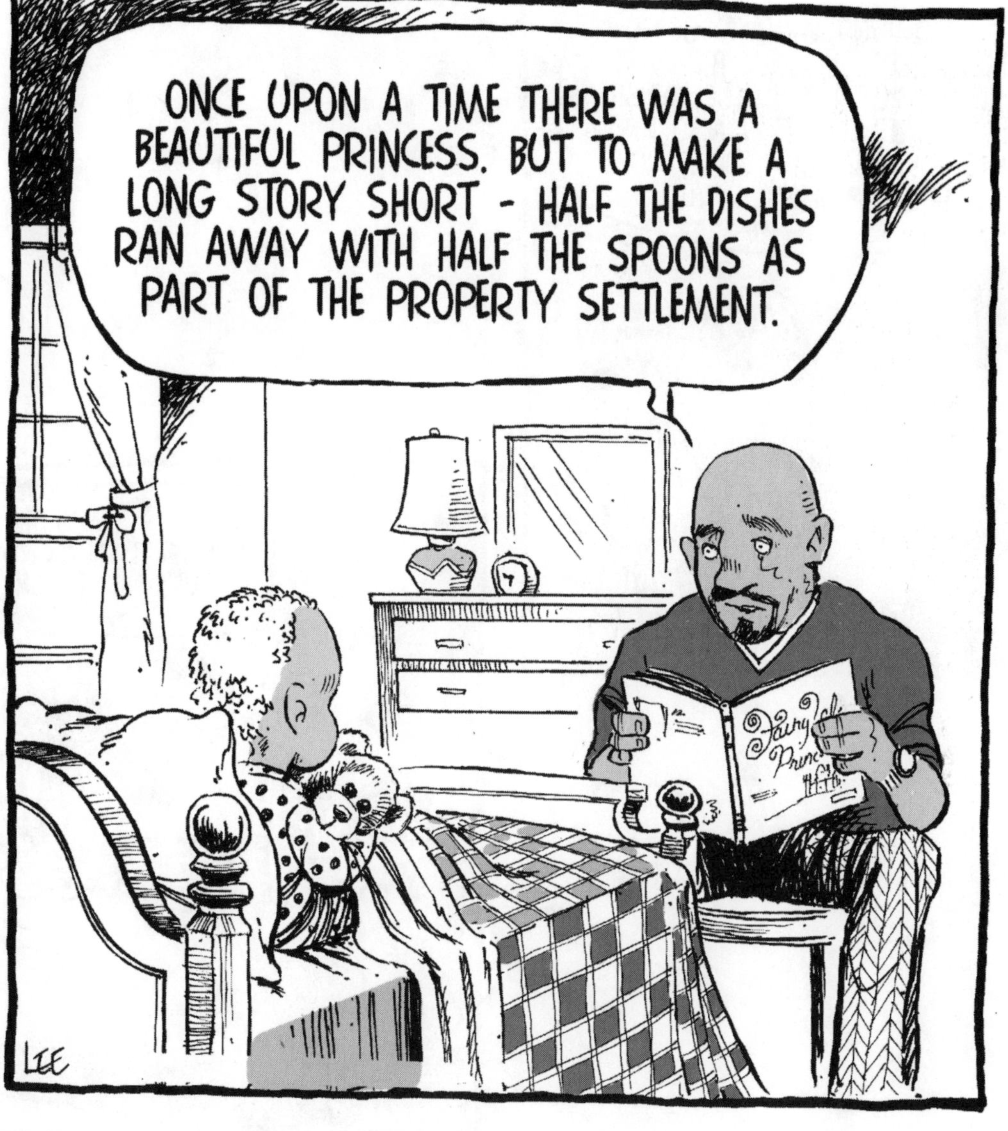
ONCE UPON A TIME THERE WAS A BEAUTIFUL PRINCESS. BUT TO MAKE A LONG STORY SHORT - HALF THE DISHES RAN AWAY WITH HALF THE SPOONS AS PART OF THE PROPERTY SETTLEMENT.
LEE

I SOOO DIDN'T WANT TO GO TO THIS PARTY - I KNEW THERE'D BE NOTHING BUT A BUNCH OF BORISH SELF-CENTERED EGOISTS. I ALSO KNEW THAT IF I DIDN'T GO, PEOPLE MIGHT THINK I WASN'T INVITED.
LEE

NO, NO - THAT'S THE WAY THEY DID IT ON 'SCRUBS'. DO IT LIKE THEY DID ON 'ER'.
LEE

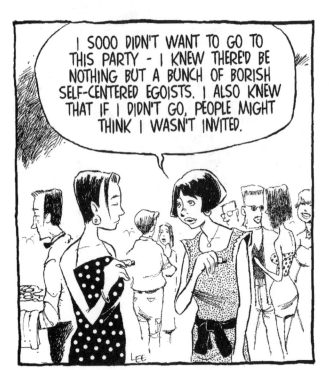

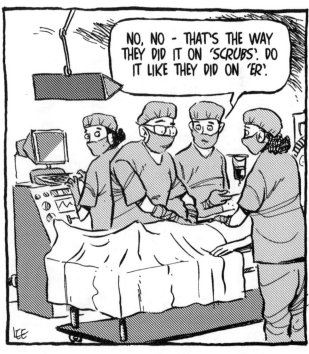

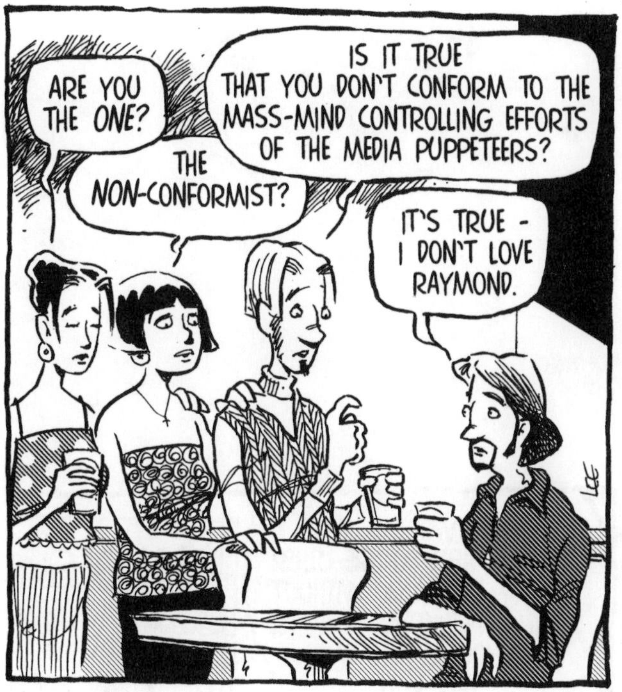

ARE YOU THE ONE?
THE NON-CONFORMIST?
IS IT TRUE THAT YOU DON'T CONFORM TO THE MASS-MIND CONTROLLING EFFORTS OF THE MEDIA PUPPETEERS?
IT'S TRUE - I DON'T LOVE RAYMOND.
LEE

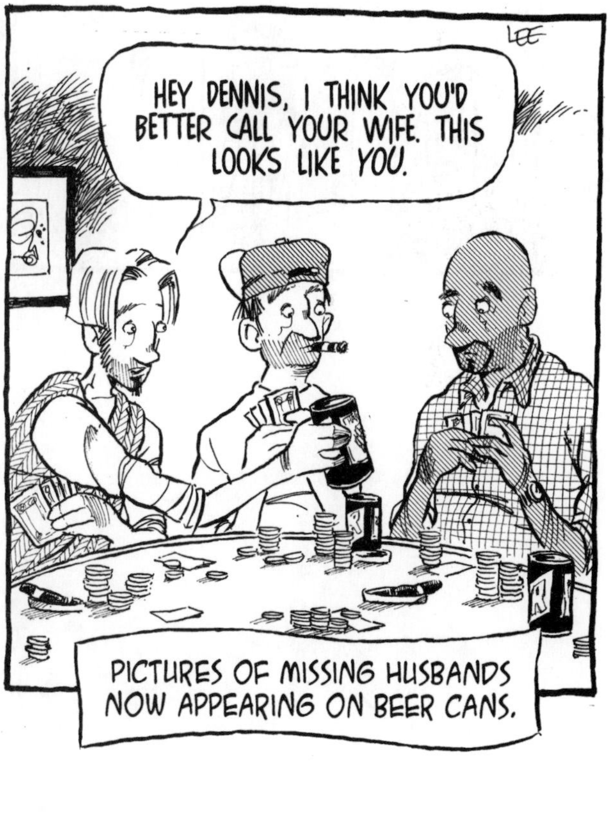

LEE
HEY DENNIS, I THINK YOU'D BETTER CALL YOUR WIFE. THIS LOOKS LIKE YOU.
PICTURES OF MISSING HUSBANDS NOW APPEARING ON BEER CANS.

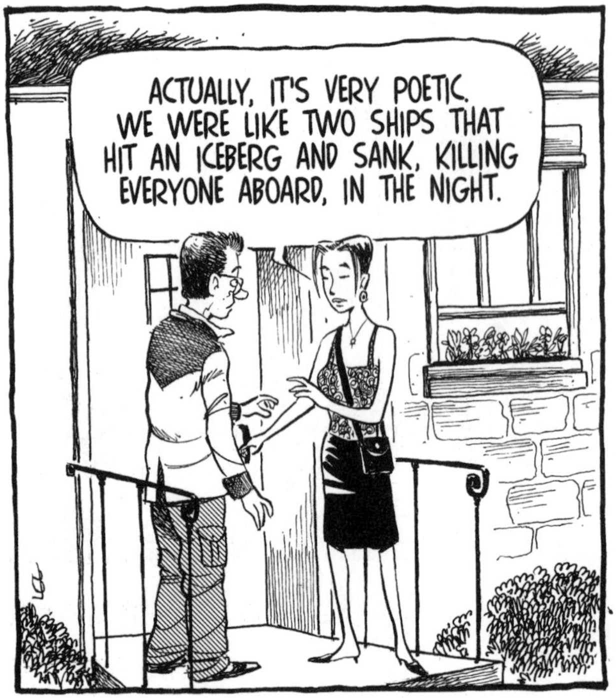
ACTUALLY, IT'S VERY POETIC. WE WERE LIKE TWO SHIPS THAT HIT AN ICEBERG AND SANK, KILLING EVERYONE ABOARD, IN THE NIGHT.
LEE

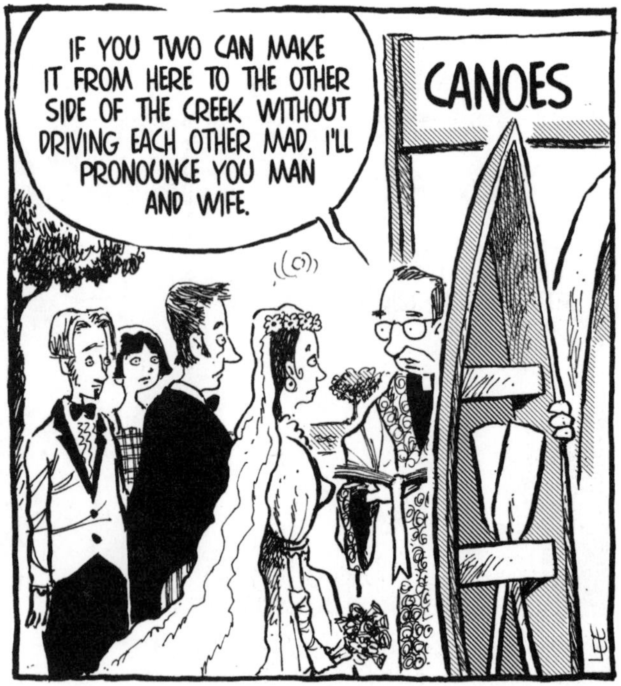
IF YOU TWO CAN MAKE IT FROM HERE TO THE OTHER SIDE OF THE CREEK WITHOUT DRIVING EACH OTHER MAD, I'LL PRONOUNCE YOU MAN AND WIFE.
CANOES
LEE

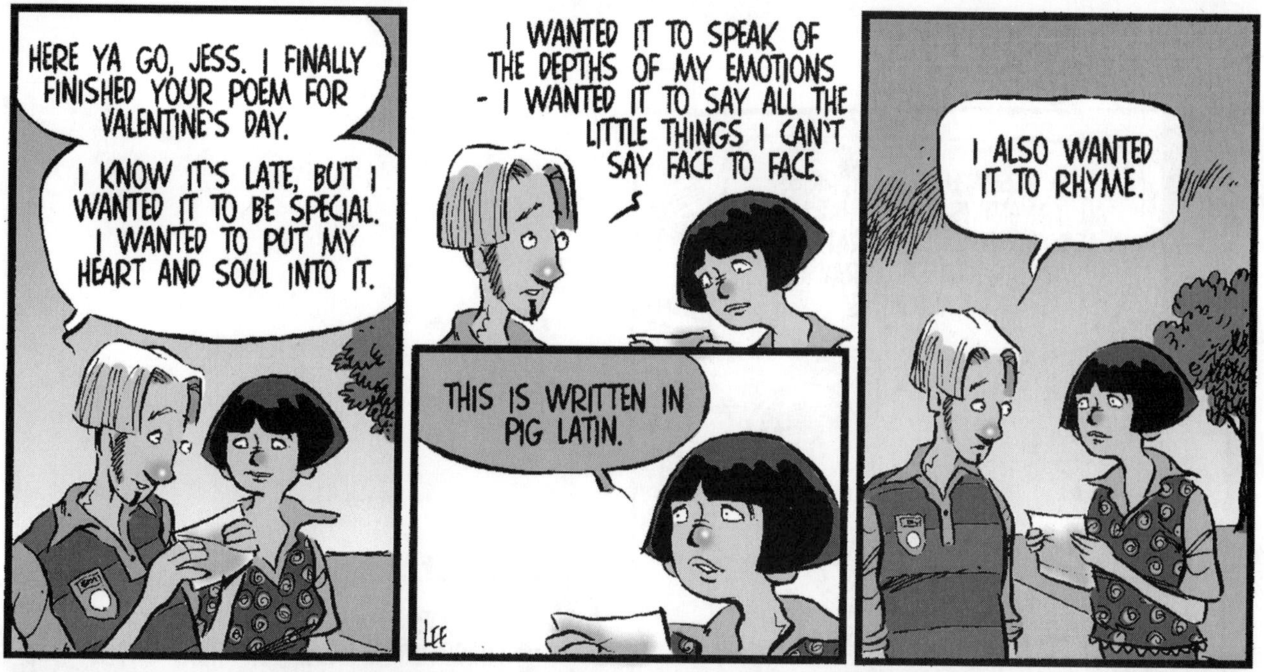
HERE YA GO, JESS. I FINALLY FINISHED YOUR POEM FOR VALENTINE'S DAY.
I KNOW IT'S LATE, BUT I WANTED IT TO BE SPECIAL. I WANTED TO PUT MY HEART AND SOUL INTO IT.
I WANTED IT TO SPEAK OF THE DEPTHS OF MY EMOTIONS - I WANTED IT TO SAY ALL THE LITTLE THINGS I CAN'T SAY FACE TO FACE.
THIS IS WRITTEN IN PIG LATIN.
LEE
I ALSO WANTED IT TO RHYME.

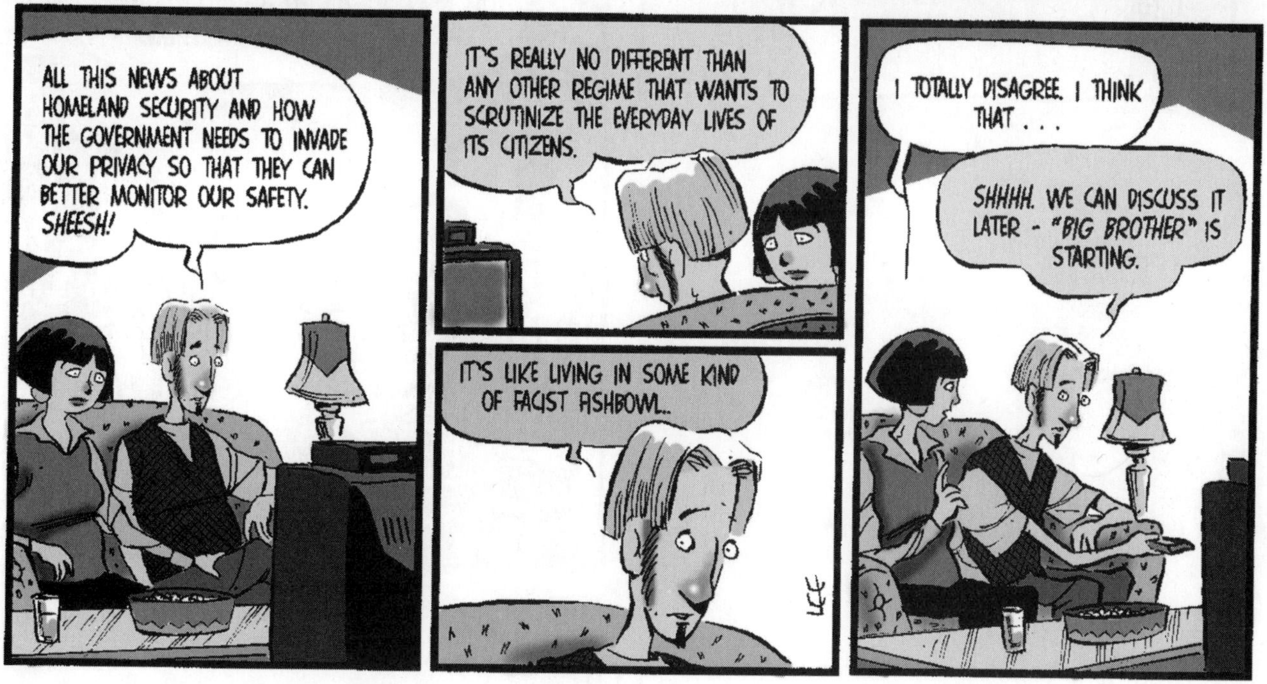
ALL THIS NEWS ABOUT HOMELAND SECURITY AND HOW THE GOVERNMENT NEEDS TO INVADE OUR PRIVACY SO THAT THEY CAN BETTER MONITOR OUR SAFETY. *SHEESH!*
IT'S REALLY NO DIFFERENT THAN ANY OTHER REGIME THAT WANTS TO SCRUTINIZE THE EVERYDAY LIVES OF ITS CITIZENS.
IT'S LIKE LIVING IN SOME KIND OF FACIST FISHBOWL..
LEE
I TOTALLY DISAGREE. I THINK THAT . . .
SHHHH. WE CAN DISCUSS IT LATER - *"BIG BROTHER"* IS STARTING.

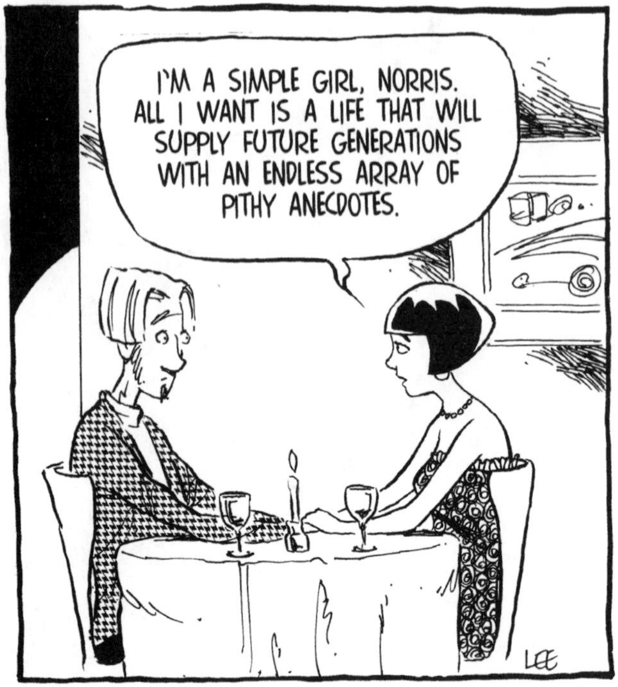
I'M A SIMPLE GIRL, NORRIS. ALL I WANT IS A LIFE THAT WILL SUPPLY FUTURE GENERATIONS WITH AN ENDLESS ARRAY OF PITHY ANECDOTES.
LEE

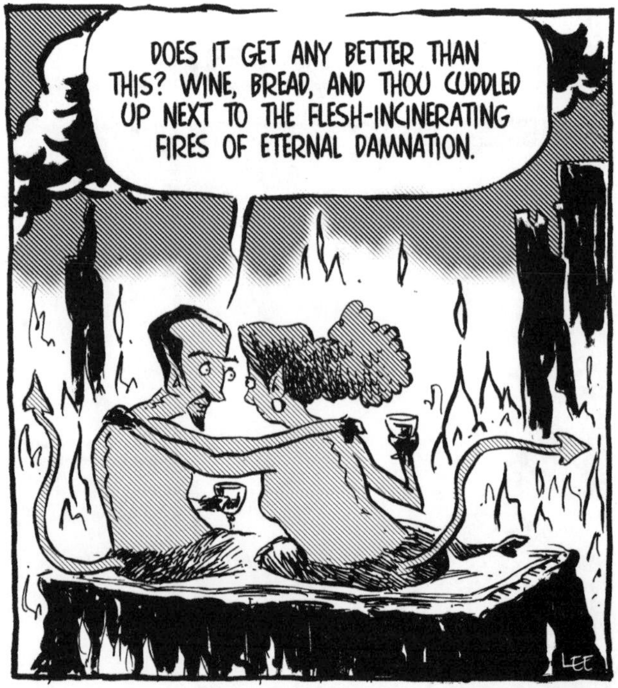
DOES IT GET ANY BETTER THAN THIS? WINE, BREAD, AND THOU CUDDLED UP NEXT TO THE FLESH-INCINERATING FIRES OF ETERNAL DAMNATION.
LEE

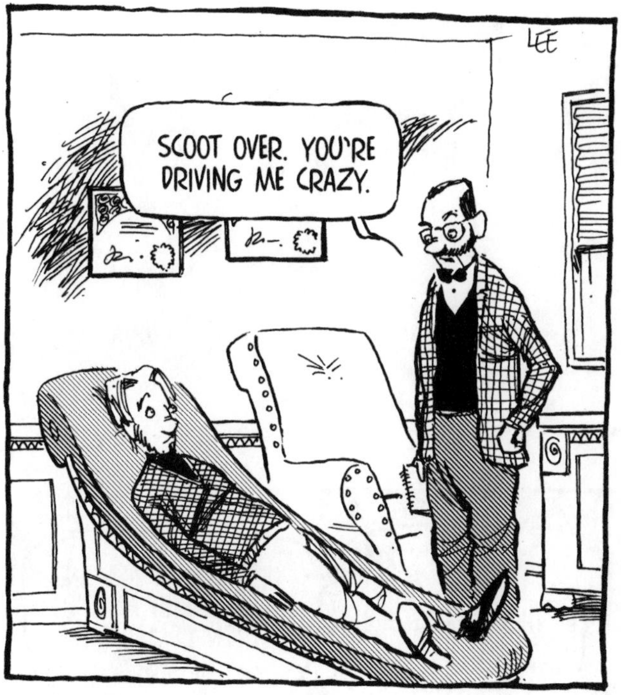
LEE
SCOOT OVER. YOU'RE DRIVING ME CRAZY.

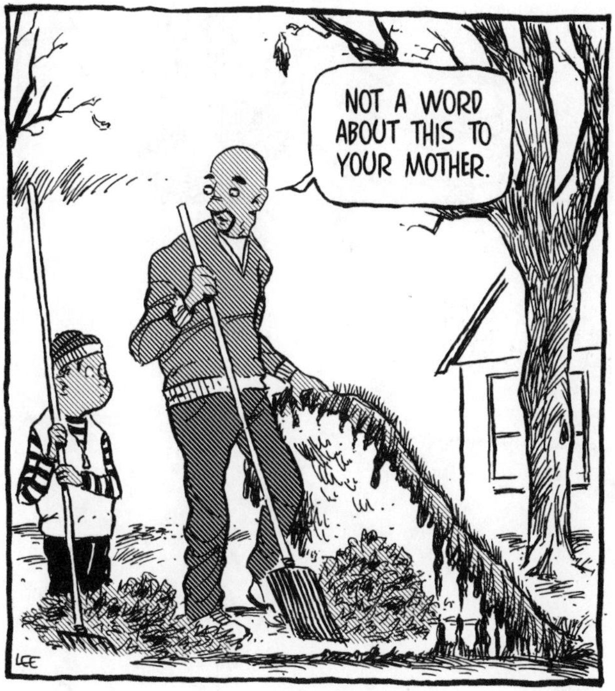
NOT A WORD ABOUT THIS TO YOUR MOTHER.
LEE

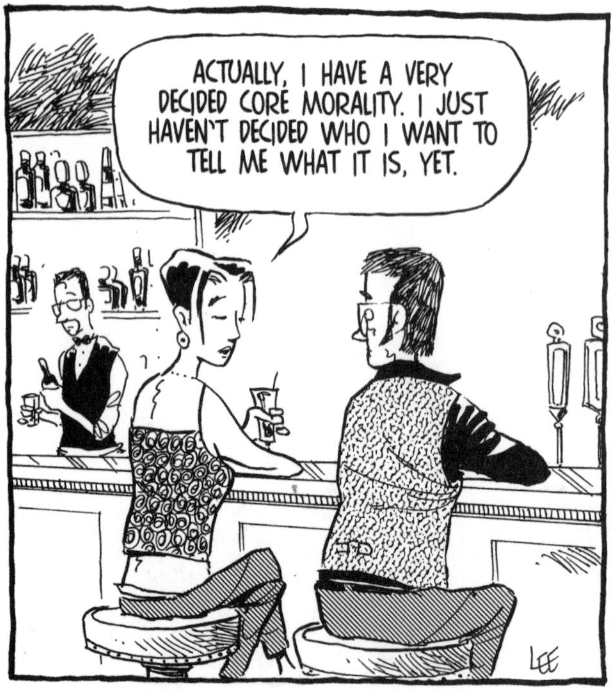
ACTUALLY, I HAVE A VERY DECIDED CORE MORALITY. I JUST HAVEN'T DECIDED WHO I WANT TO TELL ME WHAT IT IS, YET.
LEE

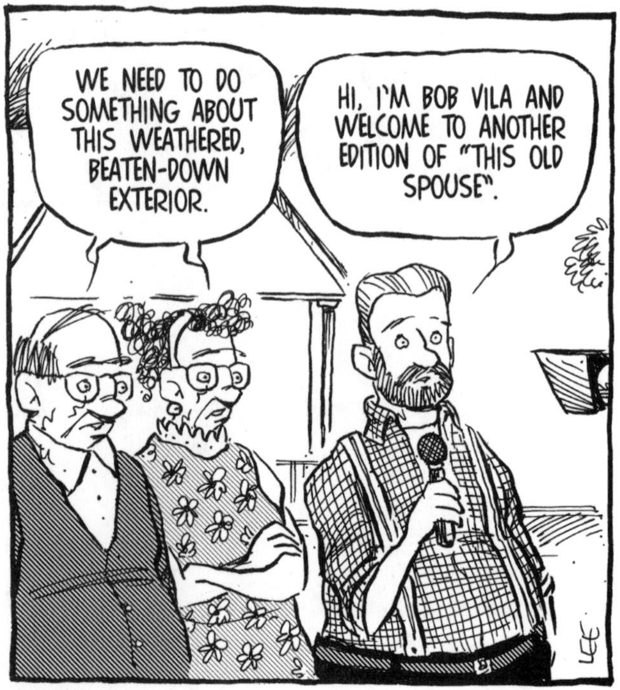
HI, I'M BOB VILA AND WELCOME TO ANOTHER EDITION OF "THIS OLD SPOUSE".
WE NEED TO DO SOMETHING ABOUT THIS WEATHERED, BEATEN-DOWN EXTERIOR.
LEE

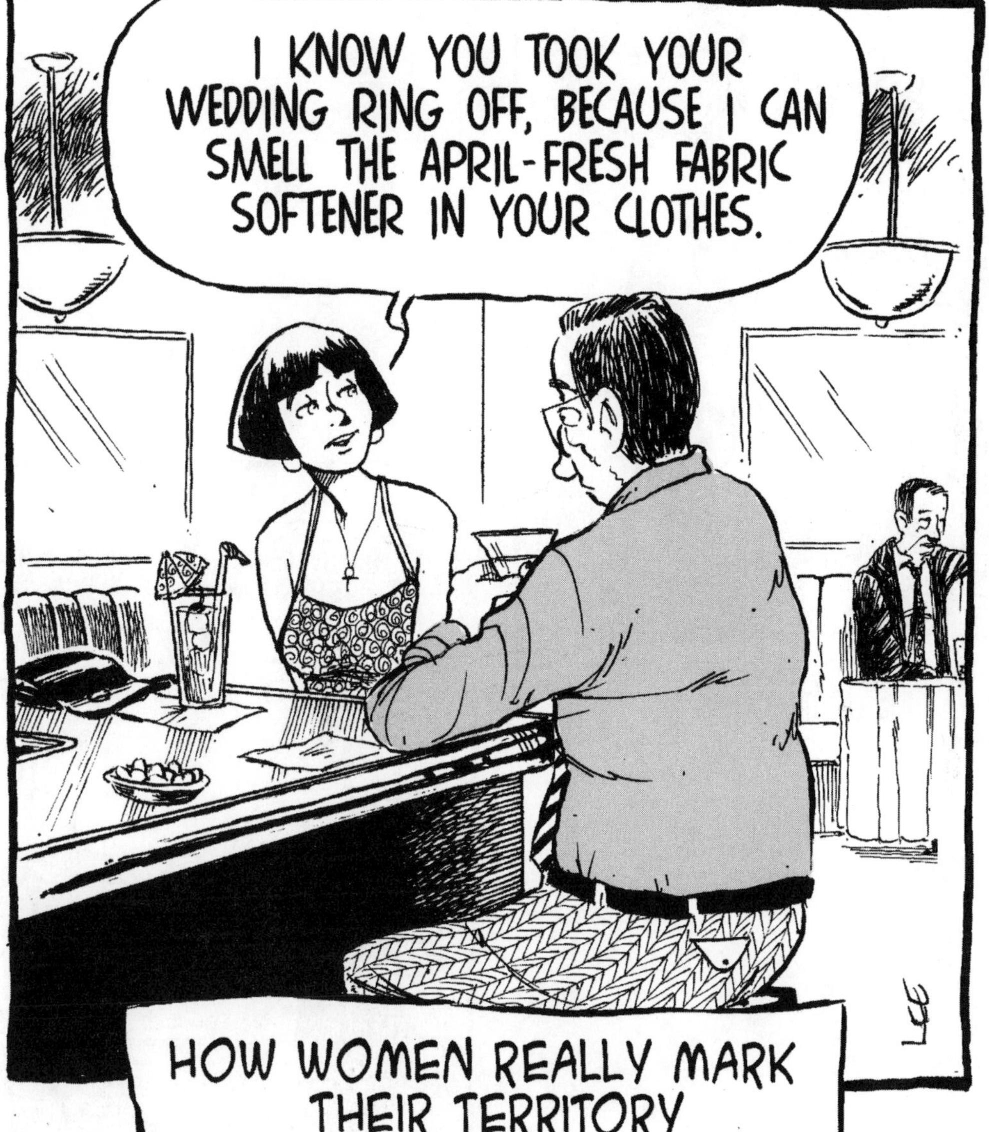
I KNOW YOU TOOK YOUR WEDDING RING OFF, BECAUSE I CAN SMELL THE APRIL-FRESH FABRIC SOFTENER IN YOUR CLOTHES.
LEE

HOW WOMEN REALLY MARK THEIR TERRITORY

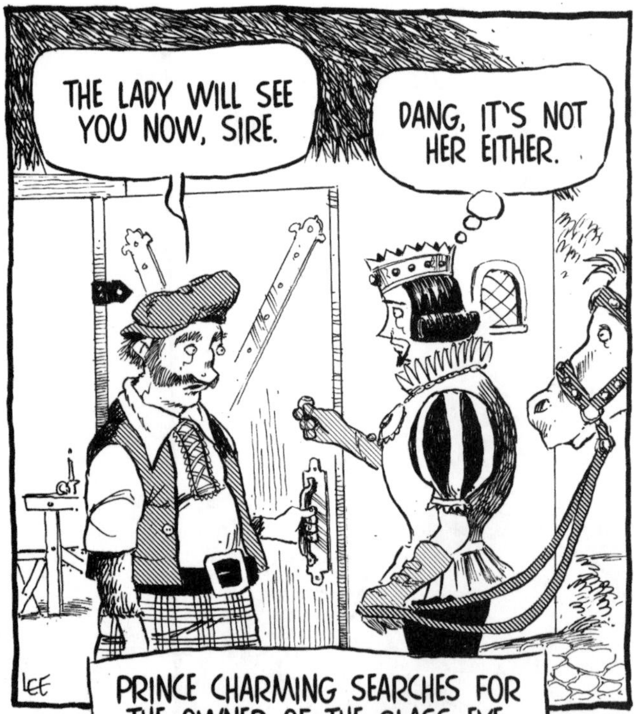
THE LADY WILL SEE YOU NOW, SIRE.
DANG, IT'S NOT HER EITHER.
LEE

PRINCE CHARMING SEARCHES FOR THE OWNER OF THE GLASS EYE.

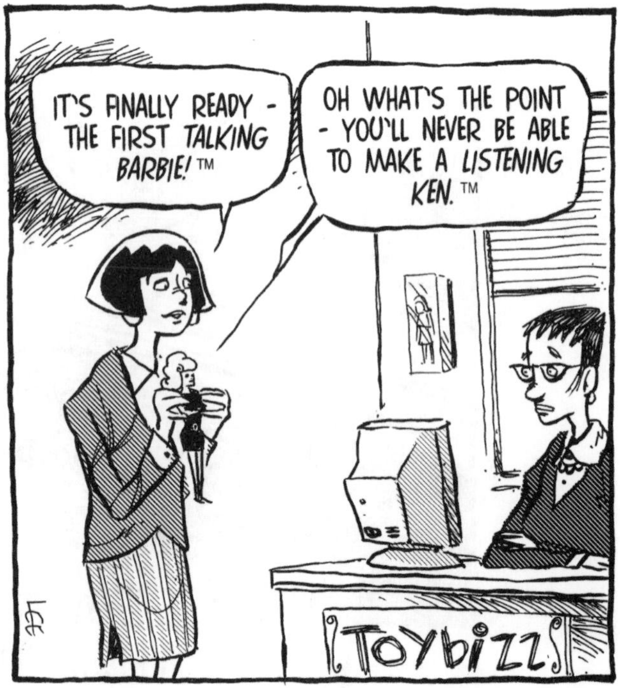
IT'S FINALLY READY - THE FIRST *TALKING BARBIE!* ™
OH WHAT'S THE POINT - YOU'LL NEVER BE ABLE TO MAKE A *LISTENING KEN.* ™
TOYBIZZ
LEE

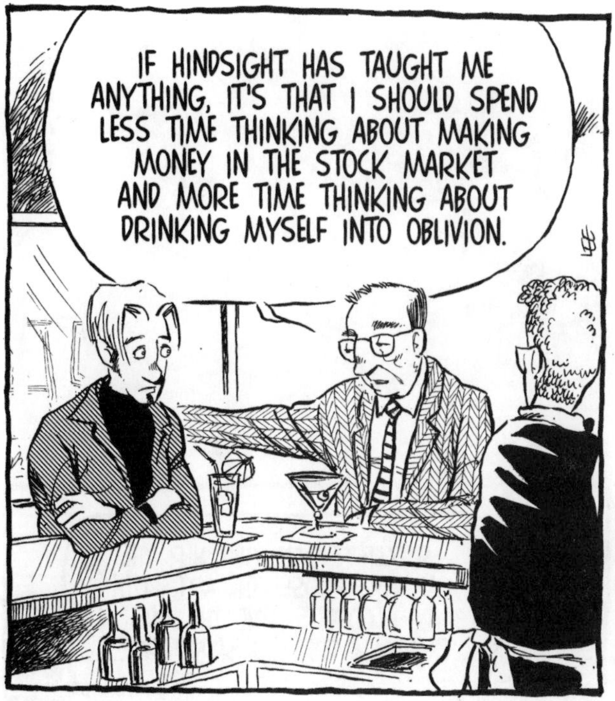
IF HINDSIGHT HAS TAUGHT ME ANYTHING, IT'S THAT I SHOULD SPEND LESS TIME THINKING ABOUT MAKING MONEY IN THE STOCK MARKET AND MORE TIME THINKING ABOUT DRINKING MYSELF INTO OBLIVION.

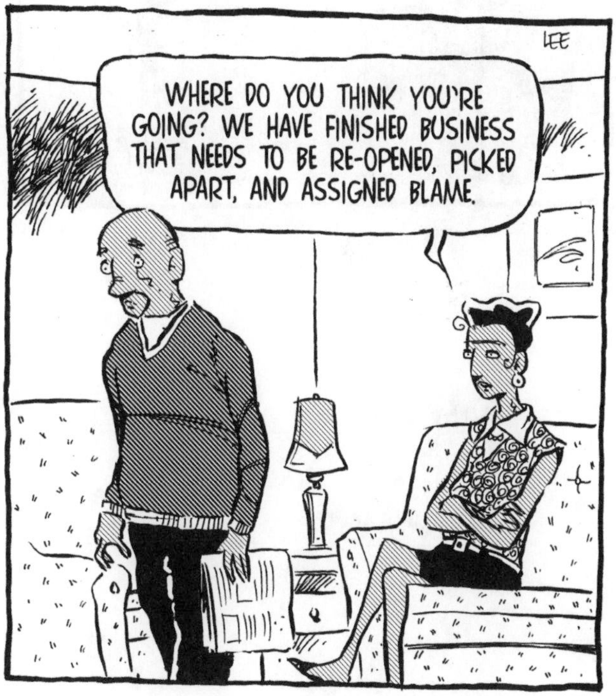
WHERE DO YOU THINK YOU'RE GOING? WE HAVE FINISHED BUSINESS THAT NEEDS TO BE RE-OPENED, PICKED APART, AND ASSIGNED BLAME.

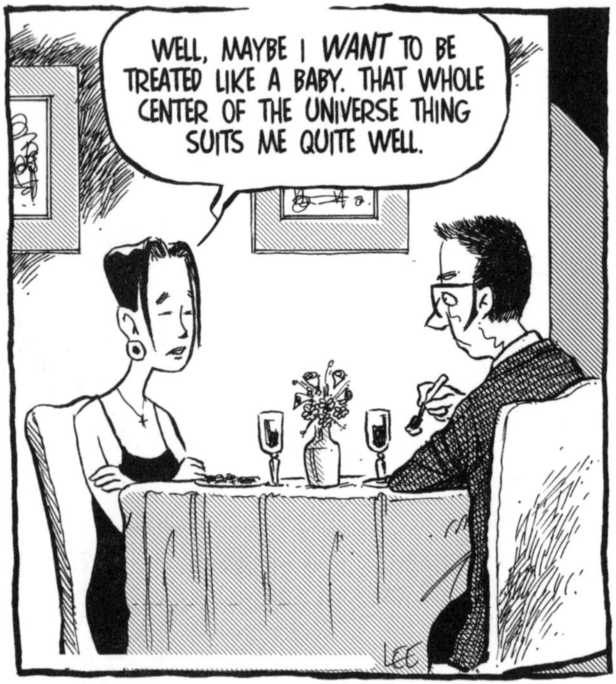
WELL, MAYBE I *WANT* TO BE TREATED LIKE A BABY. THAT WHOLE CENTER OF THE UNIVERSE THING SUITS ME QUITE WELL.
LEE

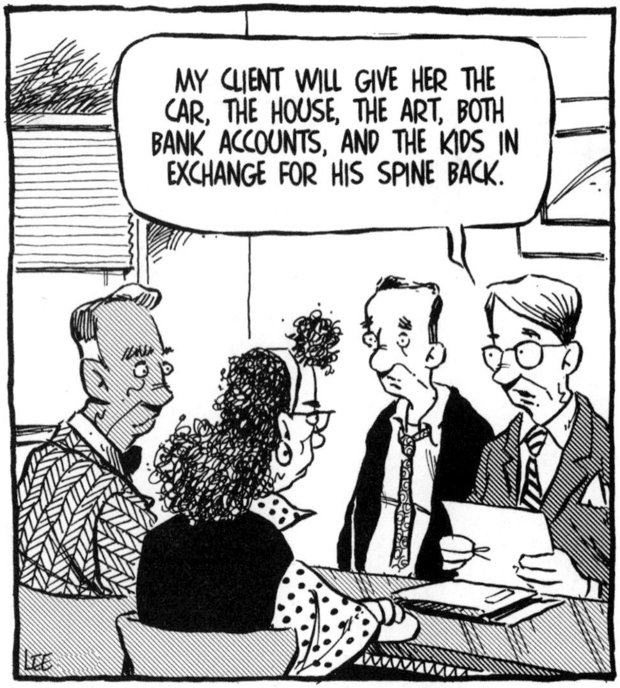
MY CLIENT WILL GIVE HER THE CAR, THE HOUSE, THE ART, BOTH BANK ACCOUNTS, AND THE KIDS IN EXCHANGE FOR HIS SPINE BACK.
LEE

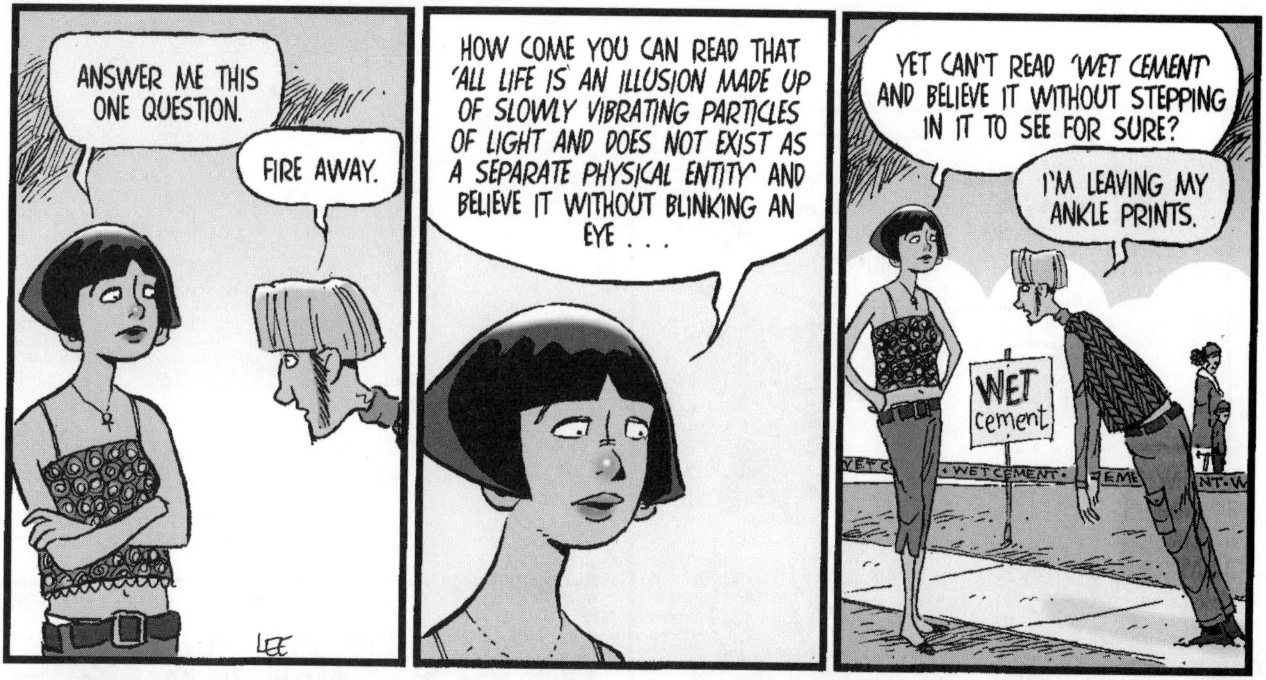
ANSWER ME THIS ONE QUESTION.
FIRE AWAY.
LEE
HOW COME YOU CAN READ THAT 'ALL LIFE IS AN ILLUSION MADE UP OF SLOWLY VIBRATING PARTICLES OF LIGHT AND DOES NOT EXIST AS A SEPARATE PHYSICAL ENTITY' AND BELIEVE IT WITHOUT BLINKING AN EYE . . .
YET CAN'T READ 'WET CEMENT' AND BELIEVE IT WITHOUT STEPPING IN IT TO SEE FOR SURE?
I'M LEAVING MY ANKLE PRINTS.
WET cement
WET CEMENT

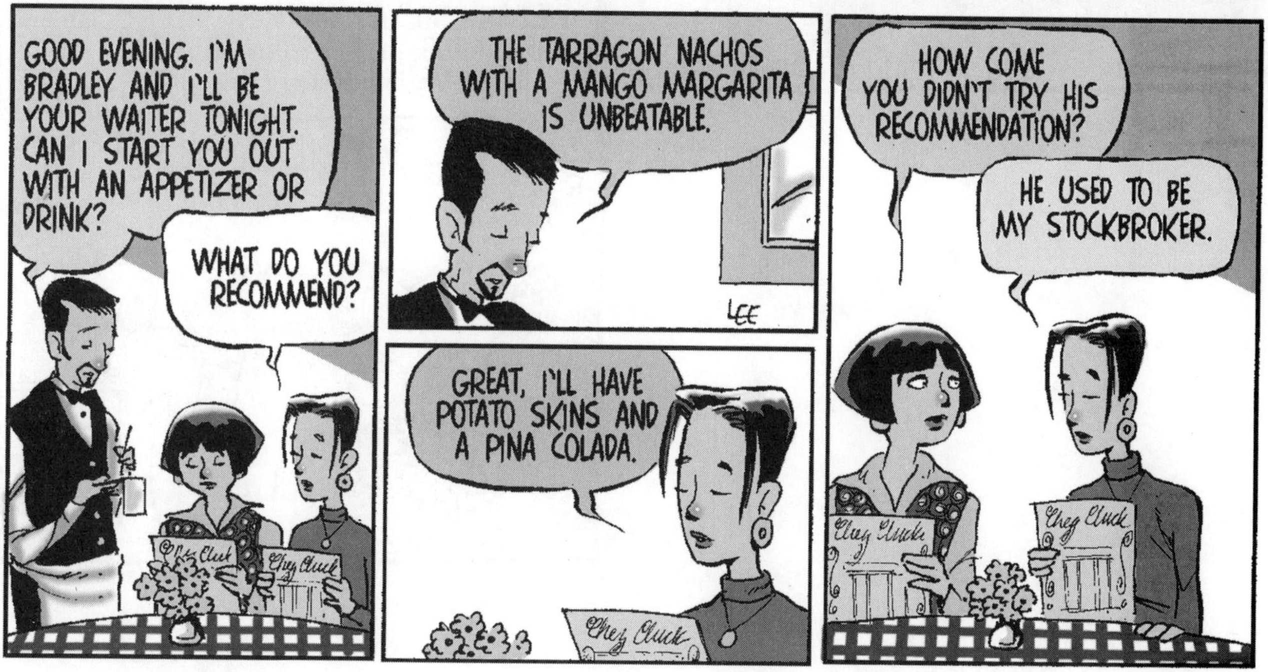
GOOD EVENING. I'M BRADLEY AND I'LL BE YOUR WAITER TONIGHT. CAN I START YOU OUT WITH AN APPETIZER OR DRINK?
WHAT DO YOU RECOMMEND?
THE TARRAGON NACHOS WITH A MANGO MARGARITA IS UNBEATABLE.
LEE
GREAT, I'LL HAVE POTATO SKINS AND A PINA COLADA.
Chez Cluck
HOW COME YOU DIDN'T TRY HIS RECOMMENDATION?
HE USED TO BE MY STOCKBROKER.

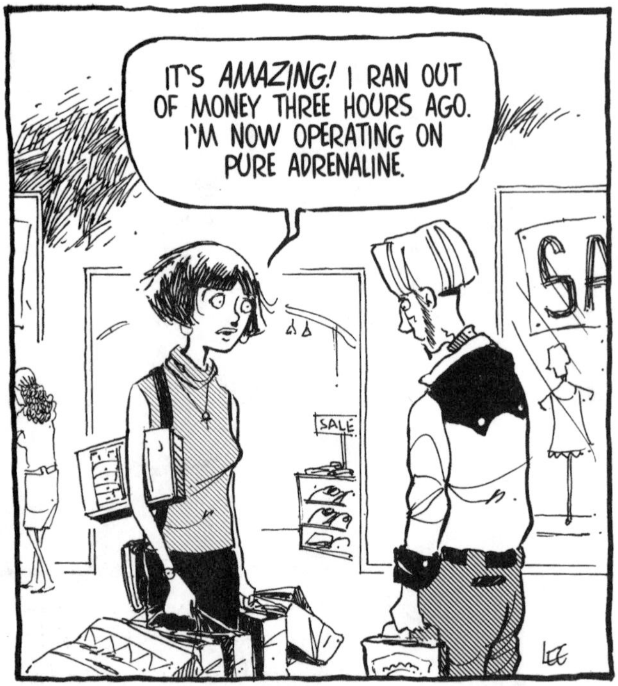
IT'S AMAZING! I RAN OUT OF MONEY THREE HOURS AGO. I'M NOW OPERATING ON PURE ADRENALINE.
SALE
LEE

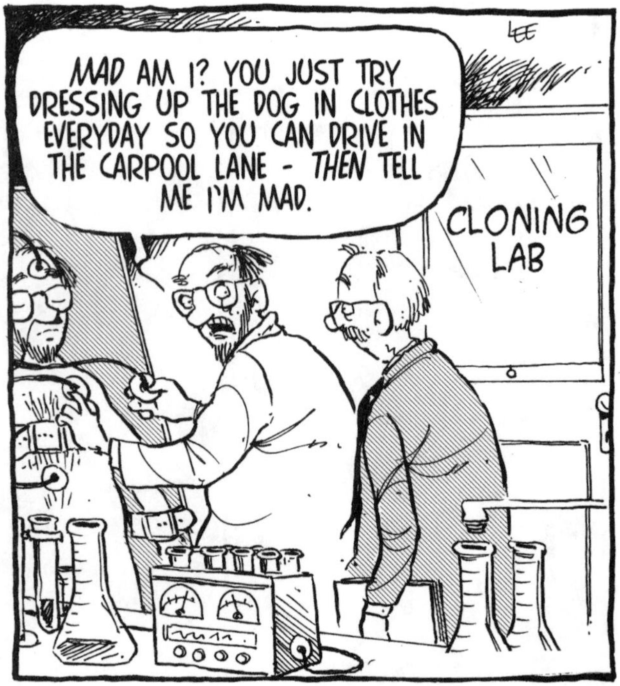
LEE
MAD AM I? YOU JUST TRY DRESSING UP THE DOG IN CLOTHES EVERYDAY SO YOU CAN DRIVE IN THE CARPOOL LANE - THEN TELL ME I'M MAD.
CLONING LAB

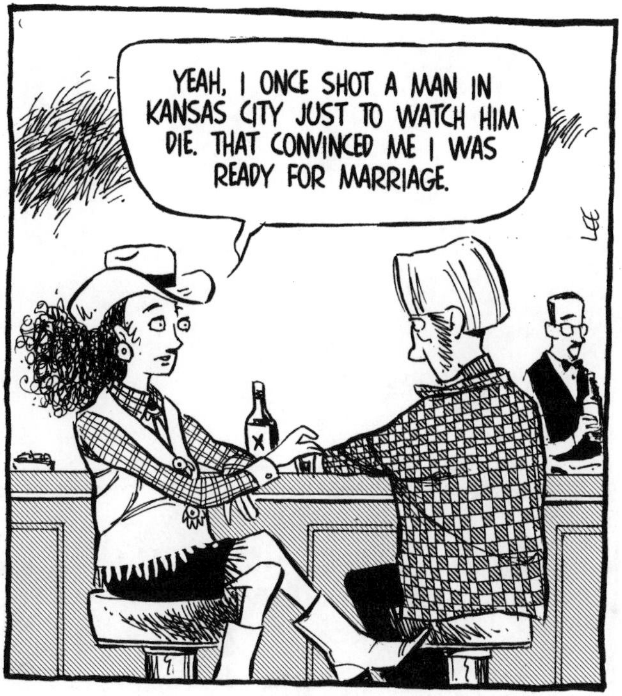
YEAH, I ONCE SHOT A MAN IN KANSAS CITY JUST TO WATCH HIM DIE. THAT CONVINCED ME I WAS READY FOR MARRIAGE.
LEE

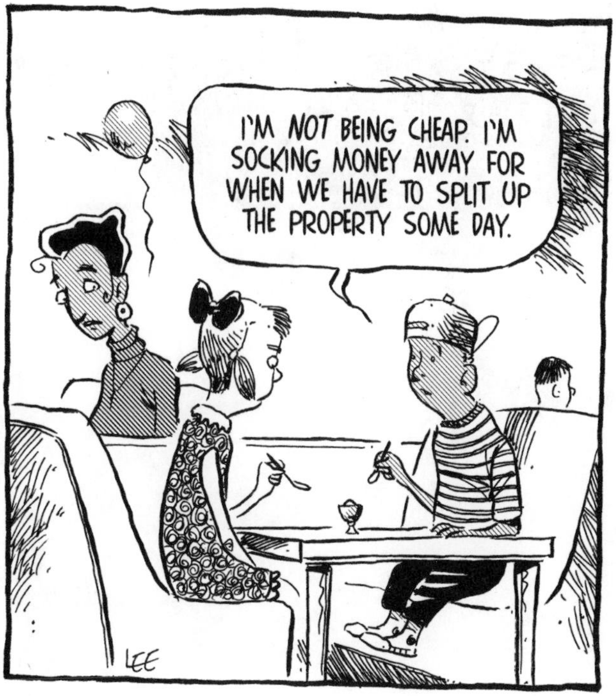
I'M *NOT* BEING CHEAP. I'M SOCKING MONEY AWAY FOR WHEN WE HAVE TO SPLIT UP THE PROPERTY SOME DAY.
LEE

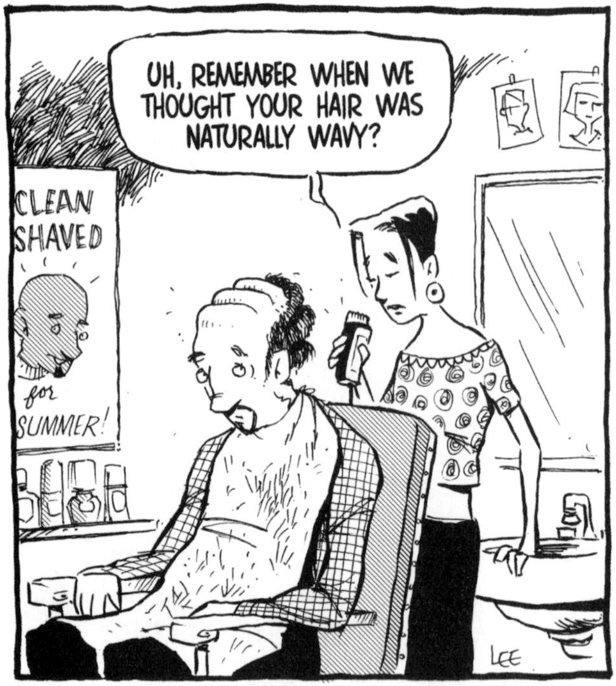
UH, REMEMBER WHEN WE THOUGHT YOUR HAIR WAS NATURALLY WAVY?
CLEAN SHAVED for SUMMER!
LEE

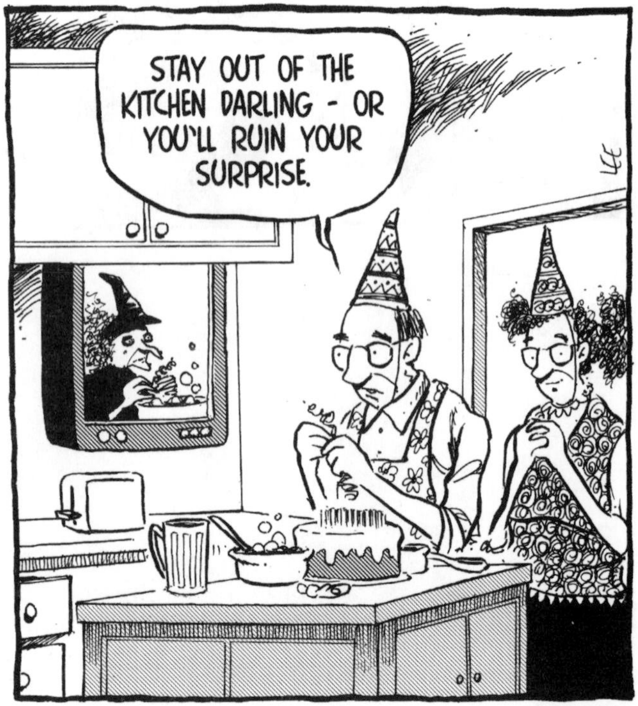
STAY OUT OF THE KITCHEN DARLING - OR YOU'LL RUIN YOUR SURPRISE.
LEE

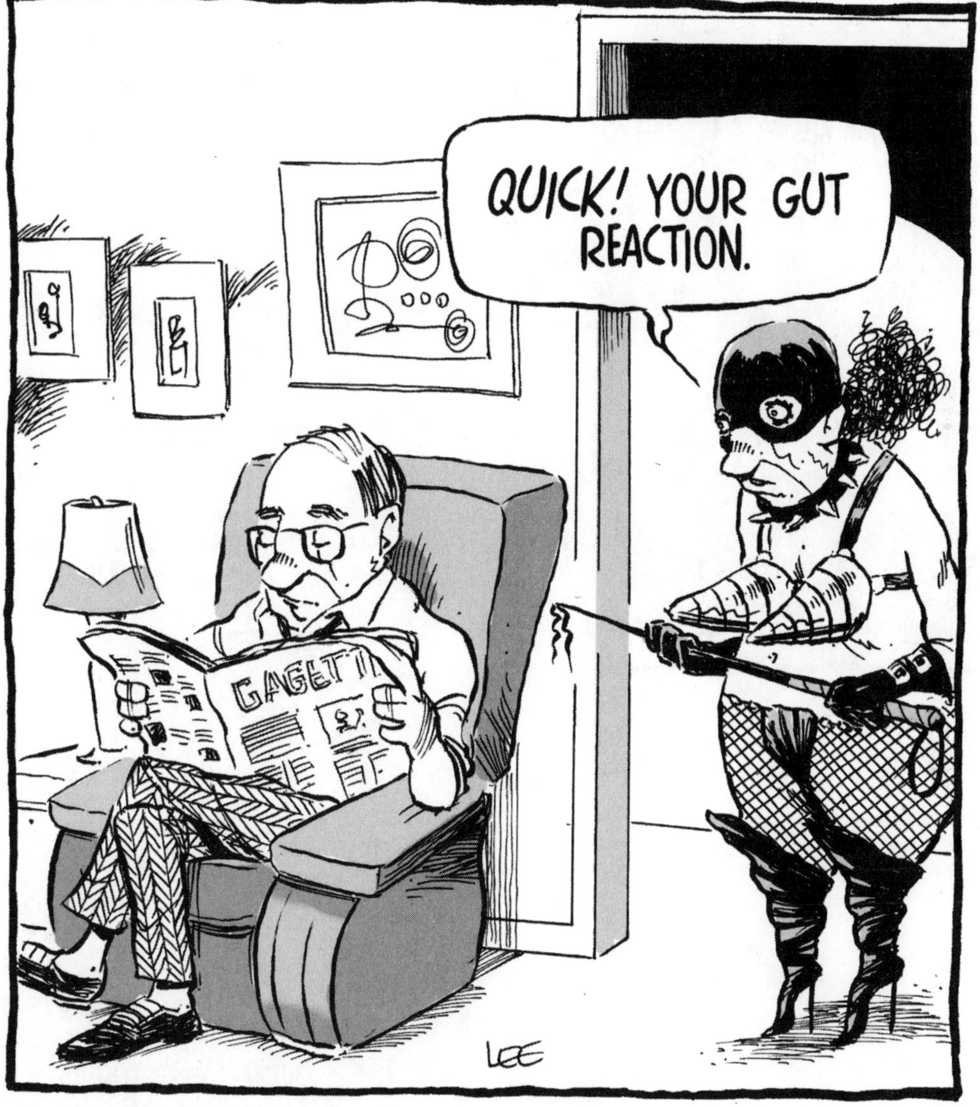
QUICK! YOUR GUT REACTION.
GAGETT
LEE

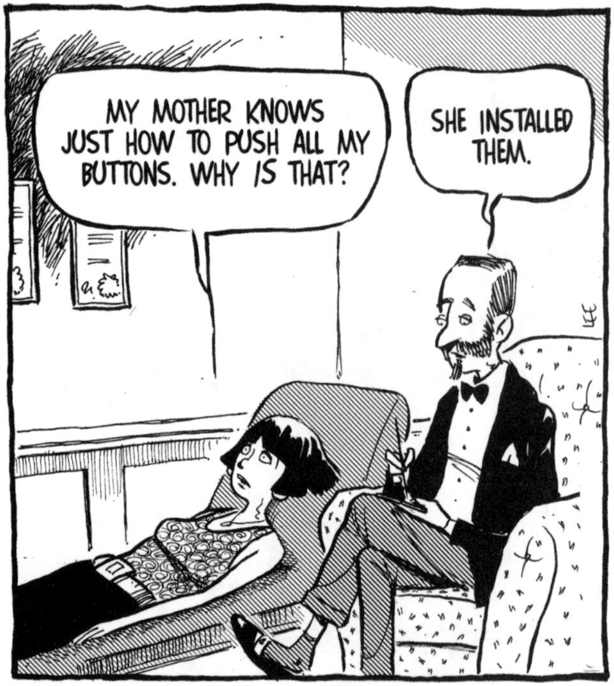
MY MOTHER KNOWS JUST HOW TO PUSH ALL MY BUTTONS. WHY IS THAT?
SHE INSTALLED THEM.
LEE

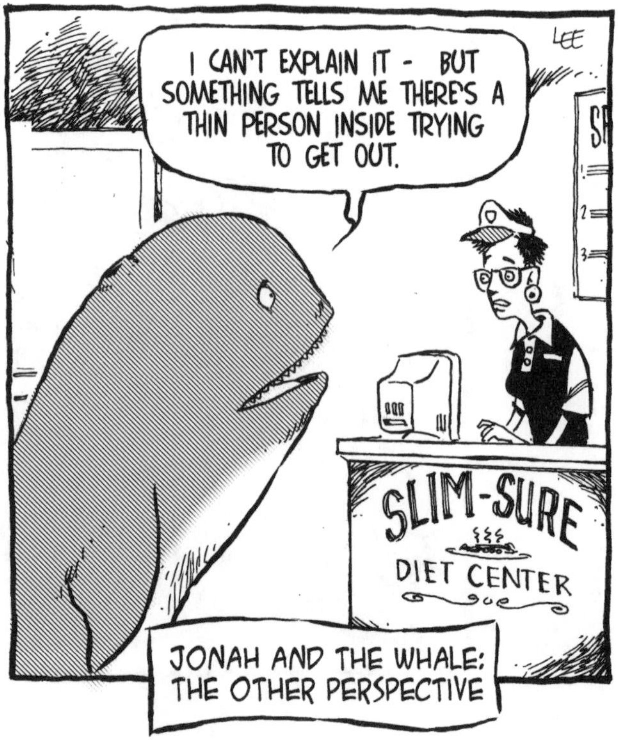
I CAN'T EXPLAIN IT - BUT SOMETHING TELLS ME THERE'S A THIN PERSON INSIDE TRYING TO GET OUT.
SLIM-SURE
DIET CENTER
LEE
JONAH AND THE WHALE: THE OTHER PERSPECTIVE

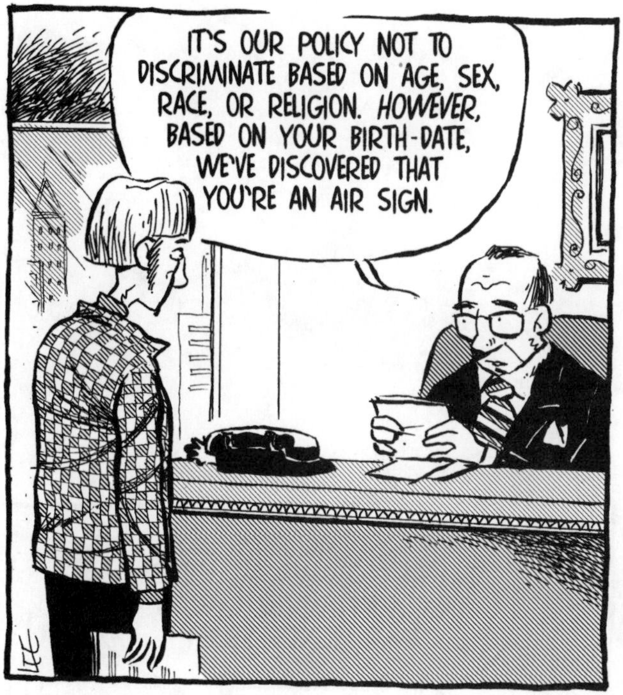
IT'S OUR POLICY NOT TO DISCRIMINATE BASED ON AGE, SEX, RACE, OR RELIGION. *HOWEVER*, BASED ON YOUR BIRTH-DATE, WE'VE DISCOVERED THAT YOU'RE AN AIR SIGN.
LEE

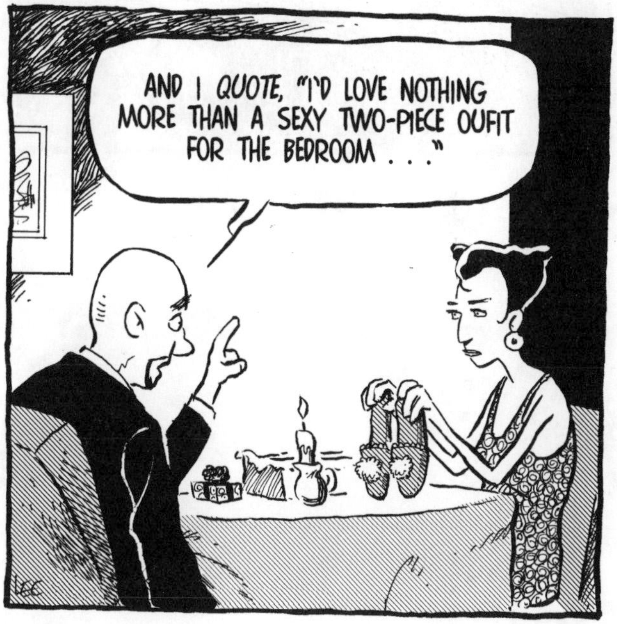
AND I *QUOTE*, "I'D LOVE NOTHING MORE THAN A SEXY TWO-PIECE OUFIT FOR THE BEDROOM . . ."
LEE

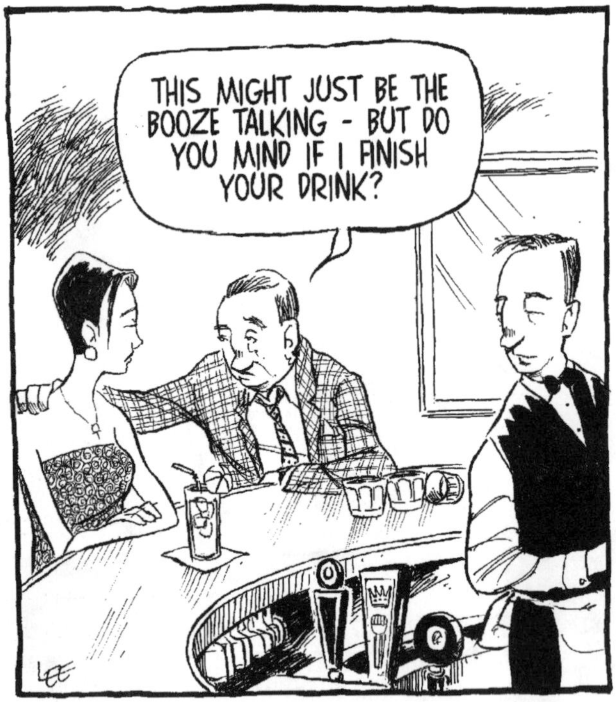
THIS MIGHT JUST BE THE BOOZE TALKING - BUT DO YOU MIND IF I FINISH YOUR DRINK?
LEE

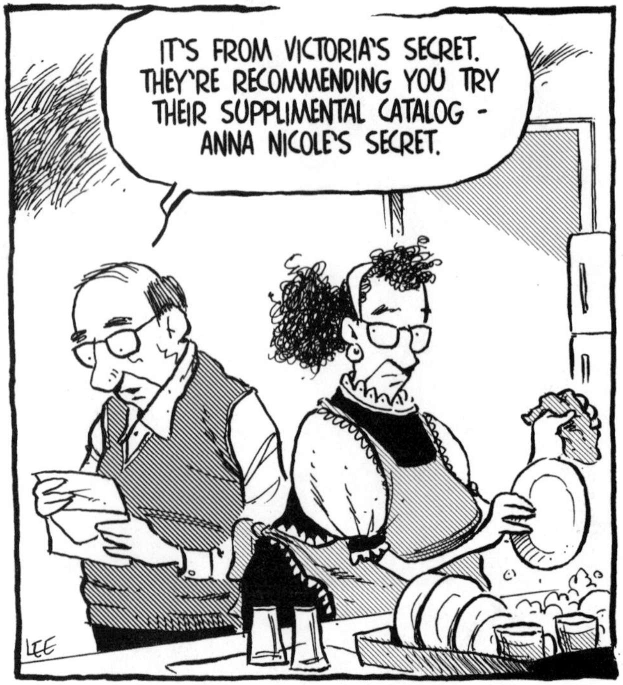
IT'S FROM VICTORIA'S SECRET. THEY'RE RECOMMENDING YOU TRY THEIR SUPPLIMENTAL CATALOG - ANNA NICOLE'S SECRET.
LEE

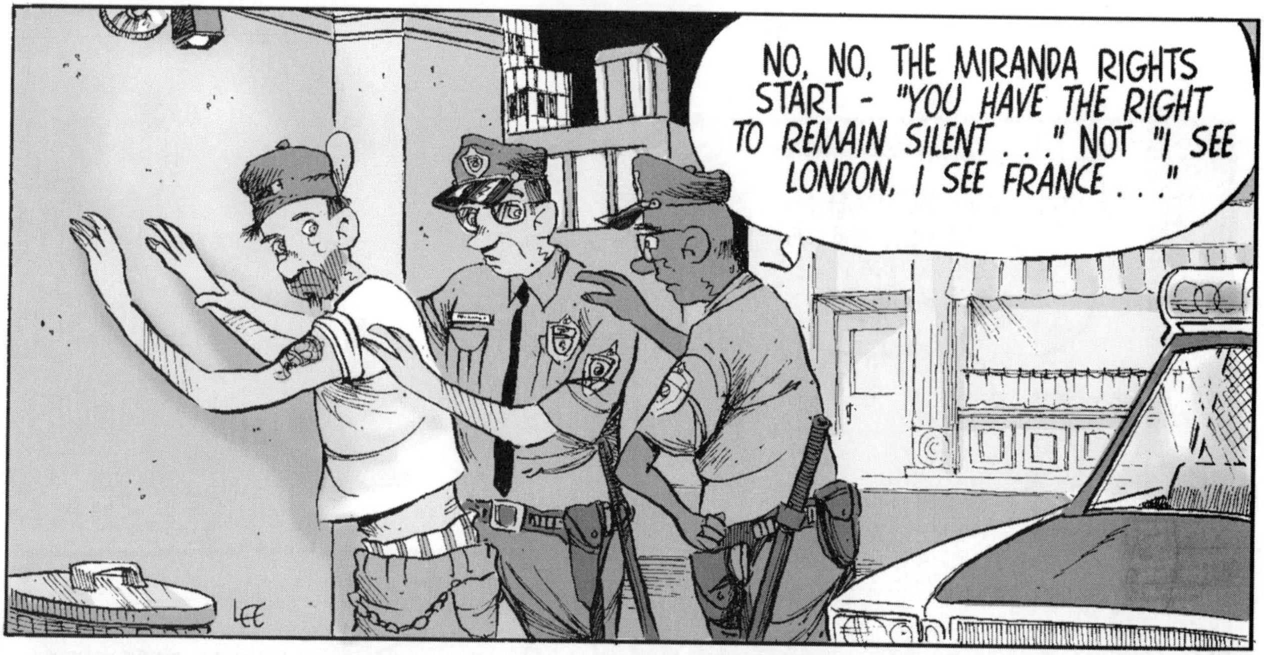
NO, NO, THE MIRANDA RIGHTS START - "YOU HAVE THE RIGHT TO REMAIN SILENT . . ." NOT "I SEE LONDON, I SEE FRANCE . . ."
LEE

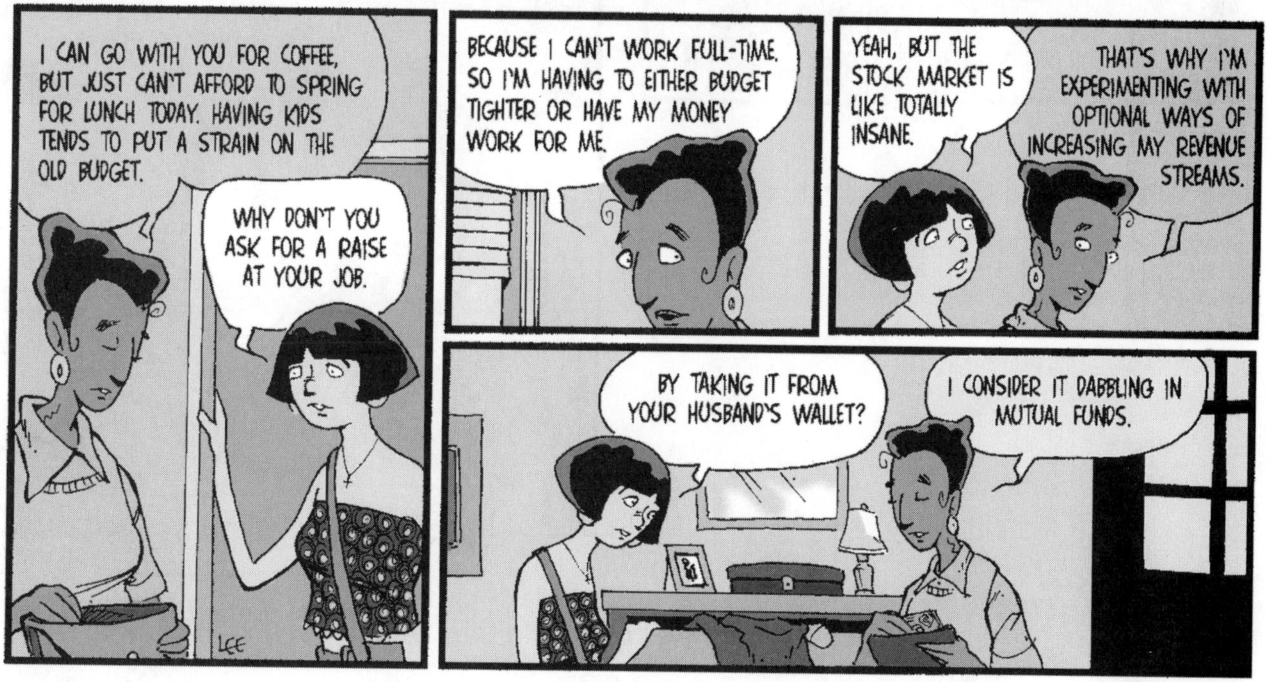
I CAN GO WITH YOU FOR COFFEE, BUT JUST CAN'T AFFORD TO SPRING FOR LUNCH TODAY. HAVING KIDS TENDS TO PUT A STRAIN ON THE OLD BUDGET.
WHY DON'T YOU ASK FOR A RAISE AT YOUR JOB.
LEE
BECAUSE I CAN'T WORK FULL-TIME. SO I'M HAVING TO EITHER BUDGET TIGHTER OR HAVE MY MONEY WORK FOR ME.
YEAH, BUT THE STOCK MARKET IS LIKE TOTALLY INSANE.
THAT'S WHY I'M EXPERIMENTING WITH OPTIONAL WAYS OF INCREASING MY REVENUE STREAMS.
BY TAKING IT FROM YOUR HUSBAND'S WALLET?
I CONSIDER IT DABBLING IN MUTUAL FUNDS.

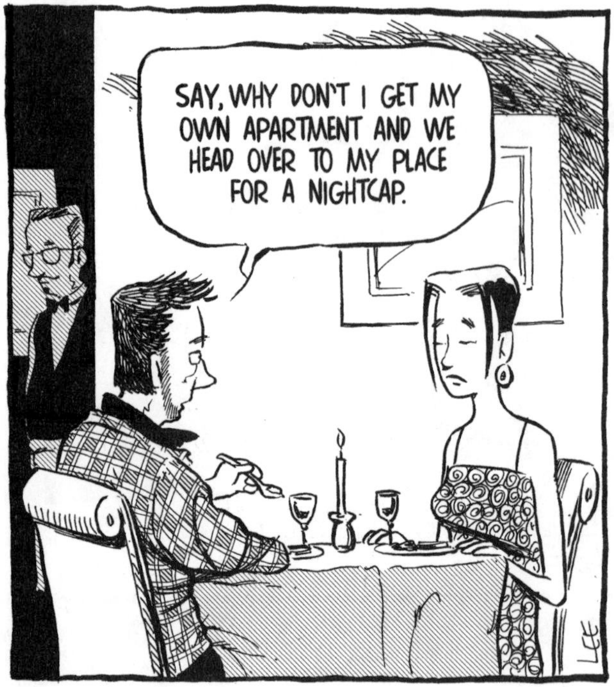
SAY, WHY DON'T I GET MY OWN APARTMENT AND WE HEAD OVER TO MY PLACE FOR A NIGHTCAP.
LEE

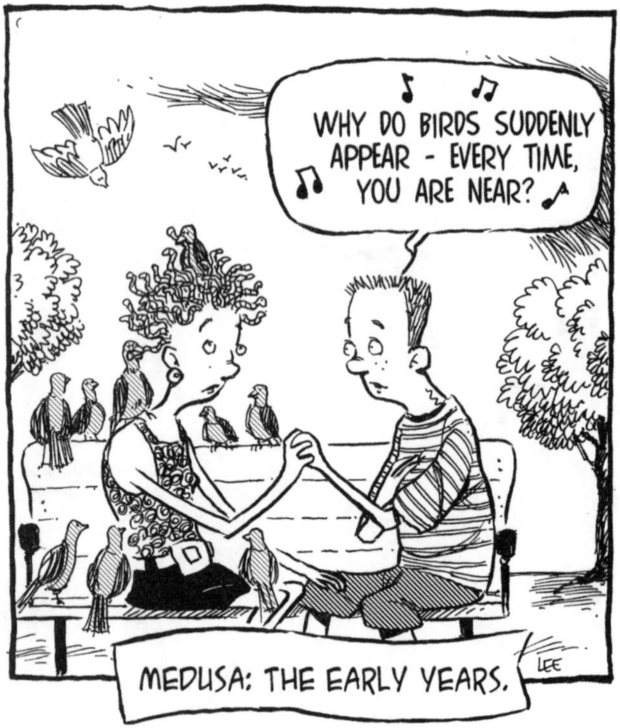
WHY DO BIRDS SUDDENLY APPEAR - EVERY TIME, YOU ARE NEAR?
MEDUSA: THE EARLY YEARS.
LEE

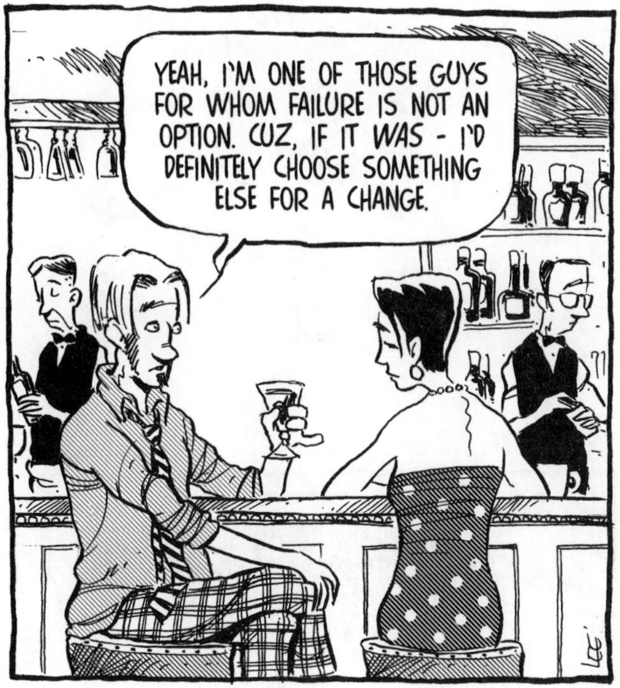
YEAH, I'M ONE OF THOSE GUYS FOR WHOM FAILURE IS NOT AN OPTION. CUZ, IF IT WAS - I'D DEFINITELY CHOOSE SOMETHING ELSE FOR A CHANGE.

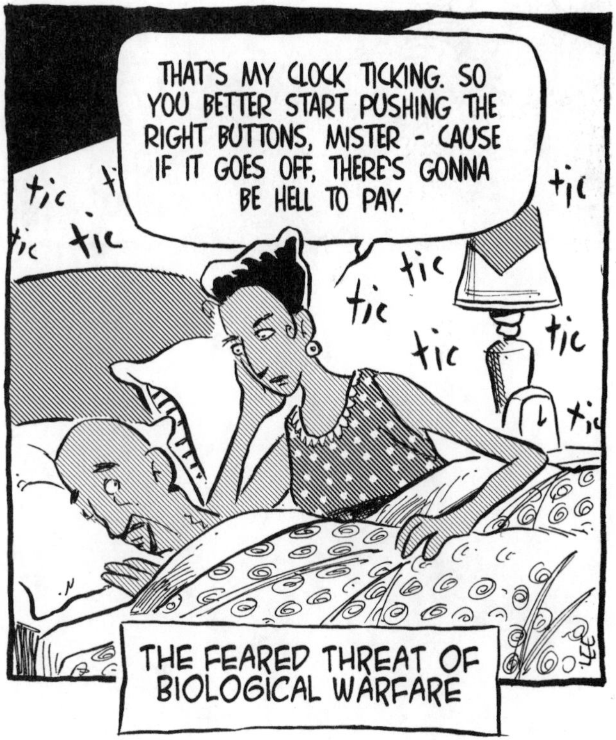
THAT'S MY CLOCK TICKING. SO YOU BETTER START PUSHING THE RIGHT BUTTONS, MISTER - CAUSE IF IT GOES OFF, THERE'S GONNA BE HELL TO PAY.
tic
tic
tic
tic
tic
tic
tic
tic
THE FEARED THREAT OF BIOLOGICAL WARFARE

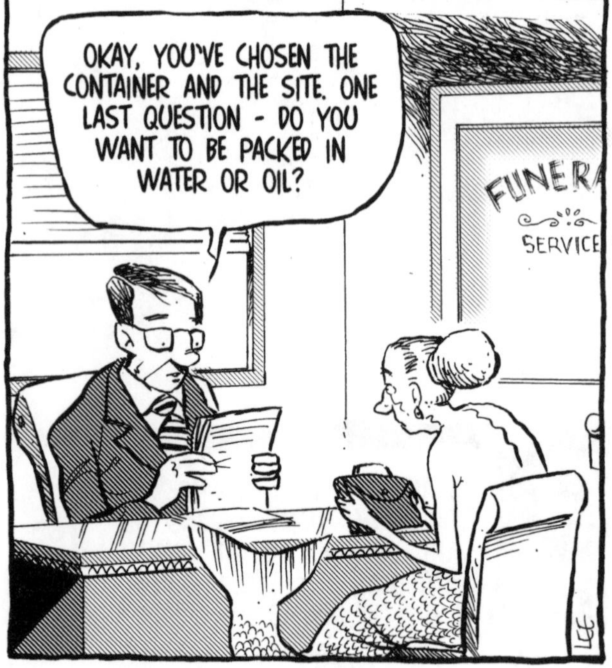
OKAY, YOU'VE CHOSEN THE CONTAINER AND THE SITE. ONE LAST QUESTION - DO YOU WANT TO BE PACKED IN WATER OR OIL?
FUNERA
SERVICE

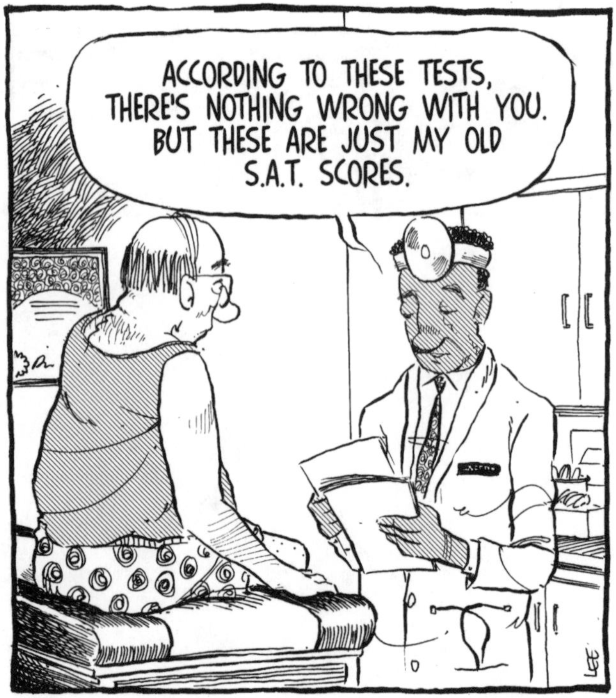
ACCORDING TO THESE TESTS, THERE'S NOTHING WRONG WITH YOU. BUT THESE ARE JUST MY OLD S.A.T. SCORES.

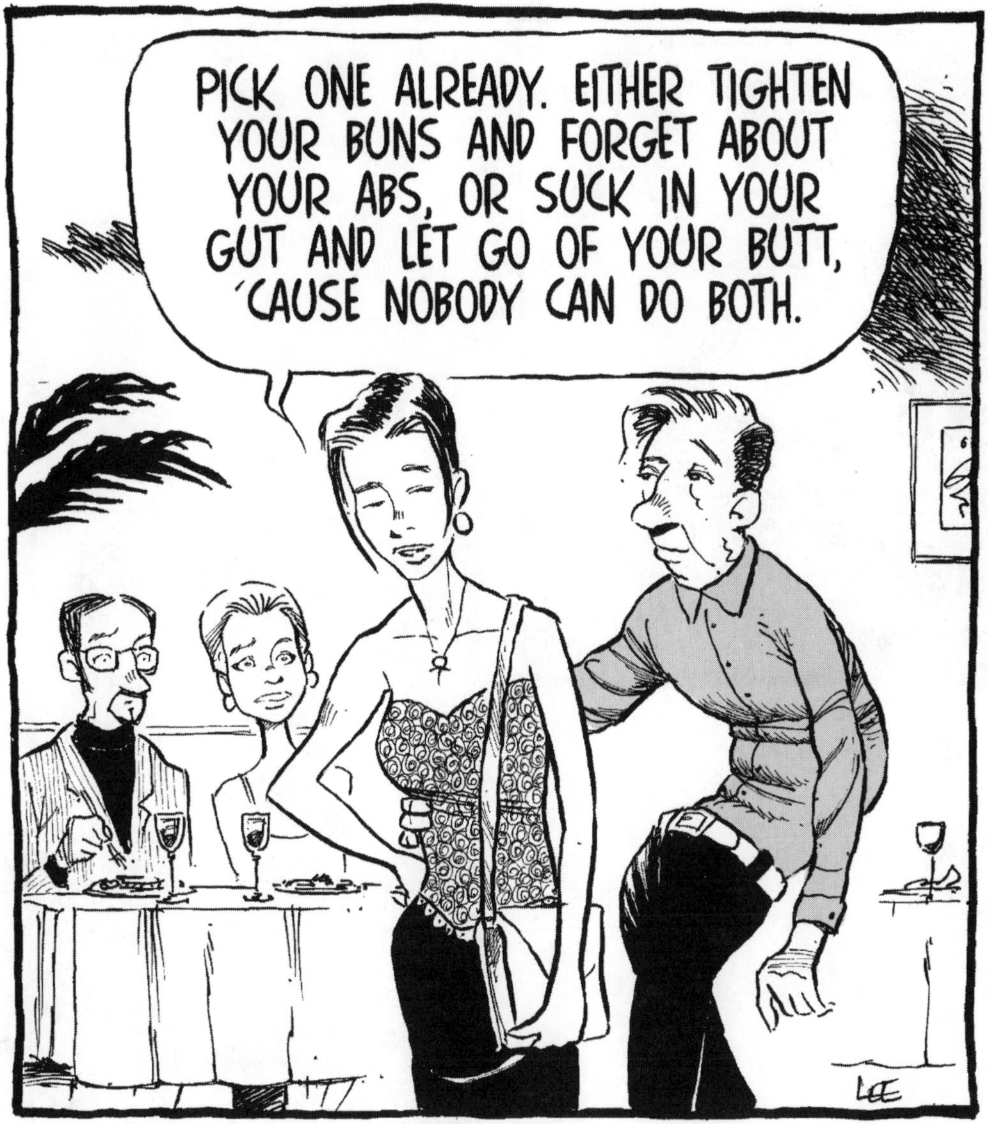
PICK ONE ALREADY. EITHER TIGHTEN YOUR BUNS AND FORGET ABOUT YOUR ABS, OR SUCK IN YOUR GUT AND LET GO OF YOUR BUTT, 'CAUSE NOBODY CAN DO BOTH.
LEE

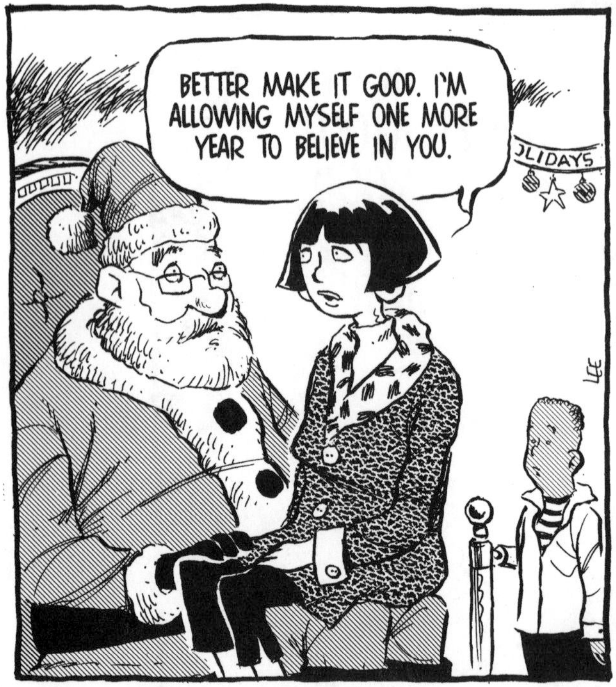
BETTER MAKE IT GOOD. I'M ALLOWING MYSELF ONE MORE YEAR TO BELIEVE IN YOU.
LEE

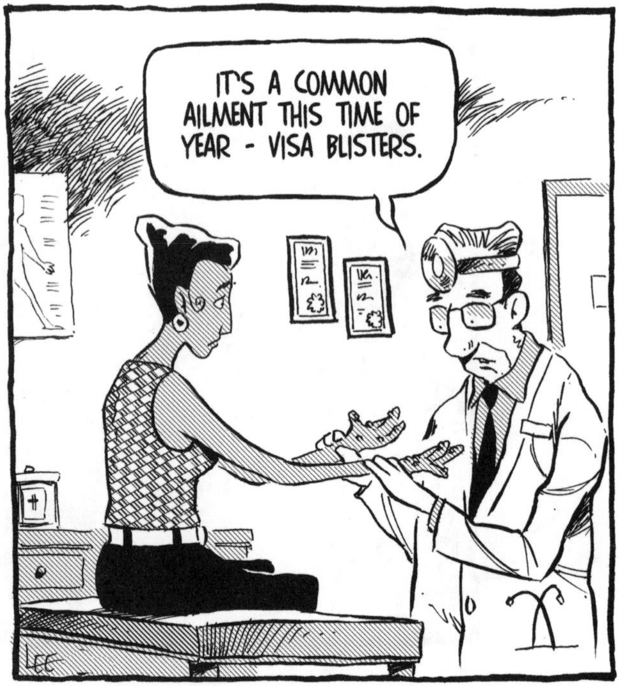
IT'S A COMMON AILMENT THIS TIME OF YEAR - VISA BLISTERS.
LEE

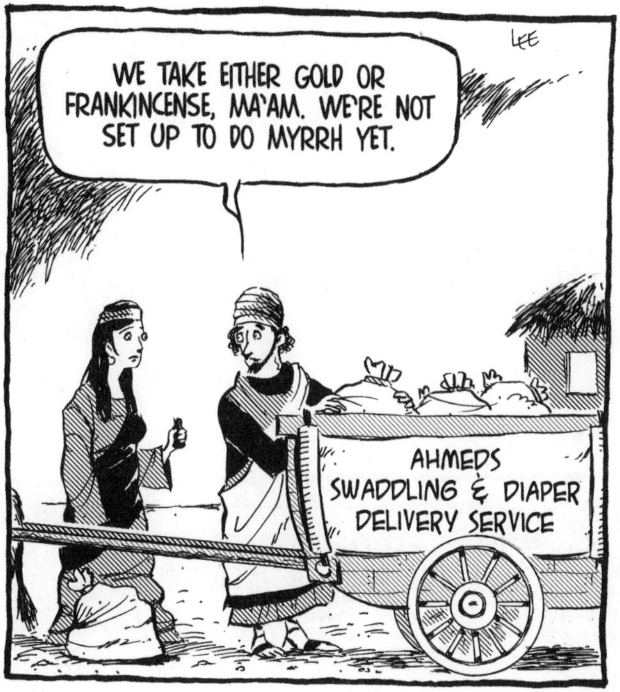
LEE
WE TAKE EITHER GOLD OR FRANKINCENSE, MA'AM. WE'RE NOT SET UP TO DO MYRRH YET.
AHMEDS SWADDLING & DIAPER DELIVERY SERVICE

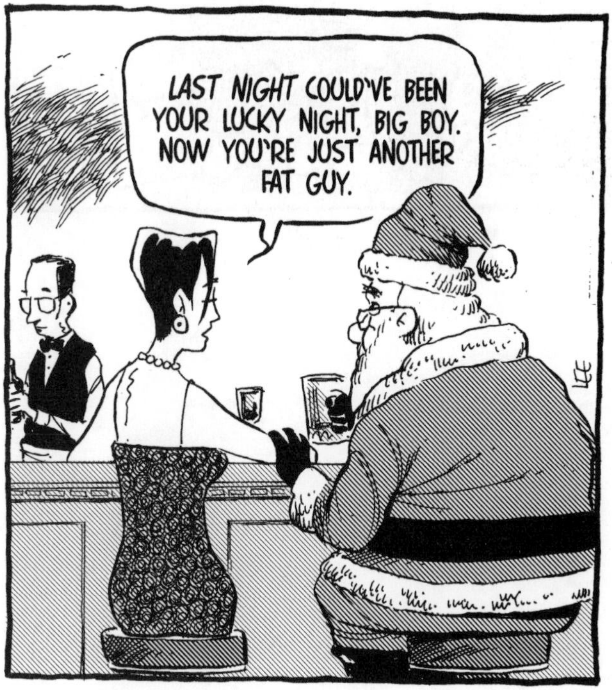
LAST NIGHT COULD'VE BEEN YOUR LUCKY NIGHT, BIG BOY. NOW YOU'RE JUST ANOTHER FAT GUY.
LEE

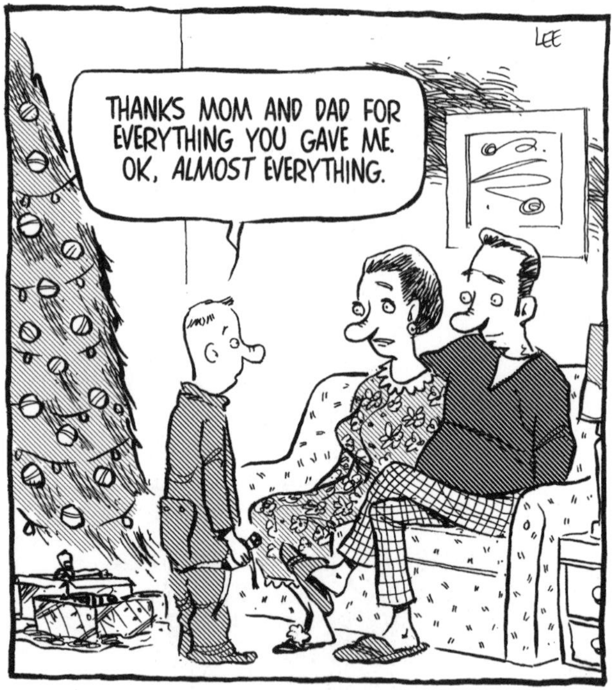
LEE
THANKS MOM AND DAD FOR EVERYTHING YOU GAVE ME. OK, *ALMOST* EVERYTHING.

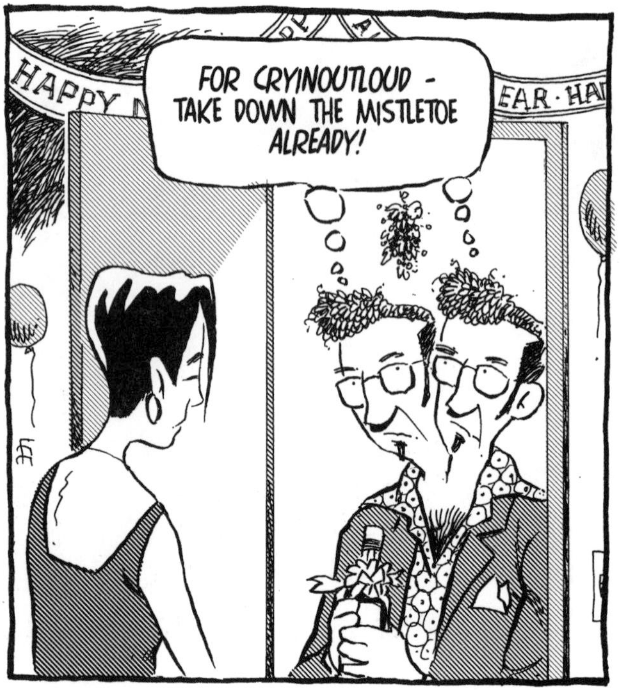
HAPPY
EAR·HA
FOR CRYINOUTLOUD - TAKE DOWN THE MISTLETOE *ALREADY!*
LEE

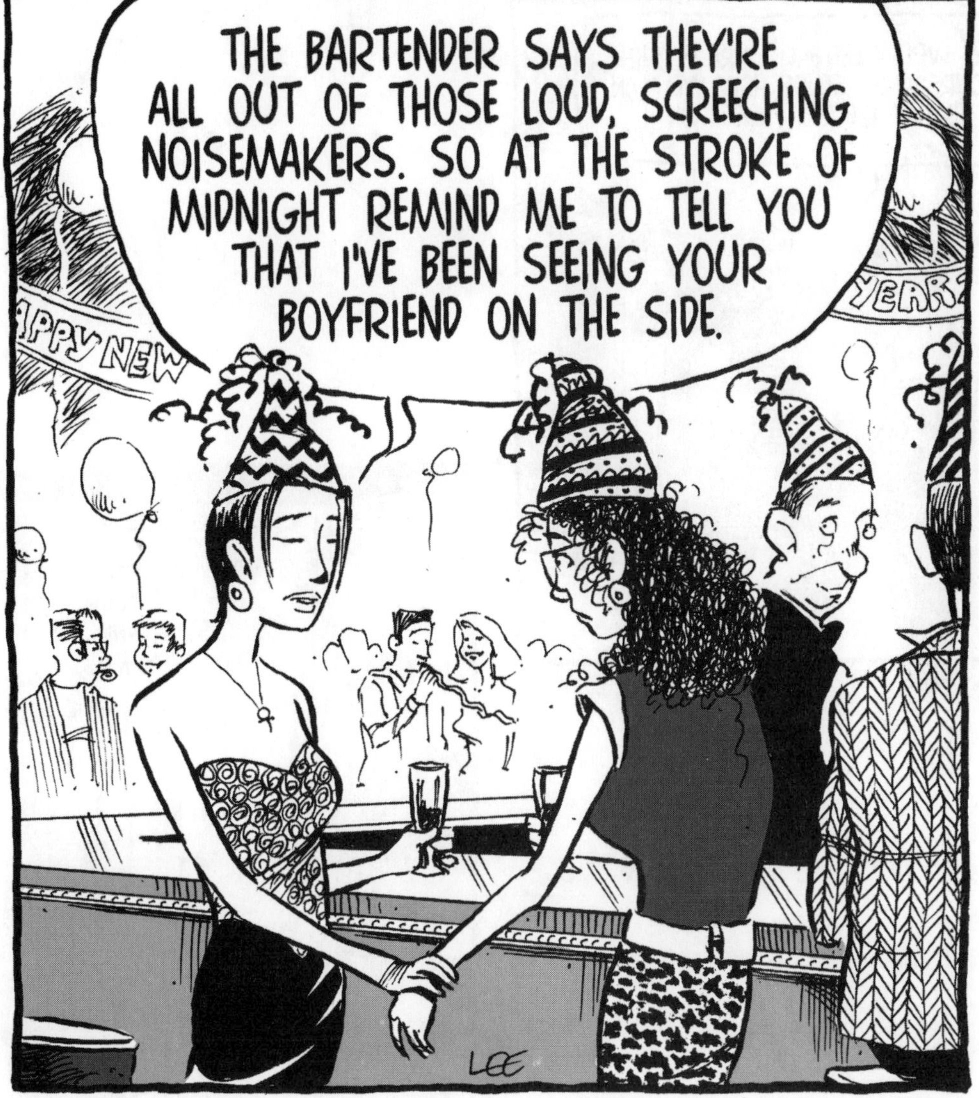
THE BARTENDER SAYS THEY'RE ALL OUT OF THOSE LOUD, SCREECHING NOISEMAKERS. SO AT THE STROKE OF MIDNIGHT REMIND ME TO TELL YOU THAT I'VE BEEN SEEING YOUR BOYFRIEND ON THE SIDE.
LEE

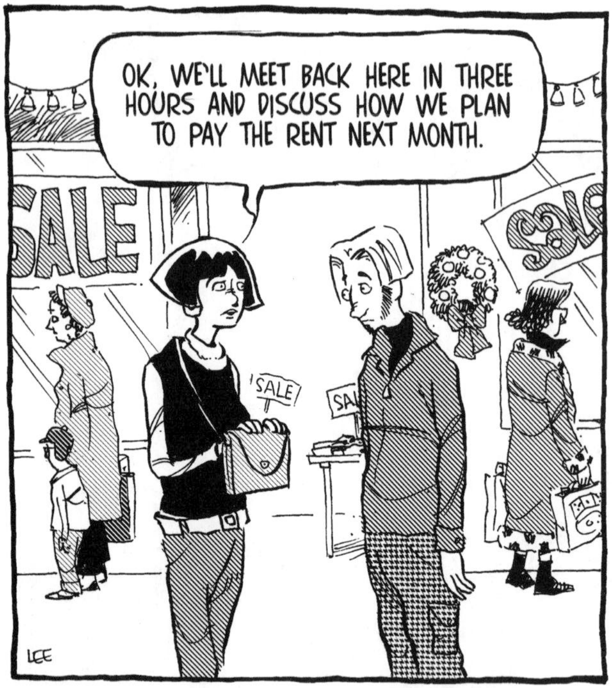
OK, WE'LL MEET BACK HERE IN THREE HOURS AND DISCUSS HOW WE PLAN TO PAY THE RENT NEXT MONTH.
SALE
SALE
LEE

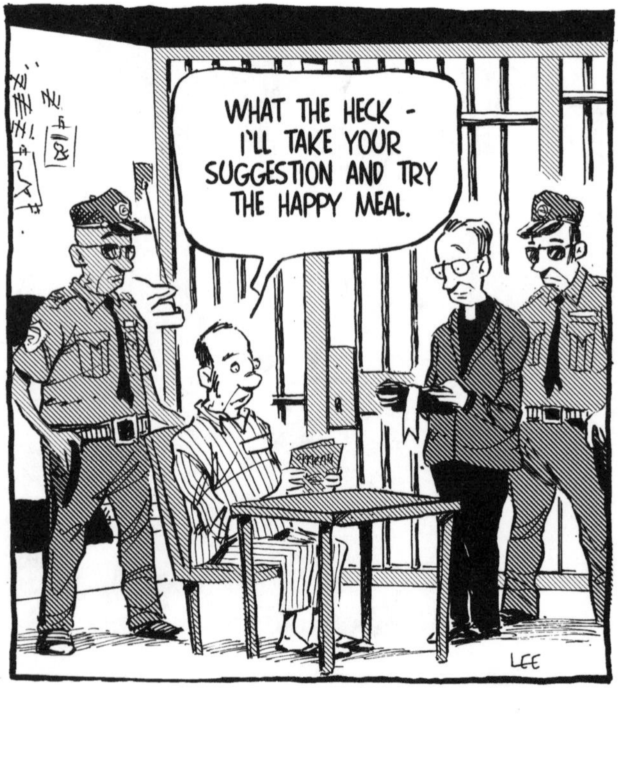
WHAT THE HECK - I'LL TAKE YOUR SUGGESTION AND TRY THE HAPPY MEAL.
LEE

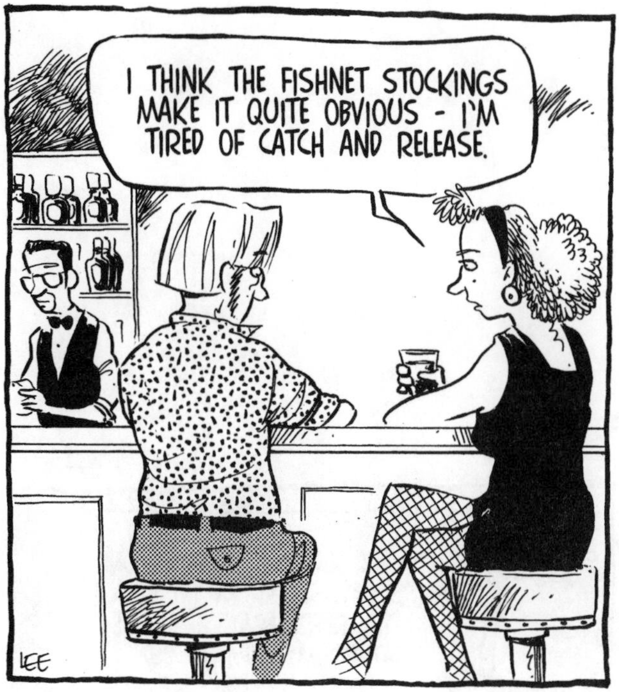
I THINK THE FISHNET STOCKINGS MAKE IT QUITE OBVIOUS - I'M TIRED OF CATCH AND RELEASE.
LEE

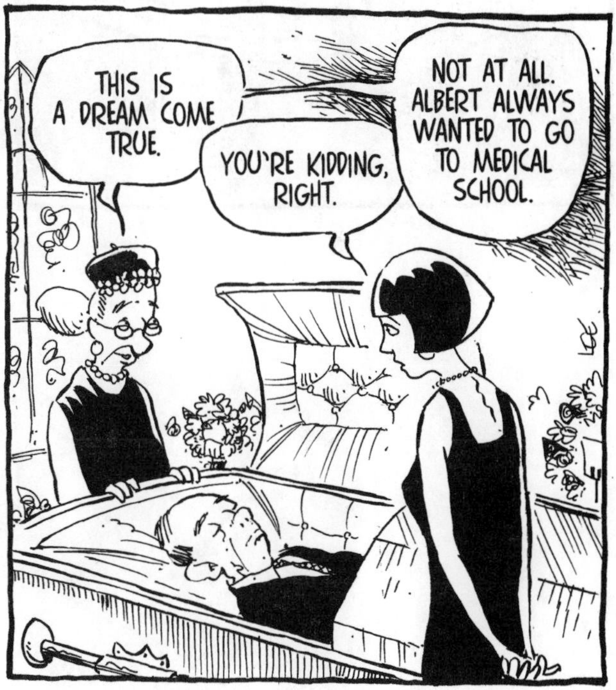
THIS IS A DREAM COME TRUE.
YOU'RE KIDDING, RIGHT.
NOT AT ALL. ALBERT ALWAYS WANTED TO GO TO MEDICAL SCHOOL.
LEE

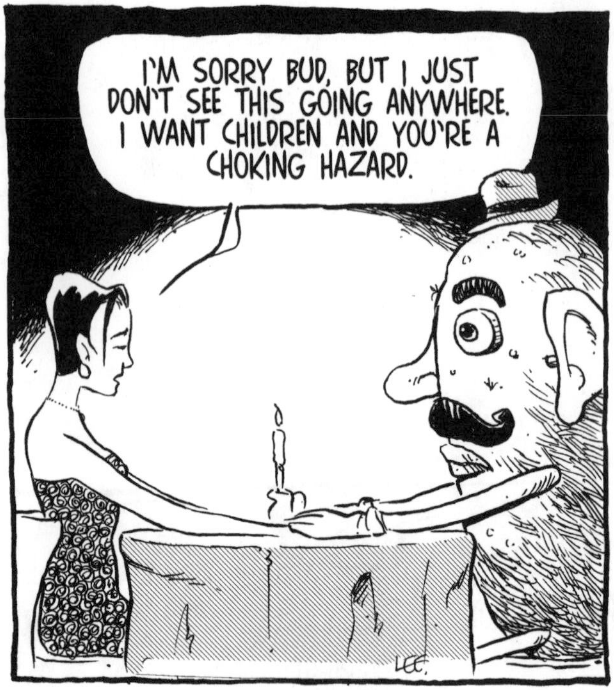
I'M SORRY BUD, BUT I JUST DON'T SEE THIS GOING ANYWHERE. I WANT CHILDREN AND YOU'RE A CHOKING HAZARD.
LEE

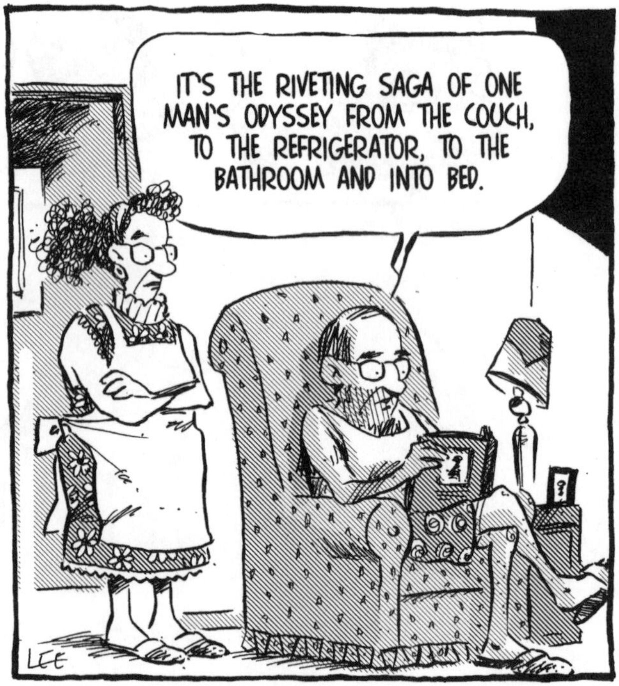
IT'S THE RIVETING SAGA OF ONE MAN'S ODYSSEY FROM THE COUCH, TO THE REFRIGERATOR, TO THE BATHROOM AND INTO BED.
LEE

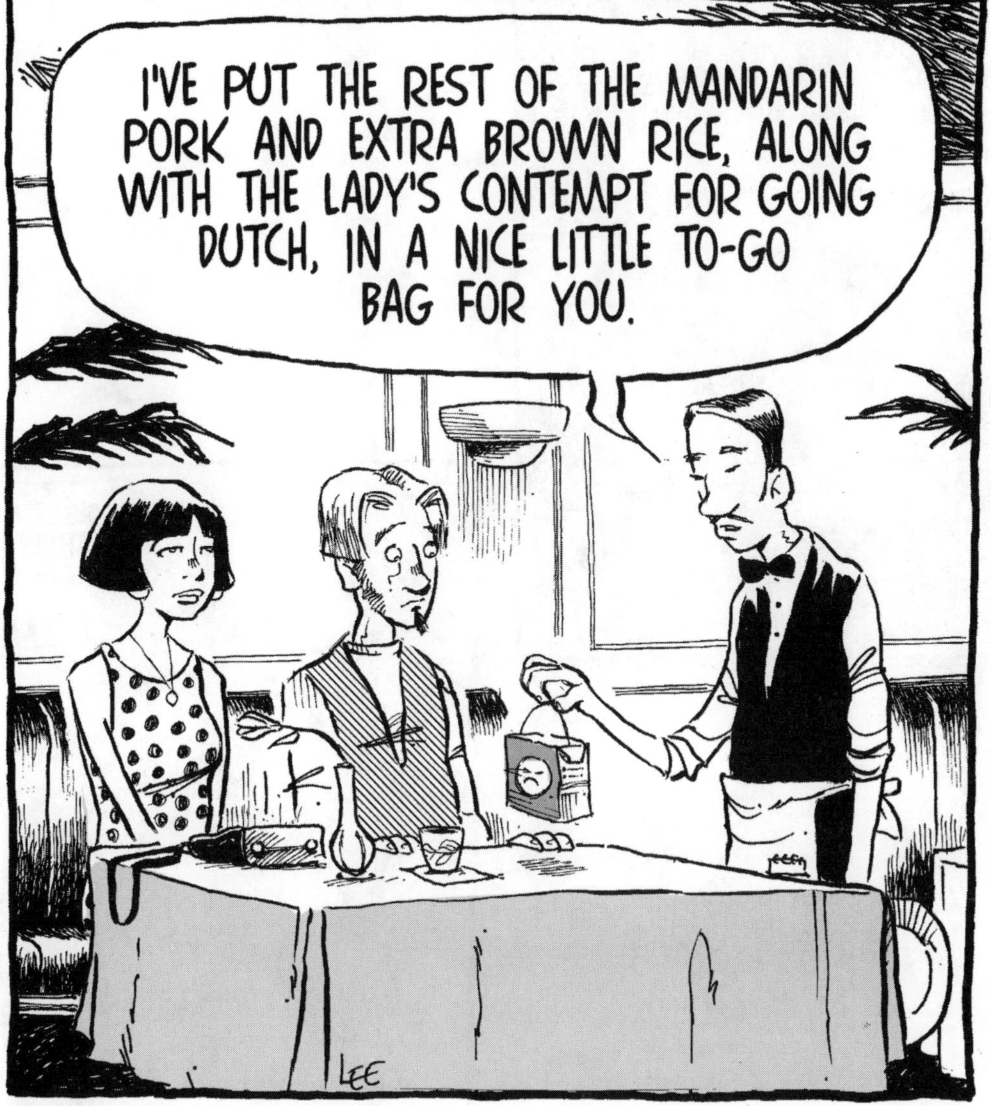
I'VE PUT THE REST OF THE MANDARIN PORK AND EXTRA BROWN RICE, ALONG WITH THE LADY'S CONTEMPT FOR GOING DUTCH, IN A NICE LITTLE TO-GO BAG FOR YOU.
LEE

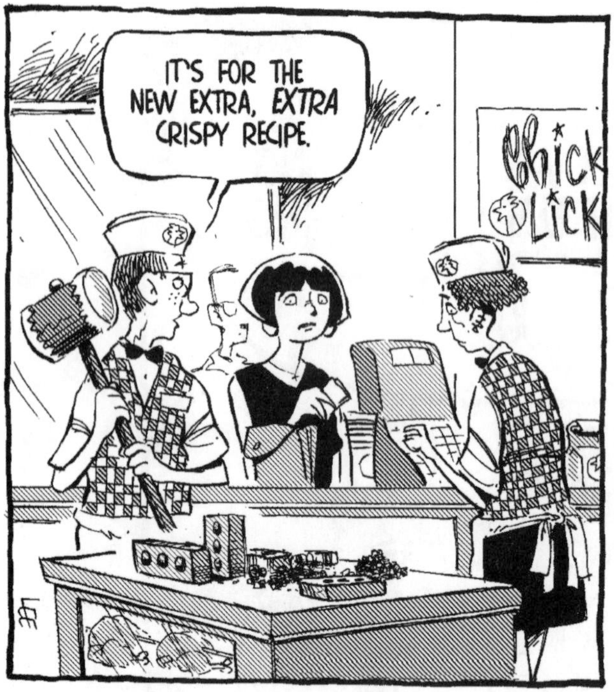
IT'S FOR THE NEW EXTRA, *EXTRA* CRISPY RECIPE.
Chick Lick
LEE

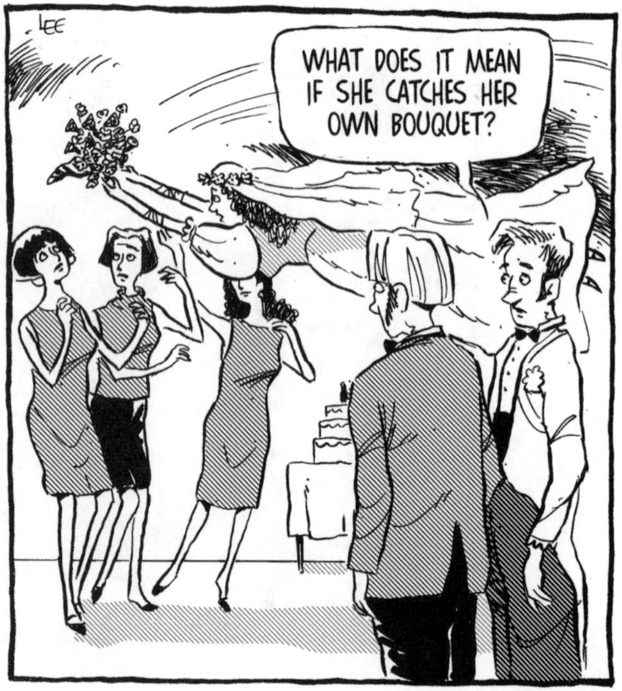
LEE
WHAT DOES IT MEAN IF SHE CATCHES HER OWN BOUQUET?

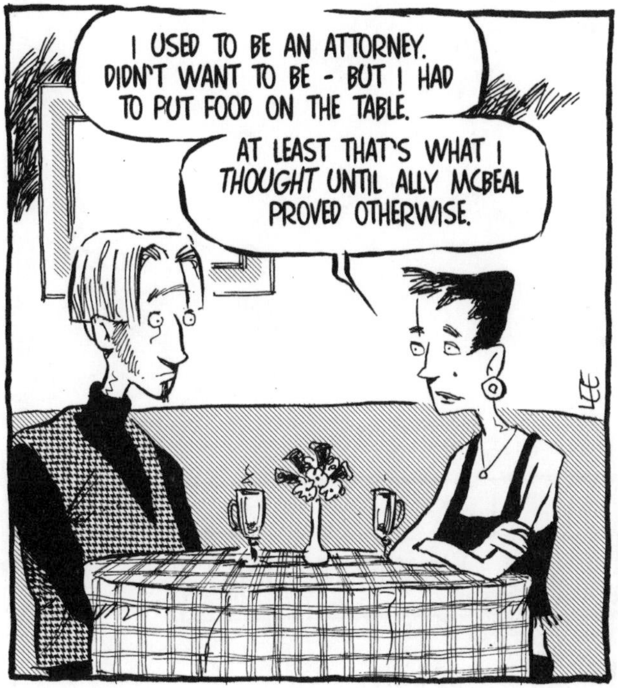
I USED TO BE AN ATTORNEY. DIDN'T WANT TO BE - BUT I HAD TO PUT FOOD ON THE TABLE.
AT LEAST THAT'S WHAT I *THOUGHT* UNTIL ALLY MCBEAL PROVED OTHERWISE.

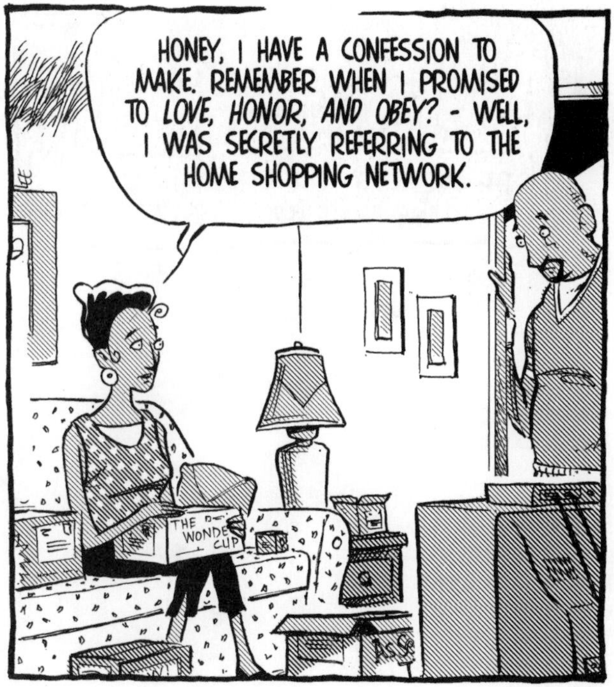
HONEY, I HAVE A CONFESSION TO MAKE. REMEMBER WHEN I PROMISED TO *LOVE, HONOR, AND OBEY?* - WELL, I WAS SECRETLY REFERRING TO THE HOME SHOPPING NETWORK.

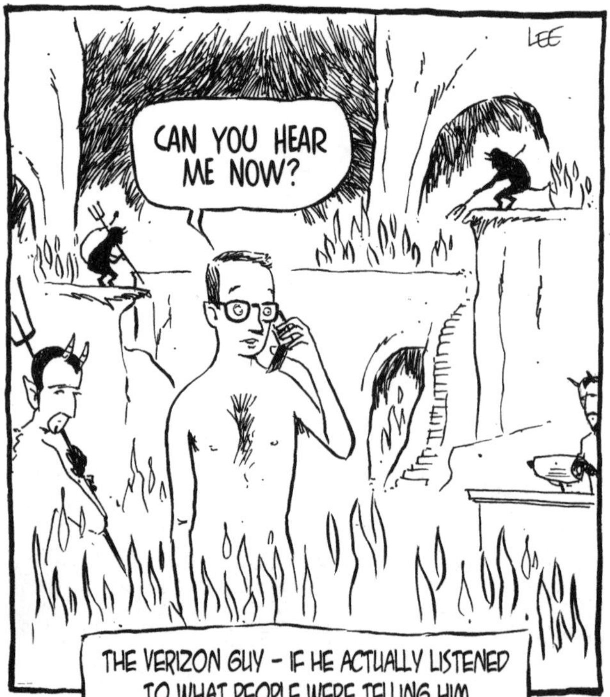
LEE
CAN YOU HEAR ME NOW?

THE VERIZON GUY – IF HE ACTUALLY LISTENED TO WHAT PEOPLE WERE TELLING HIM

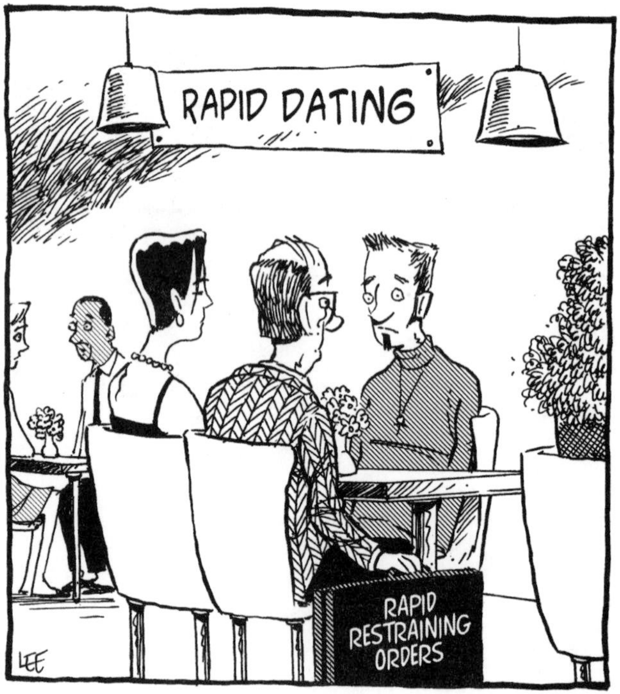
RAPID DATING
RAPID RESTRAINING ORDERS
LEE

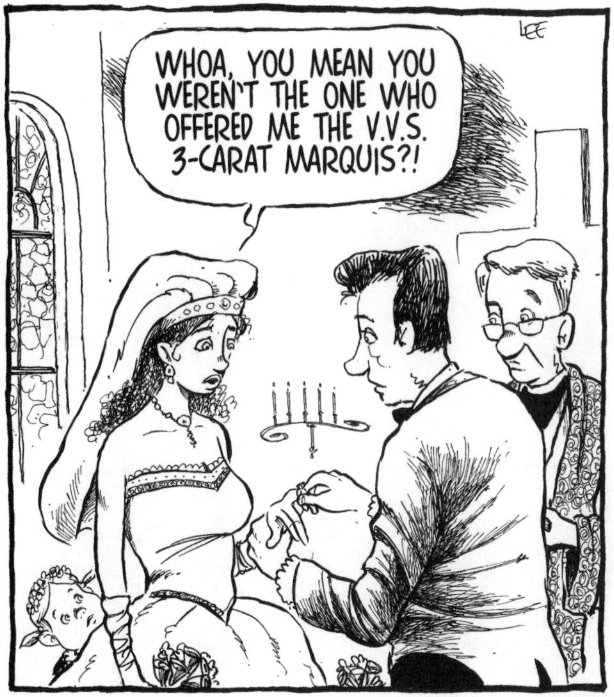
LEE
WHOA, YOU MEAN YOU WEREN'T THE ONE WHO OFFERED ME THE V.V.S. 3-CARAT MARQUIS?!

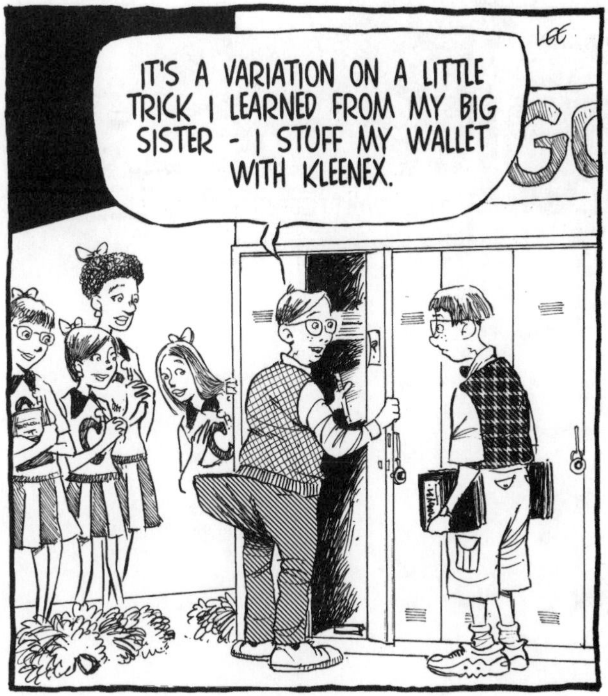
LEE
IT'S A VARIATION ON A LITTLE TRICK I LEARNED FROM MY BIG SISTER - I STUFF MY WALLET WITH KLEENEX.

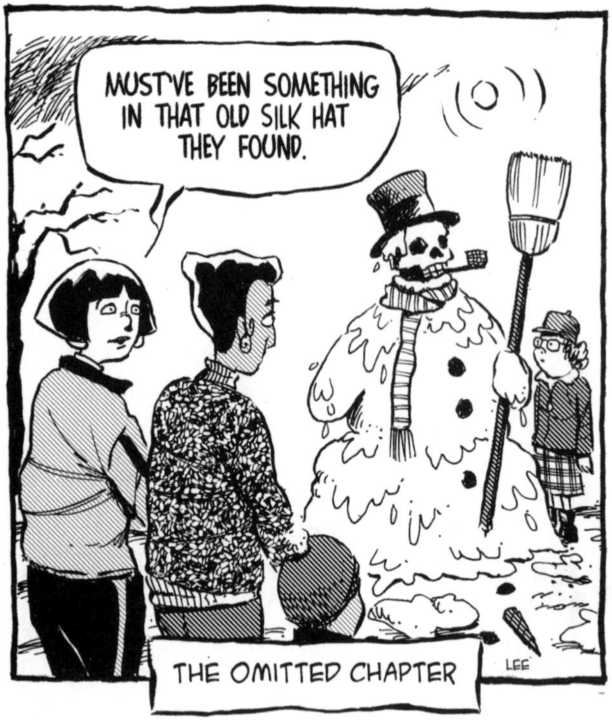
MUST'VE BEEN SOMETHING IN THAT OLD SILK HAT THEY FOUND.
THE OMITTED CHAPTER
LEE

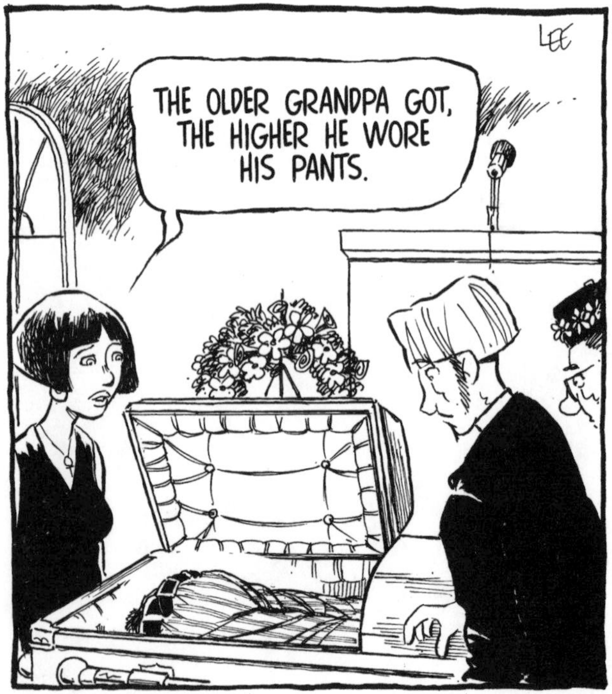
LEE
THE OLDER GRANDPA GOT, THE HIGHER HE WORE HIS PANTS.